THE AMERICAN FRONTIER

OPPOSING VIEWPOINTS®

Other Books in the American History Series:

THE AMERICAN FRONTIER

OPPOSING VIEWPOINTS®

David L. Bender, *Publisher*
Bruno Leone, *Executive Editor*

Teresa O'Neill, *Series Editor*
John C. Chalberg, Ph.D., professor of history,
    Normandale Community College, *Consulting
    Editor*

Mary Ellen Jones, Ph.D., associate professor of
    English, Wittenberg University,
    Springfield, Ohio, *Book Editor*

AMERICAN HISTORY SERIES

Cover photos: Library of Congress (top and both middle), National Archives (bottom)

Library of Congress Cataloging-in-Publication Data

The American frontier : opposing viewpoints / Mary Ellen Jones, book editor.
    p.   cm. — (American history series)
    Includes bibliographical references and index.
    ISBN 1-56510-086-7 (lib.) — ISBN 1-56510-085-9 (paper)
    1. Frontier thesis. 2. Frontier and pioneer life—United States.
3. United States—Territorial expansion. 4. West (U.S.)—History.
I. Jones, Mary Ellen, 1937-   . II. Series: American history series
(San Diego, Calif.)
E179.5.A47733   1994   93-29898
978'.02—dc20   CIP

For Bob,
  as always:
  this book's for you.

In memory, too, of Jody Grosh.

Sincere thanks also to
  Lynn Downey of Levi Strauss & Co.,
  Terry O'Neill of Greenhaven Press,
  Yvonne Schieberl of the Tulare County
    (California) Free Library,
  and, most especially, to Lori Judy of Thomas
    Library, Wittenberg University.

Contents

Foreword

Aboard the *Arbella* as it lurched across the cold, gray Atlantic, John Winthrop was as calm as the waters surrounding him were wild. With the confidence of a born leader, Winthrop gathered his Puritan passengers around him. It was time to offer a sermon. England lay behind them, and years of strife and persecution for their religious beliefs were over, he said. But the Puritan abandonment of England, he reminded his followers, did not mean that England was beyond redemption. Winthrop wanted his followers to remember England even as they were leaving it behind. Their goal should be to create a new England, one far removed from the authority of the Anglican church and King Charles I. In Winthrop's words, their settlement in the New World ought to be a model society, a city upon a hill. He hoped his band would be able to create a just society in America for corrupt England to imitate.

Unable to find either peace or freedom within their home country, these Puritans were determined to provide England with a living example of a community that valued both. Across the hostile Atlantic Ocean would shine the bright light of a just, harmonious, and God-serving society. England may have been beset by sin and corruption, but Winthrop and the colonists believed they could still save England—and themselves. Together, they would coax out of the rocky New England soil not only food for their tables but many thriving communities dedicated to achieving harmony and justice.

One June 8, 1630, John Winthrop and his company of refugees had their first glimpse of what they came to call New England. High on the surrounding hills stood a welcoming band of fir trees whose fragrance drifted to the *Arbella* on a morning breeze. To Winthrop, the "smell off the shore [was] like the smell of a garden."

This new world would, in fact, often be compared to the Garden of Eden. In it, John Winthrop would have his opportunity to start life over again. So would his family and his shipmates. So would all those who would come after them. Victims of conflict in old England hoped to find peace in New England.

Winthrop, for one, had experienced much conflict in his life. As a Puritan, he was opposed to Catholicism and Anglicanism, both of which, he believed, were burdened by distracting rituals and distant hierarchies. A parliamentarian by conviction, he despised Charles I, who had spurned Parliament and created a private army to do his bidding. He believed in individual responsibility and fought against the loss of religious and political freedom. A gentleman landowner, he feared the rising economic power of a merchant class that seemed to value only money. Once Winthrop stepped aboard the *Arbella*, he hoped conflict would not be a part of his American future.

But his Puritan religion told Winthrop that human beings are fallen creatures and that perfection, whether communal or individual, is unachievable on this earth. Therefore, he was presented with a dilemma: On the one hand, his religion demanded that he attempt to live a perfect life in an imperfect world. On the other hand, it told him that he was destined to fail.

Soon after Winthrop disembarked from the *Arbella*, he came face-to-face with this maddening dilemma. He found himself presiding not over a utopia—an ideal community—but over a colony caught up in disputes as troubling as any that he had confronted in his English past.

John Winthrop, it seems, was not the only Puritan with a dream of perfection, with a vision of a heaven on earth. Others in the community saw the dream differently. They wanted greater political and religious freedom than their leader was prepared to grant. Often, Winthrop was able to handle this conflict diplomatically. He expanded, for example, participation in elections and allowed the voters of Massachusetts Bay greater power.

But religious conflict was another matter because it was a conflict of competing visions of the Puritan utopia. In Roger Williams and Anne Hutchinson, two of his fellow colonists, John Winthrop faced rivals unprepared to accept his definition of the perfect community. To Williams, perfection demanded that he separate himself from the Puritan institutions in his community and create an even "purer" church. Winthrop, however, disagreed and exiled Williams to Rhode Island. Hutchinson presumed that she could interpret God's will without a minister. Again, Winthrop did not agree. Hutchinson was tried on charges of heresy, convicted, and banished from Massachusetts.

John Winthrop's Massachusetts colony was the first, but far from the last, American attempt to build a unified, peaceful community that, in the end, only provoked a discord. This glimpse at its history reveals what Winthrop confronted: the unavoidable presence of conflict in American life.

American Assumptions

From America's origins in the early seventeenth century, Americans have often held several interrelated assumptions about their country. First, people believe that to be American is to be free. Second, because Americans did not have to free themselves from feudal lords or an entrenched aristocracy, conflict is often considered foreign to American life. Finally, America has been seen as a perpetual haven from the troubles and disputes that are found in the Old World.

John Winthrop, for one, lived his life as though all of these assumptions were true. But the opposing viewpoints presented in the American History Series should reveal that for many Americans, these assumptions were and are myths. Indeed, for numerous Americans, liberty has not always been guaranteed, and conflict has been a necessary, sometimes welcome aspect of their life. To these Americans, the United States is less a sanctuary than it is one more battleground for old and new ideas.

Our American landscape has been torn apart again and again by a great variety of clashes—theological, ideological, political, economic, geographical, racial, gender-based, and class-based. But to discover such a landscape is not necessarily to come upon a hopelessly divided country. If the editors desire to prove anything during the course of this series, it is not that America has been enlivened, enriched, and even strengthened by exchanges destroyed by conflict but rather that America has been between Americans who have disagreed with one another.

Observers of American life, however, often see a country in which its citizens behave as though all of the basic questions of life have been settled. Over the years, they see a generation after generation of Americans who seem to blithely agree with one another. In the nineteenth century, French traveler Alexis de Tocqueville called the typical American a "venturesome conservative." According to Tocqueville, this American was willing to risk money in the marketplace but otherwise presented the drab front of someone who thought, dressed, and acted just like everyone else. To Tocqueville, Americans were individualistic risk takers when it came to playing the game of capitalism but were victims of public opinion (which he defined as the "tyranny of the majority") when it came to otherwise expressing themselves.

In the twentieth century, sociologist David Riesman has registered his agreement with Tocqueville. He has defined the modern American as "other-directed." Perhaps willing to leap into the economic arena, this American is unwilling to take risks in the marketplace of ideas. The result is either silence or assent, either because this person is unsure of his or her own beliefs or because the mass media dictate beliefs—or a bit of both. The other-directed American is fearful of standing apart from the crowd.

The editors of this series would like to suggest that Tocqueville and Riesman were too narrow in their assessment of Americans. They have found innumerable Americans who have been willing to take the trouble to disagree.

The American Individual

Thomas Jefferson was one of the least confrontational of Americans, but he boldly and irrevocably enriched American life with his individualistic views. Like John Winthrop before him, he had a notion of an American Eden. Like Winthrop, he offered a vision of a harmonious society. And like Winthrop, he not only became enmeshed in conflict but eventually presided over a people beset by it. But unlike Winthrop, Jefferson believed this Eden was not located in a specific community but in each individual American. His Declaration of Independence from Great Britain could also be read as a declaration of independence for each individual in American society.

Jefferson's ideal world was composed of "yeoman farmers," each of whom was roughly equal to the other in society's eyes, each of whom was free from the restrictions of both government and his fellow citizens. Throughout his life, Jefferson offered a continuing challenge to Americans: advance individualism and equality or see the death of the American experiment. Jefferson believed that the strength of this experiment depended upon a society of autonomous individuals and a society without great gaps between rich and poor. His challenge to his fellow Americans to create—and sustain—such a society has itself produced both economic and political conflict.

A society whose guiding document is the Declaration of Independence is a society assured of the freedom to dream—and to disagree. We know that Jefferson himself hated conflict, whether personal or political. His tendency was to avoid confrontations of any sort, to squirrel himself away and write rather than to stand up and speak his mind. It is only through his written words that we can grasp Jefferson's utopian dream of a society of independent farmers, all pursuing their private dreams and all leading lives of sufficient prosperity.

This man of wealth and intellect lived an essentially happy life in accord with his view that Americans ought to have the right to pursue "happiness." But Jefferson's public life was much more troublesome. From the first rumblings of the American Revolution in the 1760s to the North-South skirmishes of the 1820s that ultimately produced the Civil War, Jefferson was at or near the center of American political history. The issues were almost too many—and too crucial—for one lifetime. Jefferson had to choose between supporting or rejecting the path of revolution. During and after the ensuing war, he was at the forefront of the battle for religious liberty. After endorsing the Constitution, he opposed the economic plans of Alexander Hamilton. At the end of the century, he fought the infamous Alien and Sedition Acts, which limited civil liberties. As president, he opposed the Federalist court, conspiracies to divide the union, and calls for a new war against England.

Throughout his life, Thomas Jefferson, slaveholder, pondered the conflict between American freedom and American slavery. And from retirement at his Monticello retreat, he frowned at the rising spirit of commercialism that he feared was dividing Americans and destroying his dream of American harmony.

No matter the issue, however, Thomas Jefferson invariably supported the rights of the individual. Worried as he was about the excesses of commercialism, he accepted them because his main concern was to live in a society where liberty and individualism could flourish. To Jefferson, Americans had to be free to worship as they desired. They also deserved to be free from an over-reaching government. To Jefferson, Americans should also be free to possess slaves.

Harmony, an Elusive Goal

Before reading the articles in this anthology, the editors ask readers to ponder the lives of John Winthrop and Thomas Jefferson. Each held a utopian vision, one based upon the demands of community and the other on the autonomy of the individual. Each dreamed of a country of perpetual new beginnings. Each found himself thrust into a position of leadership and found that conflict could not be avoided. And each lived long enough to face and express many opposing views. Harmony, whether communal or individual, was a forever elusive goal.

The opposing visions of Winthrop and Jefferson have been at the heart of many differences among Americans from many backgrounds through the whole of American history. Moreover, their visions have provoked important responses that have helped shape American society, the American character, and many an American battle.

Is the theme of community versus the individual the single defining theme in American history? No, but it is a recurring theme that provides us with a useful point of departure for showing that Americans have been more rambunctious and contentious than Tocqueville or Riesman found them to be, that blandness has not been the defining characteristic for all Americans.

In this age of mass media, the danger exists that the real issues that divide Americans will be, at best, distorted or, at worst, ignored. But by thinking honestly about the past, the real issues and real differences have often been of critical, even of life-and-death, importance to Americans. And they continue to be so today.

The editors of the American History Series have done extensive research to find representative opinions on the issues included in these volumes. They found numerous outstanding opposing viewpoints from people of all times, classes, and genders in American history. From those, they selected commentaries that best fit the nature and flavor of the period under consideration. Every attempt was made to include the most important and relevant viewpoints in each chapter. Obviously, not every notable viewpoint could be included. Therefore, a bibliography has been provided at the end of each book to aid readers in seeking out for themselves additional information.

The editors are confident that as this series reveals past conflicts, it will help revitalize the reader's views of the American present. In that spirit, the American History Series is dedicated to the proposition that American history is more complicated, more fascinating, and more troubling than John Winthrop, Thomas Jefferson, Alexis de Tocqueville, or David Riesman ever dared to imagine.

John C. Chalberg
Consulting Editor

Introduction

"Many historians would say the frontier experience is the single most important factor in determining who we are today, the keystone in the edifice of America."

Perhaps once every generation there occurs an event or pattern of events so momentous that those living through it are never the same again. This defining moment shapes the generation, provides a bond tighter than family for those who share its experiences, and initiates its participants to a collective identity that others can only imagine. For survivors of the Great Depression, the Holocaust, or the Vietnam War, for example, life afterward was immeasurably, irrevocably changed. Though formative events are often catastrophic, they need not be. President John Kennedy's vision of a new Camelot united a generation in hope, made idealism viable once more, and, despite assassin's bullets and gossips' tongues, left those who were touched by that shining moment ready to serve in a way incomprehensible to the generation that followed.

A nation's character is forged over many generations. Yet as a nation we can point to defining attitudes and experiences: the personal courage and intellectual integrity of the founding fathers, the bloodshed and adherence to principle during the cataclysmic clashes of the Civil War, and the movement of our people west with the frontier. Of them all, many historians would say the frontier experience is the single most important factor in determining who we are today, the keystone in the edifice of America.

Unlike the Civil War, for instance, which rises to nearly equal dimensions of mythic and psychological importance, the frontier experience was repeated over and over again. It marked not one generation, but many. And as the frontier advanced and the experience was relived generation after generation, from Massachusetts to Indiana, from Virginia to Kentucky, and then to Missouri and thence on to California and Oregon, it pressed ever deeper into our national consciousness. Traces of it can be seen clearly today, just as physical signs remain along the Oregon Trail, for instance, where ruts are still clearly visible, worn into rock by the wheels of wagon after wagon after wagon. In addition, the frontier experience, more than any other, is nearly all-encompassing. Almost every dimension of our history touches on or is touched by the frontier: economics and politics, immigration and relations with the native American, technology and religion, foreign affairs and regional literature, the noblest heroism and the cruelest butchery.

Though quintessentially American, the frontier experience is also part of a larger pattern of events. Some historians argue that America—and its frontier—are part of a centuries-long process; the ocean was for European pioneers what the Appalachians were for late eighteenth-century Americans: a barrier to be crossed in the quest for something better. Certainly that goal of the "West," reached from whatever direction, is central to the American immigration experience. Europeans came west, Mexicans went to "El Norte," Chinese traveled to "Gam Sahn," lying far to the east, and Russian fur traders traveled south. Direction mattered little; the dream was all.

Only a century after the Proclamation of 1763 had attempted to pen up all this hope to the east of the Appalachians by placing a firm boundary between the lands white settlers could appropriate and those of the natives, the Pacific had been reached and the interior was being flooded with settlers. Within a generation—as small homesteaders turned to industrial farms, the telegraph provided almost instant knowledge about the markets, and the railroads offered easy transportation—this nation of westerers began to export its agricultural bounty. And, as this nation of immigrants began to feed our original homelands, we exported parts of our culture as well. Around the world, fascination with the West grew. Buffalo Bill Cody took his Wild West Show abroad to audiences including Queen Victoria, and a German, Karl May, began writing Western novels.

But if the frontier provided entertainment and opportunity for the rest of the world, it also gave those nations a means for interpreting our behavior. Europeans watched with horror that series of assassinations—of John Kennedy and his brother Bobby and Martin Luther King—and, struggling to understand, mused, "It must be the frontier. Americans love their guns. They are a nation of cowboys."

This mixture of hope and horror reflects the nature of the frontier experience. From the very beginning, the frontier has been a complex place, ambiguous in its goals and evoking ambivalent responses. Even Frederick Jackson Turner, writing of the character traits that emerged because of the frontier, recognized that

> To the frontier the American intellect owes its striking characteristics. That coarseness and strength combined with acuteness

and inquisitiveness; that practical, inventive turn of mind, quick to find expedients; that masterful grasp of material things, lacking in the artistic but powerful to effect great ends; that restless, nervous energy; that dominant individualism, working for good and for evil, and withal that buoyancy and exuberance which comes with freedom—these are the traits of the frontier.

These are not all ideal traits; Turner recognizes the boorish as well as the brave, the renegade as well as the pathfinder.

Repeatedly one can observe these complexities and contradictions. On the fur and gold frontiers, for example, we are used to thinking of the individual at work, perhaps with a partner, attempting to wrest riches from nature; on both, however, the individual was soon supplanted by the corporation, which had adequate capital to turn a haphazard operation into an efficient one. We are used to thinking of the frontier as an antisocial, certainly nonurban environment. Yet trappers' rendezvous and settlers' wagon trains provided opportunities for socializing as well as personal safety and, very early on, mining towns flourished, however briefly, and railheads and termini for cattle drives made urban beachheads amidst open country. Moreover, while some fled the constraints of society—and perhaps the long arm of the law—others, not only teachers and missionaries, steadfastly carried civilization west with them.

Generalizations become impossible. For example, although conflict is typically viewed as the archetypal pattern for Indian-white relations, neither race behaved monolithically. Indians, preferring French concepts of land use over British ones during colonial times, were drawn into European wars played out in American settings. Tribes chose sides and fought against each other. Over a hundred years later, the fratricidal pattern was repeated. On the Plains, because of the pressures resulting from the relocation of eastern tribes west, some, such as the Crows, saw the United States government as the lesser of two evils and joined forces with it against the Sioux. Similarly, it is impossible to generalize about the Western woman. Who *was* she? The Madonna of the Trail; the trapper's squaw; the New England wife of a forty-niner who stayed in California to make a mini-fortune baking pies when her husband fled back to the comforts of civilization; the entertainer, like Lola Montez and her Spider Dance; the missionary who married solely so she could go west to convert the Indians; or the female captive of the Indians who, when "rescued," refused to return to white society? Finally, it is impossible even to generalize about the dream. For while, to many, the frontier itself was a utopia, for others the forces it set in motion created the climate of despair or desperation that often spawns utopian visions.

Dreams may be the product of denial. And thus, the Mormon founding of the state of Deseret was a product of persecution elsewhere, the emergence of the Ghost Dance religion a response to white usurpation of Indian land, and the establishing of late nineteenth-century utopian communities an alternative to post-frontier society that no longer fulfilled promises perceived now as birthrights.

For, once the frontier had become embedded in our being, we had to make adjustments when it seemed to be gone. This is evident even in contemporary politics and culture. One of the frustrations with our modern foreign policy (in Bosnia and Somalia, for example) is that the "righteous violence" of our frontier past no longer seems viable. Since government "cowboys" led us into defeat in "Indian country" in Vietnam, it no longer seems possible for the United States, as solitary gunslinger, to right the world's wrongs. Teddy Roosevelt, borrowing traits from his friend Owen Wister's creation, the Virginian, could recommend "Walk softly but carry a big stick" and lead his Rough Riders up San Juan Hill. But modern presidents need to seek international consensus to do what seems right. This frustrating inability to act, to achieve clear and obvious solutions, may be one reason for the resurgence of popularity of Western films such as *Unforgiven* and *Posse*. While they may be more politically correct than earlier Westerns, as they integrate new views on race and gender, they still provide an affirmation that right triumphs and that the bad guys can not only be identified but defeated.

This book will concentrate on the social history of the frontier. However important they may be, dates and battles and treaties are not the sole stuff of history. Equally important are the artifacts of society: the Mormon handcart songs, unique cattle brands and twists of barbed wire, women's bloomers, the Montgomery Ward catalogue that was for homesteaders a "dream book" before becoming toilet paper, Sharp's rifles, Sibley tents, Wild West shows and dime novels and movies, letters and diaries and business documents. And while not all the selections in this book are overtly argumentative, points of view emerge clearly. Francis Chardon's monthly rat count, for example, speaks volumes about the harshness of life on the frontier; his frostbitten fingers de-romanticize the West; his was not a Thoreau-like return to the comfortable nature of Walden Pond. Similarly in Elaine Goodale Eastman's anguished description of Wounded Knee one can find the tortured self-doubt of good people of the time: How can an ostensibly civilized, benevolent society wreak such havoc on those it means to help?

The frontier is a topic of epic proportions. Its influence is widespread and long-lasting, even as modern historians examine aspects of which earlier historians were scarcely cognizant. Thus this book can promise its reader only to blaze a trail into the wilderness. The real journey of discovery must be a personal one, pushing further and further into the unknown. Each step leads to a new vista. And, as it was for many who advanced the frontier westward, the reward may not be in land or gold, but in the experience itself.

Mary Ellen Jones
Book Editor

CHAPTER 1

The Frontier Thesis

Chapter Preface

In 1893, the World's Columbian Exposition opened in Chicago. The fair, called by one critic "a creation . . . nearly allied in beauty to festal and imperial Rome," entertained throngs of visitors with the extraordinary and exciting: the best of architecture, technology, and city planning; a seventy-five-foot-high statue from France called "the Republic"; the miracle of public illumination by electricity; and the Darling of the Nile, the belly dancer Little Egypt.

Onto this stage stepped a young historian, Frederick Jackson Turner, to present to the American Historical Association his essay "The Significance of the Frontier in American History." Historian Henry Nash Smith later called it "the most influential piece of writing about the West produced during the nineteenth century." The essay's thesis was startlingly simple: "The existence of an area of free land, its continuous recession, and the advance of American settlement westward, explain American development. . . . The frontier is the line of most rapid and effective Americanization." This thesis directly countered the views of two then-dominant schools of historians, those interpreting U.S. history in terms of the slavery controversy and those explaining U.S. institutions as products of English—or Teutonic—"germs" planted in the New World.

Although the essay initially may have been overshadowed by the excitement of the exposition, it soon propelled Turner into a select group of historians of the ensuing century, historians like Henry Nash Smith, Howard Mumford Jones, Alfred W. Crosby, Jr. and Patricia Nelson Limerick, whose generalizations are sweepingly concrete, whose prose frequently borders on poetry, and whose ideas have the brilliant originality and elegant simplicity that compel the reader to utter with admiration and envy, "Why didn't *I* think of that?"

The essay also propelled Turner into a maelstrom of debate that has lasted through most of this century. Some, like Smith, admired Turner's thesis, seeing it as "moving from the plane of the economist's abstractions to a plane of metaphor, and even of myth," a myth of "rebirth, a regeneration, a rejuvenation of man and society." Smith cites a speech Turner made in 1896:

> [In the frontier] Americans had a safety valve for social danger, a bank account on which they might continually draw to meet losses. This was the vast unoccupied domain that stretched from the borders of the settled areas to the Pacific Ocean. . . . No grave social problem could exist while the wilderness at the

21

edge of civilizations opened wide its portals to all who were oppressed, to all who with strong arms and stout heart desired to hew out a home and a career for themselves. Here was an opportunity for social development continually to begin over again, wherever society gave signs of breaking into classes. Here was a magic fountain of youth in which America continually bathed and was rejuvenated.

But Turner had his critics as well. The very fact that he spent much of his career reworking and amplifying his thesis was for some the basis for criticism. For others, it was the substance of his ideas that posed problems. Howard Lamar in 1968, for instance, objected to the implications that a "discontinuity existed between America's rural past and its urban-industrial present." This, Lamar argued, made the thesis "useless as a guide for the present and future." In short, he believed that Turner's emphasis on pre-industrial America made his ideas irrelevant to modern, urban America. In 1987 Patricia Nelson Limerick observed that Turner's thesis, which appeared to unify the American experience, actually excluded more than it included:

Turner was, to put it mildly, ethnocentric and nationalistic. English-speaking white men were the stars of his story; Indians, Hispanics, French-Canadians, and Asians were at best supporting actors and at worst invisible. Nearly as invisible were women, of all ethnicities.

Turner, of course, was writing in and of his time; the catalytic event stimulating his thought was the 1890 declaration by the Bureau of the Census that no more free land existed; in effect, the frontier was closed. To some, this clearly punctuated conclusion of the first phase of American history was too precise; the Turner model was too tidy. Limerick, for example, suggests that if one "selects a defining characteristic of the frontier and then an associated event," there may be alternative termini for the frontier. For instance, if the criterion is the acquisition of contiguous lands, 1848, with the acquisition of Oregon and the Mexican territories, marks the end of the frontier. Or, if the criterion is the "workability of the West as a refuge for distinctive societies," the 1890 Mormon concession to the majority on the issue of polygamy marks the closing of the frontier. Such observations, of course, do not invalidate Turner's thesis. They do, however, demonstrate the rich variety of historical thought stimulated by his provocative idea.

Whatever the debate about the modern viability of Turner's thesis, its function as a catalyst for subsequent thought on the nature of American society has been invaluable. Decade by decade over the past century, Turner's ideas—and those of his critics and advocates—have led to new insights. This, as much as his original thesis, is the value of Turner's writing. For, as he proposed in 1891:

Each age writes the history of the past anew with reference to the conditions uppermost in its own time. . . . The aim of history, then, is to know the elements of the present by understanding what came into the present from the past. For the present is simply the developing past, the past the undeveloped present. . . . The antiquarian strives to bring back the past for the sake of the past; the historian strives to show the present to itself by revealing its origin from the past. The goal of the antiquarian is the dead past; the goal of the historian is the living present.

VIEWPOINT 1

"This perennial rebirth, this fluidity of American life, this expansion westward with its new opportunities, its continuous touch with the simplicity of primitive society, furnish the forces dominating American character."

The Significance of the Frontier in American History

Frederick Jackson Turner (1861-1932)

Frederick Jackson Turner was one of the most provocative of American historians. His essay "The Significance of the Frontier in American History" was read to the American Historical Society meeting in 1893. His premise was that "the existence of an area of free land, its continuous recession, and the advance of the American settlement westward, explained American development." This concept has since provided the basis for dialogue among historians of the American West.

———

In a recent bulletin of the Superintendent of the Census for 1890 appear these significant words: "Up to and including 1880 the country had a frontier of settlement, but at present the unsettled area has been so broken into by isolated bodies of settlement that there can hardly be said to be a frontier line. In the discussion of its extent, its westward movement, etc., it can not, therefore, any longer have a place in the census reports." This brief official statement marks the closing of a great historic movement. Up to our own day American history has been in a large degree the history of the colonization of the Great West. The existence of an area of free land, its continuous recession, and the advance of American settlement, westward, explain American development.

Behind institutions, behind constitutional forms and modifications, lie the vital forces that call these organs into life and shape them to meet changing conditions. The peculiarity of American institutions is the fact that they have been compelled to adapt themselves to the changes of an expanding people—to the changes involved in crossing a continent, in winning a wilderness, and in developing at each area of this progress out of the primitive economic and political conditions of the frontier into the complexity of city life. Said [the politician John C.] Calhoun in 1817, "We are great, and rapidly—I was about to say fearfully— growing!" So saying, he touched the distinguishing feature of American life. All peoples show development; the germ theory of politics has been sufficiently emphasized. In the case of most nations, however, the development has occurred in a limited area; and if the nation has expanded, it has met other growing peoples whom it has conquered. But in the case of the United States we have a different phenomenon. Limiting our attention to the Atlantic coast, we have the familiar phenomenon of the evolution of institutions in a limited area, such as the rise of representative government; the differentiation of simple colonial governments into complex organs; the progress from primitive industrial society, without division of labor, up to manufacturing civilization. But we have in addition to this a recurrence of the process of evolution in each western area reached in the process of expansion. Thus American development has exhibited not merely advance along a single line, but a return to primitive conditions on a continually advancing frontier line, and a new development for that area. American social development has been continually beginning over again on the frontier. This perennial rebirth, this fluidity of American life, this expansion westward with its new opportunities, its continuous touch with the simplicity of primitive society, furnish the forces dominating American character. The true point of view in the history of this nation is not the Atlantic coast, it is in the Great West. Even the slavery struggle, which is made so exclusive an object of attention by writers like Professor von Holst, occupies its important place in American history because of its relation to westward expansion.

In this advance, the frontier is the outer edge of the wave—the meeting point between savagery and civilization. Much has been written about the frontier from the point of view of border warfare and the chase, but as a field for the serious study of the economist and the historian it has been neglected.

The American frontier is sharply distinguished from the European frontier—a fortified boundary line running through dense populations. The most significant thing about the American frontier is that it lies at the hither edge of free land. In the census reports it is treated as the margin of that settlement which has a density of two or more to the square mile. . . .

The frontier is the line of most rapid and effective Americanization. The wilderness masters the colonist. It finds him a European in dress, industries, tools, modes of travel, and thought. It takes him from the railroad car and puts him in the birch canoe. It strips off the garments of civilization and arrays him in the hunting shirt and the moccasin. It puts him in the log cabin of the Cherokee and Iroquois and runs an Indian palisade around him. Before long he has gone to planting Indian corn and plowing with a sharp stick; he shouts the war cry and takes the scalp in orthodox Indian fashion. In short, at the frontier the environment is at first too strong for the man. He must accept the conditions which it furnishes, or perish, and so he fits himself into the Indian clearings and follows the Indian trails. Little by little he transforms the wilderness, but the outcome is not the old Europe, not simply the development of Germanic germs, any more than the first phenomenon was a case of reversion to the Germanic mark. The fact is that here is a new product that is American. At first, the frontier was the Atlantic coast. It was the frontier of Europe in a very real sense. Moving westward, the frontier became more and more American. As successive terminal moraines result from successive glaciations, so each frontier leaves its traces behind it, and when it becomes a settled area the region still partakes of the frontier characteristics. Thus the advance of the frontier has meant a steady movement away from the influence of Europe, a steady growth of independence on American lines. And to study this advance, the men who grew up under these conditions, and the political, economic, and social results of it, is to study the really American part of our history.

In the course of the seventeenth century the frontier was advanced up the Atlantic river courses, just beyond the "fall line," and the tidewater region became the settled area. In the first half of the eighteenth century another advance occurred. Traders followed the Delaware and Shawnee Indians to the Ohio as early as the end of the first quarter of the century. Governor Spotswood, of Virginia, made an expedition in 1714 across the Blue Ridge.

Railroads played a major role in the expansion of the Western frontier. In this 1869 photograph, the owners of the Union Pacific and Central Pacific railroads shake hands in Promontory Point, Utah, after driving the last spike to complete the new transcontinental railroad linking East with West.

The end of the first quarter of the century saw the advance of the Scotch-Irish and the Palatine Germans up the Shenandoah Valley into the western part of Virginia, and along the Piedmont region of the Carolinas. The Germans in New York pushed the frontier of settlement up the Mohawk to German Flats. In Pennsylvania the town of Bedford indicates the line of settlement. Settlements had begun on New River, a branch of the Kanawha, and on the sources of the Yadkin and French Broad. The King attempted to arrest the advance by his proclamation of 1763, forbidding settlement beyond the sources of the rivers flowing into the Atlantic; but in vain. In the period of the Revolution the frontier crossed the Alleghenies into Kentucky and Tennessee, and the upper waters of the Ohio were settled. When the first census was taken in 1790, the continuous settled area was bounded by a line which ran near the coast of Maine, and included New England except a portion of Vermont and New Hampshire, New York along the Hudson and up the Mohawk about Schenectady, eastern and southern Pennsylvania, Virginia well across the Shenandoah Valley, and the Carolinas and eastern Georgia. Beyond this region of continuous settlement were the small settled areas of Kentucky and Tennessee, and the Ohio, with the mountains intervening between them and the Atlantic area, thus giving a new and important character to the frontier. The isolation of the region increased its peculiarly American tendencies, and the need of transportation facilities to connect it with the East called out important schemes of internal improvement, which will be noted farther on. The "West," as a self-conscious section, began to evolve.

From decade to decade distinct advances of the frontier occurred. By the census of 1820 the settled area included Ohio, southern Indiana and Illinois, southeastern Missouri, and about one-half of Louisiana. This settled area had surrounded Indian areas, and the management of these tribes became an object of political concern. The frontier region of the time lay along the Great Lakes, where [John Jacob] Astor's American Fur Company operated in the Indian trade, and beyond the Mississippi, where Indian traders extended their activity even to the Rocky Mountains; Florida also furnished frontier conditions. The Mississippi River region was the scene of typical frontier settlements.

The rising steam navigation on western waters, the opening of the Erie Canal, and the westward extension of cotton culture added five frontier states to the Union in this period. [Sociologist Francis J.] Grund, writing in 1836, declares: "It appears then that the universal disposition of Americans to emigrate to the western wilderness, in order to enlarge their dominion over inanimate nature, is the actual result of an expansive power which is inherent in them, and which by continually agitating all classes of society is constantly throwing a large portion of the whole population on the extreme confines of the State, in order to gain space for its development. Hardly is a new State or Territory formed before the same principle manifests itself again and gives rise to a further emigration; and so is it destined to go on until a physical barrier must finally obstruct its progress."

In the middle of this century the line indicated by the present eastern boundary of Indian Territory, Nebraska, and Kansas marked the frontier of the Indian country. Minnesota and Wisconsin still exhibited frontier conditions, but the distinctive frontier of the period is found in California, where the gold discoveries had sent a sudden tide of adventurous miners, and in Oregon, and the settlements in Utah. As the frontier had leaped over the Alleghenies, so now it skipped the Great Plains and the Rocky Mountains; and in the same way that the advance of the frontiersman beyond the Alleghenies had caused the rise of important questions of transportation and internal improvement, so now the settlers beyond the Rocky Mountains needed means of communication with the East, and in the furnishing of these arose the settlement of the Great Plains and the development of still another kind of frontier life. Railroads, fostered by land grants, sent an increasing tide of immigrants into the Far West. The United

States Army fought a series of Indian wars in Minnesota, Dakota, and the Indian Territory.

By 1880 the settled area had been pushed into northern Michigan, Wisconsin, and Minnesota, along Dakota rivers, and in the Black Hills region, and was ascending the rivers of Kansas and Nebraska. The development of mines in Colorado had drawn isolated frontier settlements into that region, and Montana and Idaho were receiving settlers. The frontier was found in these mining camps and the ranches of the Great Plains. The superintendent of the census for 1890 reports, as previously stated, that the settlements of the West lie so scattered over the regions that there can no longer be said to be a frontier line.

Frontiers Reflect Natural Boundaries

In these successive frontiers we find natural boundary lines which have served to mark and to affect the characteristics of the frontiers, namely: the "fall line"; the Allegheny Mountains; the Mississippi; the Missouri where its direction approximates north and south; the line of arid lands, approximately the ninety-ninth meridian; and the Rocky Mountains. The fall line marked the frontier of the seventeenth century; the Alleghenies that of the eighteenth; the Mississippi that of the first quarter of the nineteenth; the Missouri that of the middle of this century (omitting the California movement); and the belt of the Rocky Mountains and the arid tract, the present frontier. Each was one by a series of Indian wars.

At the Atlantic frontier one can study the germs of processes repeated at each successive frontier. We have the complex European life sharply precipitated by the wilderness into the simplicity of primitive conditions. The first frontier had to meet its Indian question, its question of the disposition of the public domain, of the means of intercourse with older settlements, of the extension of political organization, of religious and educational activity. And the settlement of these and similar questions for one frontier served as a guide for the next. The American student . . . may study the origin of our land policies in the colonial land policy; he may see how the system grew by adapting the statutes of the customs of the successive frontiers. He may see how the mining experience in the lead regions of Wisconsin, Illinois, and Iowa was applied to the mining laws of the Sierras, and how our Indian policy has been a series of experimentations on successive frontiers. Each tier of new States has found in the older ones material for its constitutions. Each frontier has made similar contributions to American characters. . . .

But with all these similarities there are essential differences, due to the place element and the time element. It is evident that the farming frontier of the Mississippi Valley presents different conditions from the mining frontier of the Rocky Mountains. The frontier reached by the Pacific Railroad, surveyed into rectangles, guarded by the United States Army, and recruited by the daily immigrant ship, moves forward at a swifter pace and in a different way than the frontier reached by the birch canoe or the pack horse. . . .

The United States lies like a huge page in the history of society. Line by line as we read this continental page from West to East we find the record of social evolution. It begins with the Indian and the hunter; it goes on to tell of the disintegration of savagery by the entrance of the trader, the pathfinder of civilization; we read the annals of the pastoral stage in ranch life; the exploitation of the soil by the raising of unrotated crops of corn and wheat in sparsely settled farming communities; the intensive culture of the denser farm settlement; and finally the manufacturing organization with city and factory system. This page is familiar to the student of census statistics, but how little of it has been used by our historians. Particularly in eastern States this page is a palimpsest. What is now a manufacturing State was in an earlier decade an area of intensive farming. Earlier yet it had been a wheat area, and still earlier the "range" had attracted the cattle-herder. Thus Wisconsin, now developing manufacture, is a State with varied agricultural interests. But earlier it was given over to almost exclusive grain-raising, like North Dakota at the present time.

Each of these areas has had an influence in our economic and political history; the evolution of each into a higher stage has worked political transformations. . . .

Successive Waves of Human Frontiers

The Atlantic frontier was compounded of fisherman, fur-trader, miner, cattle-raiser, and farmer. Excepting the fisherman, each type of industry was on the march toward the West, impelled by an irresistible attraction. Each passed in successive waves across the continent. Stand at Cumberland Gap and watch the procession of civilization marching single file—the buffalo following the trail to the salt springs, the Indian, the fur-trader and hunter, the cattle-raiser, the pioneer farmer—and the frontier has passed by. Stand at South Pass in the Rockies a century later and see the same procession with wider intervals between. The unequal rate of advance compels us to distinguish the frontier into the trader's frontier, the rancher's frontier, or the miner's frontier, and the farmer's frontier. When the mines and the cowpens were still near the fall line the traders' pack trains were tinkling across the Alleghenies, and the French on the Great Lakes were fortifying their posts, alarmed by the British trader's birch canoe. When the trappers scaled the Rockies, the farmer was still near the mouth of the Missouri.

Why was it that the Indian trader passed so rapidly across the continent? What effects followed from the trader's frontier? The trade was coeval with American discovery. The Norsemen, Vespuccius, Verrazani, Hudson, John Smith, all trafficked for furs. The Plymouth Pilgrims settled in Indian cornfields, and their first return cargo was of beaver and lumber. The records of the various New England colonies show how steadily exploration was carried into the wilderness by this trade. What is true for New England is, as would be expected, even plainer for the rest of the colonies. All along the coast from Maine to Georgia the Indian trade opened up the river courses. Steadily the trader passed westward, utilizing the older lines of French trade. The Ohio, the Great Lakes, the Mississippi, and the Platte, the lines of western advance, were ascended by traders. They found the passes in the Rocky Mountains and guided Lewis and Clark, Frémont, and Bidwell. The explanation of the rapidity of this advance is connected with the effects of the trader on the Indian. The trading post left the unarmed tribes at the mercy of those that had purchased firearms—a truth which the Iroquois Indians wrote in blood, and so the remote and unvisited tribes gave eager welcome to the trader. "The savages," wrote La Salle, "take better care of us French than of their own children; from us only can they get guns and goods." This accounts for the trader's power and rapidity of his advance. Thus the disintegrating forces of civilization entered the wilderness. Every river valley and Indian trail became a fissure in Indian society, and so that society became honeycombed. Long before the pioneer farmer appeared on the scene, primitive Indian life had passed away. The farmers met Indians armed with guns. The trading frontier, while steadily undermining Indian power by making the tribes ultimately dependent on the whites, yet, through its sale of guns, gave to the Indian increased power of resistance to the farming frontier. French colonization was dominated by its trading frontier; English colonization by its farming frontier. There was an antagonism between the two frontiers as between the two nations. Said Duquesne to the Iroquois, "Are you ignorant of the difference between the king of England and the king of France? Go see the forts that our king has established and you will see that you can still hunt under their very walls. They have been placed for your advantage in places which you frequent. The English, on the contrary, are no sooner in possession of a place than the game is driven away. The forest falls before them as they advance, and the soil is laid bare so that you can scarce find the wherewithal to erect a shelter for the night."

31

And yet, in spite of this opposition of the interests of the trader and the farmer, the Indian trade pioneered the way for civilization. The buffalo trail became the Indian trail, and this became the trader's "trace"; the trails widened into roads, and the roads into turnpikes, and these in turn were transformed into railroads. The same origin can be shown for the railroads of the South, the Far West, and the Dominion of Canada. The trading posts reached by these trails were on the sites of Indian villages which had been placed in positions suggested by nature; and these trading posts, situated so as to command the water systems of the country, have grown into such cities as Albany, Pittsburgh, Detroit, Chicago, St. Louis, Council Bluffs, and Kansas City. Thus civilization in America has followed the arteries made by geology, pouring an ever richer tide through them, until at last the slender paths of aboriginal intercourse have been broadened and interwoven into the complex mazes of modern commercial lines; the wilderness has been interpenetrated by lines of civilization growing ever more numerous. It is like the steady growth of a complex nervous system for the originally simple, inert continent. If one would understand why we are today one nation, rather than a collection of isolated States, he must study this economic and social consolidation of the country. . . .

New Order of Americanism

From the time the mountains rose between the pioneer and the seaboard, a new order of Americanism arose. The West and the East began to get out of touch of each other. The settlements from the sea to the mountains kept connection with the rear and had a certain solidarity. But the over-mountain men grew more independent. The East took a narrow view of American advance, and nearly lost these men. Kentucky and Tennessee history bears abundant witness to the truth of this statement. The East began to try to hedge and limit westward expansion. Though Webster could declare that the were no Alleghenies in his politics, yet in politics in general they were a very solid factor.

The exploitation of the beasts took hunter and trader to the west, the exploitation of the grasses took the rancher west, and the exploitation of the virgin soil of the river valleys and prairies attracted the farmer. Good soils have been the most continuous attraction to the farmer's frontier. The land hunger of the Virginians drew them down the rivers into Carolina, in early colonial days; the search for soils took the Massachusetts men to Pennsylvania and to New York. As the eastern lands were taken up migration flowed across them to the west. Daniel Boone, the great backwoodsman, who combined the occupations of hunter, trader, cattle-raiser, farmer, and surveyor—learning, probably from the traders, of the fertility of the lands of the upper Yadkin, where the traders were wont to rest as they took their way to the Indians—left his Pennsylvania home with his father, and passed down the Great Valley road to that stream. Learning from a trader of the game and rich pastures of Kentucky, he pioneered the way for the farmers to that region. Thence he passed to the frontier of Missouri, where his settlement was long a landmark on the frontier. Here again he helped to open the way for civilization, find salt licks, and trails, and land. His son was among the earliest trappers in the passes of the Rocky Mountains, and his party are said to have been the first to camp on the present site of Denver. His grandson, Colonel A. J. Boone, of Colorado, was a power among the Indians of the Rocky Mountains, and was appointed an agent by the government. Kit Carson's mother was a Boone. Thus this family epitomizes the backwoodsmen's advance across the continent.

The Gift Outright

The land was ours before we were the land's.
She was our land more than a hundred years
Before we were her people. She was ours
In Massachusetts, In Virginia,
But we were England's, still colonials,
Possessing what we still were unpossessed by,
Possessed by what we now no more possessed.
Something we were withholding made us weak
Until we found out that it was ourselves
We were withholding from our land of living.
And forthwith found salvation in surrender.
Such as we were we gave ourselves outright
(The deed of gift was many deeds of war)
To the land vaguely realizing westward,
But still unstoried, artless, unenhanced,
Such as she was, such as she would become.

From *The Poetry of Robert Frost*, edited by Edward Connery Lathan. Copyright © 1942 by Robert Frost. Copyright © 1970 by Lesley Frost Ballantine. Copyright © 1969 by Henry Holt and Company, Inc. Reprinted by permission of Henry Holt and Co., Inc.

The farmer's advance came in a distinct series of waves. In Peck's *New Guide to the West*, published in Boston in 1837, occurs this suggestive passage:

Generally, in all the western settlements, three classes, like the waves of the ocean, have rolled one after the other. First comes the pioneer, who depends for the subsistence of his family chiefly upon the natural growth of vegetation, called the "range," and the proceeds of hunting. His implements of agriculture are rude, chiefly of his own make, and his efforts directed mainly to a crop of corn and a "truck patch." The last is a rude garden for growing cabbage, beans, corn for roasting ears, cucumbers, and potatoes. A log cabin, and, occasionally, a stable and corn-crib, and a field of a dozen acres, the timber girdled or "deadened," and fenced, are enough for his occupancy. It is quite immaterial whether he ever becomes the owner of the soil. He is the occupant for the time being, pays no rent, and feels as independent as the "lord of the manor." With a horse, cow, and one or two breeders of swine, he strikes into the woods with his family, and becomes the founder of a new county, or perhaps state. He builds his cabin, gathers around him a few other families of similar tastes and habits, and occupies till the range is somewhat subdued, and hunting a little precarious, or, which is more frequently the case, till the neighbors crowd around, roads, bridges, and fields annoy him, and he lacks elbow room. The preemption law enables him to dispose of his cabin and cornfield to the next class of emigrants; and, to employ his own figures, he "breaks for the high timber," "clears out for the New Purchase," or migrates to Arkansas or Texas, to work the same process over.

The next class of emigrants purchase the lands, add field to field, clear out the roads, throw rough bridges over the streams, put up hewn log houses with glass windows and brick or stone chimneys, occasionally plant orchards, build mills, schoolhouses, courthouses, etc., and exhibit the picture and forms of plain, frugal, civilized life.

Another wave rolls on. The men of capital and enterprise come. The settler is ready to sell out and take the advantage of the rise in property, push farther into the interior and become, himself, a man of capital, and enterprise in turn. The small village rises to a spacious town or city; substantial edifices of brick, extensive fields, orchards, gardens, colleges, and churches are seen. Broad cloths, silks, leghorns, crapes, and all the refinements, luxuries, elegancies, frivolities, and fashions are in vogue. Thus wave after wave is rolling westward; the real El Dorado is still farther on. . . .

Consequences of the Frontier

Omitting those of the pioneer farmers who move from the love of adventure, the advance of the more steady farmer is easy to understand. Obviously the immigrant was attracted by the cheap lands of the frontier, and even the native farmer felt their influence strongly. Year by year the farmers who lived on soil whose returns were diminished by unrotated crops were offered the virgin soil of the frontier at nominal prices. Their growing families demanded more lands, and these were dear. The competition of the unexhausted, cheap, and easily tilled prairie lands compelled the farmer either to go west and continue the exhaustion of the soil on a new frontier, or to adopt intensive culture. Thus the census of 1890 shows, in the Northwest, many counties in which there is an absolute or a relative decrease of population. These States have been sending farmers to advance the frontier on the plains, and have themselves begun to turn to intensive farming and to manufacture. A decade before this, Ohio had shown the same transition stage. Thus the demand for land and the love of wilderness freedom drew the frontier ever onward.

Having now roughly outlined the various kinds of frontiers, and their modes of advance, chiefly from the point of view of the frontier itself, we may next inquire what were the influences on the East and on the Old World. A rapid enumeration of some of the more noteworthy effects is all that I have time for.

First, we note that the frontier promoted the formation of a composite nationality for the American people. The coast was preponderantly English, but the later tides of continental immigration flowed across the free lands. This was the case from the earlier colonial days. The Scotch-Irish and the Palatine Germans, or "Pennsylvania Dutch," furnished the dominant element in the stock of the colonial frontier. With these peoples were also the freed indentured servants, or redemptioners, who at the expiration of their time of service passed to the frontier. Governor Spotswood of Virginia writes in 1717, "The inhabitants of our frontiers are composed generally of such as have been transported hither as servants, and being out of their time, settle themselves where land is to be taken up and that will produce the neccessarys of life with little labour." Very generally these redemptioners were of non-English stock. In the crucible of the frontier the immigrants were Americanized, liberated, and fused into a mixed race, English in neither nationality nor characteristics. . . .

In another way the advance of the frontier decreased our dependence on England. The coast, particularly of the South, lacked diversified industries, and was dependent on England for the bulk of its supplies. In the South there was even dependence on the Northern colonies for articles of food. Governor Glenn, of South Carolina, writes in the middle of the eighteenth century: "Our trade with New York and Philadelphia was of this sort, draining us of all the little money and bills we could gather from other places for their bread, flour, beer, hams, bacon, and other things of their produce, all which, except beer, our new townships begin to supply us with, which are settled with the very industrious and thriving Germans. This no doubt diminishes the number of shipping and the appearance of our trade, but it is far from being a detriment to us." Before long the frontier created a demand for merchants. As it retreated from the coast it became less and less possible for England to bring her supplies directly to the consumer's wharfs, and carry away staple crops, and staple crops began to give way to diversified agriculture for a time. The effect of this phase of the frontier action upon the northern section is perceived when we realize how the advance of the frontier aroused seaboard cities like Boston, New York, and Baltimore to engage in rivalry for what Washington called "the extensive and valuable trade of a rising empire."

Frontier-Inspired Legislation

The legislation which most developed the powers of the national government, and played the largest part in its activity, was conditioned on the frontier. Writers have discussed the subjects of tariff, land, and internal improvement, as subsidiary to the slavery question. But when American history comes to be rightly viewed it will be seen that the slavery question is an incident. In the period from the end of the first half of the present century to the close of the Civil War, slavery rose to primary, but far from exclusive, importance. But this does not justify Dr. von Holst (to take an example) in treating our constitutional history in its formative period down to 1828 in a single volume, giving six volumes chiefly to the history of slavery from 1828 to 1861, under the title "Constitutional History of the Untied States." The growth of nationalism and the evolution of the American political institutions were dependent on the advance of the frontier. Even so recent a writer as Rhodes, in his "History of the United States since the Compromise of 1850," has treated the legislation called out by the western advance as incidental to the slavery struggle.

This is a wrong perspective. The pioneer needed the goods of the coast, and so the grand series of internal improvement and railroad legislation began, with potent nationalizing effects. Over internal improvements occurred great debates, in which grave constitutional questions were discussed. Sectional groupings appear in the votes, profoundly significant for the historian. Loose construction increased as the nation marched westward. But the West was not content with bringing the farm to the factory. Under the lead of [politician and orator Henry] Clay—"Harry of the West"—protective tariffs were passed, with the cry of bringing the factory to the farm. The disposition of the public lands was a third important subject of national legislation influenced by the frontier.

The public domain has been a force of profound importance in the nationalization and development of the government. The effects of the struggle of the landed and the landless States, and of the Ordinance of 1787, need no discussion. Administratively the frontier called out some of the highest and most vitalizing activities of the general government. The purchase of Louisiana was perhaps the constitutional turning point in the history of the Republic, inasmuch as it afforded both a new area for national legislation and the occasion of the downfall of the policy of strict construction. But the purchase of Louisiana was called out by frontier needs and demands. As frontier States accrued to the Union the national power grew. In a speech on the dedication of the Calhoun monument Mr. Lamar explained: "In 1789 the States were the creators of the Federal Government; in 1861 the Federal Government was the creator of a large majority of the States."

When we consider the public domain from the point of view of the sale and disposal of the public lands we are again brought face to face with the frontier. The policy of the United States in dealing with its lands is in sharp contrast with the European system of scientific administration. Efforts to make this domain a source of revenue, and to withhold it from emigrants in order that settlement might be compact, were in vain. The jealousy and the fears of the East were powerless in the face of the demands of the frontiersmen. John Quincy Adams was obliged to confess: "My own system of administration, which was to make the national domain the inexhaustible fund for progressive and unceasing internal improvement, has failed." The reason is obvious: a system of administration was not what the West demanded: it wanted land. . . .

It is safe to say that the legislation with regard to land, tariff, and internal improvements—the American system of the nationalizing Whig party—was conditioned on frontier ideas and needs. But it was not merely in legislative action that the frontier worked against the sectionalism of the coast. The economic and social characteristics of the frontier worked against sectionalism. The men of the frontier had closer resemblances to the Middle region than to either of the other sections. Pennsylvania had been the seed-plot of frontier emigration, and, although she passed on her settlers along the Great Valley into the west of Virginia and the Carolinas, yet the industrial society of these Southern frontiersmen was always more like that of the Middle region than like that of the tidewater portion of the South, which later came to spread its industrial type throughout the South.

The Middle region, entered by New York harbor, was an open door to all Europe. The tidewater part of the South represented typical Englishmen, modified by a warm climate and servile labor, and living in baronial fashion on great plantations; New England stood for a special English movement—Puritanism. The Middle region was less English than the other sections. It had a wide mixture of nationalities, a varied society, the mixed town and county system of local government, a varied economic life, many religious sects. In short, it was a region mediating between

New England and the South, and the East and the West. It represented that composite nationality which the contemporary United States exhibits, that juxtaposition of non-English groups, occupying a valley or a little settlement, and presenting reflections of the map of Europe in their variety. It was democratic and non-sectional, if not national; "easy, tolerant, and contented"; rooted strongly in material prosperity. It was typical of the modern United States. It was least sectional, not only because it lay between North and South, but also because with no barriers to shut out its frontiers from its settled region, and with a system of connecting waterways, the Middle region mediated between East and West as well as between North and South. Thus it became the typically American region. Even the New Englander, who was shut out from the frontier by the Middle region, tarrying in New York or Pennsylvania on his westward march, lost the acuteness of his sectionalism on the way. . . .

The Frontier Transformed American Democracy

It was this nationalizing tendency of the West that transformed the democracy of Jefferson into the national republicanism of Monroe and the democracy of Andrew Jackson. The West of the War of 1812, the West of Clay, and Benton and Harrison, and Andrew Jackson, shut off by the Middle States and the mountains from the coast sections, had a solidarity of its own with national tendencies. On the tide of the Father of Waters, North and South met and mingled into a nation. Interstate migration went steadily on—a process of cross-fertilization of ideas and institutions. The fierce struggle of the sections over slavery on the western frontier does not diminish the truth of this statement; it proves the truth of it. Slavery was a sectional trait that would not down, but in the West it could not remain sectional. It was the greatest of frontiersmen who declared: "I believe this Government can not endure permanently half slave and half free. It will become all of one thing or all of the other." Nothing works for nationalism like intercourse within the nation. Mobility of population is death to localism, and the western frontier worked irresistibly in unsettling population. The effect reached back from the frontier and affected profoundly the Atlantic coast and even the Old World.

But the most important effect of the frontier has been in the promotion of democracy here and in Europe. As has been indicated the frontier is productive of individualism. Complex society is precipitated by the wilderness into a kind of primitive organization based on the family. The tendency is anti-social. It produces antipathy to control, and particularly to any direct control. The tax-gatherer is viewed as a representative of oppression. Professor Osgood, in an able article, has pointed out that the frontier conditions prevalent in the colonies are important factors in the explanation of the American Revolution, where individual liberty was sometimes confused with absence of all effective government. The same conditions aid in explaining the difficulty of instituting a strong government in the period of the confederacy. The frontier individualism has from the beginning promoted democracy. . . .

So long as free land exists, the opportunity for a competency exists, and economic power secures political power. But the democracy born of free land, strong in selfishness and individualism, intolerant of administrative experience and education, and pressing individual liberty beyond its proper bounds, has its dangers as well as its benefits. Individualism in America has allowed a laxity in regard to governmental affairs which has rendered possible the spoils system and all the manifest evils that follow from the lack of a highly developed civic spirit. . . .

From the conditions of frontier life came intellectual traits of profound importance. The works of travelers along each frontier from colonial days onward describe certain common traits, and these traits have, while softening down, still persisted as survivals in the place of their origin, even when a higher social organization succeeded. The result is that to the frontier the American intellect owes its striking characteristics. That coarseness and strength combined with acuteness and inquisitiveness; that practical, inventive turn of mind, quick to find expedients; that masterful grasp of material things, lacking in the artistic but powerful to effect great ends; that restless, nervous energy; that dominant individualism, working for good and for evil, and withal that buoyancy and exuberance which comes with freedom—these are traits of the frontier, or traits called out elsewhere because of the existence of the frontier. Since the days when the fleet of Columbus sailed into the waters of the New World, America has been another name for opportunity, and the people of the United States have taken their tone from the incessant expansion which has not only been open but has even been forced upon them. He would be a rash prophet who should assert that the expansive character of American life has now entirely ceased. Movement has been its dominant fact, and, unless this training has no effect upon a people, the American energy will continually demand a wider field for its exercise. But never again will such gifts of free land offer themselves. For a moment, at the frontier, the bonds of custom are broken and unrestraint is triumphant. There is not *tabula rasa*. The stubborn American environment there with its imperious summons to accept its conditions; the inherited ways of doing things are also there; and yet, in spite of environment, and in spite of custom, each frontier did indeed furnish a new field of opportunity, a gate of escape from the bondage of the past; and freshness, and confidence, and scorn of older society, impatience of its restraints and its ideas, and indifference to its lessons, have accompanied the frontier. What the Mediterranean Sea was to the Greeks, breaking the bond of custom, offering new experiences, calling out new institutions and activities, that, and more, the ever retreating frontier has been to the United States directly, and to the nations of Europe more remotely. And now, four centuries from the discovery of America, at the end of a hundred years of life under the Constitution, the frontier has gone, and with its going has closed the first period of American history.

VIEWPOINT 2

"The frontier hypothesis needs painstaking revision. By what it fails to mention, the theory today disqualifies itself as an adequate guide to American development."

The Turner Thesis is Dated and Provincial

George Wilson Pierson (1904-)

George Wilson Pierson, long a professor at Yale University, launched one of the first significant assaults on Frederick Jackson Turner's frontier thesis. The following viewpoint, written in 1942, remains a cogent critique. Although Pierson directly criticizes Turner's "emotion," his "too-literary" style, and his "hazy thinking," his most serious objection is that Turner ignores the economic concerns of post-industrial America. Pierson questions the advisability of basing so much of the interpretation of American society on the frontier. What happens to our understanding of America, for instance, now that it is gone? he asks. He asserts that Turner should have given more credit to individual character in the shaping of America.

How much of Frederick Jackson Turner's frontier hypothesis is reliable and useful today? This problem has begun to trouble economists, sociologists, geographers, and most of all the teachers of graduate students in the field of American history.

For how shall we account for the industrial revolution by the

Excerpted from "The Frontier and American Institutions: A Criticism of the Turner Theory," by George Wilson Pierson, *New England Quarterly* 15 (June 1942): 224-55. Reprinted by permission of the author.

frontier? Do American music and architecture come from the woods? Did American cattle? Were our religions born of the contemplation of untamed nature? Has science, poetry, or even democracy, its cradle in the wilderness? Did literature grow fertile with innovation in the open spaces? Above all, what happens to intellectual history if the environment be all?

The predicament of the scholar, who has been living in a comfortable frontier philosophy, is beginning to attract some attention. Nor may we comfort ourselves with the assurance that ours is a purely academic debate. For frontier legends of one kind or another have now so permeated American thought as to threaten drastic consequences. Have not our most influential journalists and statesmen for some time been ringing *pessimistic* changes on the theme of "lost frontier," "lost safety-valve," "lost opportunity"? Such convictions can lead to legislation. In Congress the underlying issue could shortly be: was there but one economic frontier, was it really a "safety-valve," and are both now gone? The cultural historian meanwhile asks: is it true that the frontier was the "line of most rapid and effective Americanization"? More particularly, since we are now trying to define and safeguard the "American way of life," what share did the "frontier" have in its creation, and to what cultural influences must we henceforth look for its preservation?. . .

General Criticism

First, let me say emphatically that it would seem small-minded to forget or to depreciate the inspiration that these essays originally offered to historians. Nor does it seem that we, of half a century later, have yet heard arguments that would warrant us in discarding the celebrated hypothesis entirely, out of hand. Too much of Turner's interpretation still seems reasonable and corresponding to fact. . . . The poetic insights and the masterful grasp of an understanding mind are hardly to be disguised. No blanket repudiation is therefore here to be proposed.

On the other hand, Turner himself did make a number of flat-footed and dogmatic statements, did put forward some highly questionable interpretations, did on occasion guess and not verify, did exaggerate—and stick for more than twenty years to the exaggerations. Hence it would seem that, however badly the master may have been served by his students and continuers in other particulars these followers have been made the scapegoats a little too hastily. For they have not alone been responsible for the palpable errors and exaggerations that many of the rising generation recognize in the frontier theory as it is stated and applied today. At least they did not invent the safety-valve theory that now looks so dubious; they didn't misquote when they attributed political invention, and most of the reforms and the reformers, to the frontier; they weren't the first local and national patriots. In his work with his students, Turner seems to have been modest and tentative and open-minded to a degree; but in his essays he could be and was as inclusive and sweeping as any have been since.

What were the statements and attitudes which we regard as extreme or with which we would disagree?. . . Let me conclude with a brief organization of the most cogent reasons for regarding Turner's original doctrine on the frontier and American institutions as defective and in need of repair.

To begin with the details and proceed to the general, it seems first of all necessary to suggest that—whatever may later be decided about Turner's theory—his evidence and proofs leave much to be desired. I am not here referring to our difficulty in accepting Turner's reasons for believing that the frontier stimulated invention, liberal ideas, educational improvements, or humanitarian reforms—a difficulty that remains substantial enough in itself. Rather, it is the quantity of his evidence to which I would now call attention. How few were his concrete examples, and how often he would repeat them is really astonishing. . . . Undoubtedly, Turner was more interested in discovering than in proving. . . .

It is dangerous and ungenerous, I acknowledge, for a man living in a later climate of opinion to disparage the attitude of an earlier day. But since our problem concerns the *present applicability and future usefulness* of these frontier essays, certain assumptions and definitions cannot be allowed to pass without challenge.

Some Specific Objections

As has been pointed out, first of all, the essays are in a high degree unsatisfactory in clarity, or definition. Turner's Master Force is defined and used as area, as population, as process. As if such inharmonious and confusing interpretations were not sufficiently inclusive, this force is then made to cover soil and mineral resources as well—and at times everything Western, or pre-industrial, or nonEuropean! I think it fair to say that the word *frontier* has been, and will be found again, a Pandora's box of trouble to historians, when opened to such wide interpretation.

Again, there seems to be haziness in the statement of *means*, and real doubt as to many of the *results* claimed for the frontier. At moments the wilderness, and even the flow of our population westward, seem to have been destructive rather than constructive experiences. And when the rebuilding is scrutinized, the proportion of invention looks surprisingly small. In particular, the contribution of the frontier to our educational, economic, and political institutions needs cautious reappraisal.

Once again, the emotional attitudes or assumptions of the author—and of his generation?—color his essays unmistakably. It would have been strange had they not done so. No personal censure is therefore intended. On the other hand, for the interpretation of American history in 1942, the emphasis of 1893 may become a serious handicap; it may even obscure or distort the elements in the theory that are still most meaningful. To be specific, the frontier hypothesis seems—as has been indicated several times already—too optimistic, too romantic, too provincial, and too nationalistic to be reliable in any survey of world history or study in comparative civilization. And it is too narrowly sectional and materialistic—in the sense of assigning deterministic forces to physical environment—to seem any longer a satisfactory gauge for internal cause-measurements. . . .

At an earlier point in the argument, the migration factor was isolated—as a sort of foreign substance—out of the frontier concept; and it was suggested that, at the least, a comparison with city-ward movements and with migrations the world around is in order. It now seems pertinent to suggest the extension of such comparisons from migration to the *whole story of settlement* or environmental adjustment in South America, Australia, and Africa. Did comparable situations always produce comparable results? Moreover, if we repeat such comparisons *within* the American experience, do we really find much similarity between the frontiers of Colonial Massachusetts, the Mississippi Delta, the Plains, and the mining country? If not, it would appear that the applicability of Turner's frontier hypothesis is far more limited than has been supposed.

Along another line of thought, I have suggested that Turner's views were deterministic. They were almost fatalistic. Again and again one gets the impression that western man was in the grip of overpowering forces. "The people of the United States have taken their tone from the incessant expansion which has not only been open but has even been forced upon them."

Now what makes this determinism particularly questionable is the fact that it is materialistic, yet in a high degree confused and cloudy in its statement of causes. Turner has been attacked by the economic determinists for not regarding commercialism, industrialism, and capitalism as more important than the continent—and the frontier essays certainly pay far too little attention to the commercial character of nineteenth-century American society, East *or* West. This school of critics is also quite correct in labelling Turner a geographer and a sociologist rather than a champion of the Marxian dialectic or interpretation. Nevertheless Turner remains, in his own way, almost as convinced a materialist as the author of *Das Kapital* himself. Only Turner's mastering force is a multiple thing, a cluster of causes singularly disparate and inharmonious. Part of the time the essays cite the natural environment, the physical continent, the wilderness; at other moments the source of change is located in the state of society: the sparseness, mobility, or indiscipline of settlement. Admittedly, America represented both physical hardship and social opportunity. The West was rough (a geographic factor) and it was empty (a sociological force). Perhaps, then, Turner's greatest achievement was his successful marriage of these two dissimilar forces in the single phrase: *free land*. He did not invent the term or the ideas it contains. But he most certainly popularized them.

A Perverted Reading of American History

Among the voluble critics of Turner's work was Louis Hacker, a teacher of history at Columbia University. In a 1933 issue of the Nation, *he published an outspokenly critical review of Turner's later writings expounding on the frontier thesis. Hacker believed that in his focus on the shaping of the American character, Turner ignored economic considerations, especially class conflict.*

Turner undoubtedly was right in pointing out the significance that free lands played in American development. The free lands of the West were not important, however, because they made possible the creation of a unique "American Spirit"—that indefinable something that was to set the United States apart from European experiences for all time—but because their quick settlement and utilization for the extensive cultivation of foodstuffs furnished exactly those commodities with which the United States, as a debtor nation, could balance its international payments and borrow European capital in order to develop a native industrial enterprise. Thus, in the first place, agriculture, primarily the agriculture of those Western areas of which Turner made so much, was really a catspaw for industry; once having served its purpose, that is to say the capitalist development of the nation, it could be neglected politically and ultimately abandoned economically. In the second place, the presence of the frontier helps to explain the failure of American labor to preserve a continuous revolutionary tradition: class lines could not become fixed as long as the free lands existed to drain off the most spirited elements in the working and lower middle-class populations—not only as farmers, of course, but as small merchants and enterprisers, too—and to prevent the creation of a labor reserve for the purpose of thwarting the demands of organized workers.

If this sounds like a defense of Turner, it is intended rather as a clearer definition of his special materialism, which remains objectionable. And it remains so—even disregarding the untenable variations in his definition of *frontier*—because too much is attributed both to the land and to the fact that it was easy to acquire. A number of Turner's ablest friends and admirers regard his *free land* doctrine as a contribution of extraordinary insight and importance, and unquestionably it does seem impressive. Yet the modern observer cannot but be disturbed by the failure of some non-English groups, and even of a tremendous number of native Americans, to heed this call. The open spaces do not seem to have acted as a solvent on the Pennsylvania Germans or the *habitants* of Lower Canada, and the migratory New England groups were only partially disintegrated, while an increasing number of farm boys gravitated to town and city (an even stronger solvent?) instead. It will bear repeating that Turner perhaps exaggerated the importance of "free land."

(Perhaps it is unreasonable to suggest that the North American Indians ought to have profited in the same fashion from so much free land. Yet what about the Spaniards, who had the run of the whole hemisphere? Did the Mississippi Valley make them democratic, prosperous, and numerous? In a word, do not the level of culture, and the "fitness" of a society for the wilderness, matter more than the wilderness? Employing again the comparative vista, were there no unoccupied forests in medieval France? And if today a new continent were to rise out of the Pacific Ocean, are we so sure that it would encourage small freeholds, not corporation or governmental monopolies?)

On the other hand, I cannot but feel that too small a role is allowed to man's own character and ambitions, to his capacity for change, and to the traditions and momentum of the society which came to use this free land. Thus the continent masters, destroys, commands, and creates—while man is surprisingly passive. Where many of us are inclined to regard the physical environment as permissive, or limiting in its influence, Turner in his essays tends to make it mandatory. Vice versa, where sociologists are today coming to recognize the factor of tradition and habit as very powerful, and where a man's ability to master circumstance is at times conceded to be extraordinary, the frontier hypothesis tends to ignore human origins and peculiarities, at least in the composition of American traits and American institutions. Thus first causes are made to lie in real estate, not state of mind. Hence, again, the first Colonial settlers are not examined with any care, but are treated as if they were *average* Europeans. And the later developments and changes in coastal society are handled as if they could have had only two sources: either a fresh migration or influence from Europe, or the powerful influence of an innovating frontier. Native invention in New England? Improvement in New York without the stimulus of the West? Apparently not.

It remains to add two final comments. They concern contradiction and omission.

However optimistic, nationalistic, one-sided, repetitious, fatalistic, undocumented, or erroneous a number of Turner's proposals may appear, the curious fact seems to be that one of the most striking weaknesses of the essays as a whole is internal inconsistency. As has been hinted throughout this paper, the frontier theory in its full development does not hang together. The nationalism of the frontier does violence to its sectional tendencies, innovations are derived from repetition, the improvement of civilization is achieved *via* the abandonment of civilization, and materialism gives birth to idealism. Such inconsistencies do not necessarily condemn the whole theory out of hand. But they do unsettle conviction; they make it hard to remain complacent; they invite the most careful, open-minded restudy.

To this should be added the thought of what Turner did not write. Making all due allowances for the fact that the master's essays were composed in the period 1893-1920, it remains true that in the single field of economics he slighted the industrial revolution, he didn't seem to understand the commercial revolution, and he said nothing at all about the agricultural revolution. Yet it might be asserted that the last alone will be found to have produced more changes in American farming in the nineteenth century than all the frontiers put together! Again, it must be clear from our restatement that the frontier essays entirely failed to check the hypothesis by setting American experience against world experience. Because Turner was primarily a *Western* explorer, his pupils and followers have tended to neglect the all-important comparative approach. When, then, we review the questions with which this paper began, when we remember that the thirteen frontier essays treat the development of "American" and Middle-Western characteristics without reference to Romanticism, to Evangelism, to the eighteenth-century Enlightenment, to the scientific discoveries and the secularization of thought that in varying degrees have overtaken all Western peoples since the discovery of America, it may fairly be deduced that *for future purposes* these celebrated statements leave too much out.

Perhaps a conclusion may be stated in these terms:

In what it proposes, the frontier hypothesis needs painstaking revision. By what it fails to mention, the theory today disqualifies itself as an adequate guide to American development.

VIEWPOINT 3

"It was the magnitude and the unbroken continuity of the experience that gave the frontier major importance in American life. . . . Here in this movement beat the deep overtone of a nation's destiny, and to it all kept step unconsciously."

The Turner Thesis Is Universal and Relevant

Walter Prescott Webb (1888-1963)

Walter Prescott Webb, author of *The Great Plains* and *The Great Frontier*, taught for many years at the University of Texas. The following essay demonstrates not only his fundamental acceptance of Frederick Jackson Turner's frontier thesis, but, perhaps more importantly, it is an illustration of the original ideas for which Turner was the impetus. Webb argues that the American frontier was part of a much larger phenomenon, the interaction between "European civilization and the vast raw lands into which it moved." First published in 1951, Webb's essay remains a classical defense of Turner.

From "Ended: Four Hundred Year Boom: Reflections on the Age of the Frontier," by Walter Prescott Webb, *Harper's Magazine*, October 1951.

Since America led the way in evolving the frontier process, and leads the world in the study of that process, we have no choice but to examine the American experience and to note briefly how scholars came to attend it as a field of study. American historians assume that the frontier process began with the English settlement at Jamestown in 1607, and the year 1890 is usually taken to mark the date when there was no more frontier available, when the new land was no longer new. There may be some quibbling about the dates, but they do bracket the three centuries of American frontier experience and experimentation.

It was the magnitude and the unbroken continuity of the experience that gave the frontier major importance in American life. It made no difference what other tasks the Americans had on their hands at a given time, there was the additional, ever-present one of moving into and settling new country. They did it while they fought for independence, before and after; they did it while they hammered out the principles of a democratic government shaped to the needs of frontiersmen; and they did not cease doing it in the period of civil strife. They never reached the limits of the vacancy they owned before they acquired another vacancy, by purchase, by treaty, by conquest, and in every case the frontiersmen infiltrated the country before the nation acquired it. Like locusts they swarmed, always to the west, and only the Pacific Ocean stopped them. Here in this movement beat the deep overtone of a nation's destiny, and to it all kept step unconsciously.

To say that the people were unconscious of the force that moved them, and of the medium in which they moved, is to state a fact which is easy to prove but hard to explain. It may be said that they were emotionally aware of the frontier long before they were intellectually cognizant of it. People could not have as their main task for three centuries working with raw land without getting its dirt under their nails and deep into their skins. The effects were everywhere, in democratic government, in boisterous politics, in exploitative agriculture, in mobility of population, in disregard for conventions, in rude manners, and in unbridled optimism. . . .

Part of a Larger Phenomenon

What happened in America was but a detail in a much greater phenomenon, the interaction between European civilization and the vast raw lands into which it moved. An effort will be made here to portray the whole frontier, to suggest how it affected the life and institutions of Western civilization throughout the modern period; and as a basis for this exposition four propositions are submitted for consideration:

(1) Europe had a frontier more than a century before the United States was settled.

(2) Europe's frontier was much greater than that of the United States, or of any other one nation; it was the greatest of all time.

(3) The frontier of Europe was almost, if not quite, as important in determining the life and institutions of modern Europe as the frontier of America was in shaping the course of American history. Without the frontier modern Europe would have been so different from what it became that it could hardly be considered modern at all. This is almost equivalent to saying that the frontier made Europe modern.

(4) The close of the Great Frontier may mark the end of an epoch in Western civilization just as the close of the American frontier is often said to have marked the end of the first phase of American history. If the close of the Great Frontier does mark the end of an age, the modern age, then the institutions designed to function in a society dominated largely by frontier forces will find themselves under severe strain.

If we conceive of Western Europe as a unified, densely populated region with a common culture and civilization—which it has long had basically—and if we see the frontier also as a unit, a vast and vacant land without culture, we are in position to view the interaction between the two as a simple but gigantic operation extending over more than four centuries, a process that may appear to be the drama of modern civilization.

To emphasize the unity of Western Europe, and at the same time set it off in sharp contrast to its opposite, the frontier, we may call it the Metropolis. Metropolis is a good name, implying what Europe really was, a cultural center holding within it everything pertaining to Western civilization. Prior to 1500 the Metropolis comprised all the "known" world save Asia, which was but vaguely known. Its area was approximately 3,750,000 square miles, and its population is estimated to have been about 100 million people.

There is no need to elaborate the conditions under which these people lived, but it should be remembered that by modern standards the society was a static one with well-defined classes. The population pressed hard on the means of subsistence. There was not much food, practically no money, and very little freedom. What is more important, there was practically no means of escape for those people living in this closed world. The idea of progress had not been born. Heaven alone, which could be reached only through the portals of death, offered any hope to the masses of the Metropolis.

Then came the miracle that was to change everything, the emancipator bearing rich gifts of land and more land, of gold and silver, of new foods for every empty belly and new clothing stuffs for every half-naked back. Europe, the Metropolis, knocked on the door of the Great Frontier, and when the door was opened it was seen to be golden, for within there was undreamed-of treasure, enough to make the whole Metropolis rich. The long quest of a half-starved people had at last been rewarded with success beyond comprehension. . . .

Frontier Democracy

One of Turner's most ardent supporters, historian Ray Allen Billington ascribes to the populist interpretation of the West. In this excerpt from his book America's Frontier Heritage, *Billington emphasizes social democracy on the frontier. He quotes a British visitor: "You may be a son of a lord back in England, but that ain't what you are out here."*

Basically, frontier individualism stemmed from the belief that all men were equal (excluding Negroes, Indians, Orientals, and other minority groups), and that all should have a chance to prove their personal capabilities without restraint from society. This seemed fair in a land of plenty, where superabundant opportunity allowed each to rise or fall to his proper level as long as governments did not meddle. Faith in the equality of men was the great common creed of the West. Only an understanding of the depth of this belief can reveal the true nature of social democracy on successive frontiers.

To European visitors, this was the most unique feature of Western life and thought: the attitude that set that region apart from Europe or the East. "There is nothing in America," wrote one, "that strikes a foreigner so much as the real republican equality existing in the Western States, which border on the wilderness."

The Metropolis had a new piece of property and the frontier had a new owner. The Metropolitans were naturally curious about their property, and quite naturally began to ask questions about it. How big is it? Who lives on it? What is its inherent worth? What can *I* get out of it? They learned that the frontier had an area five or six times that of Europe; that it was practically vacant, occupied by a few primitive inhabitants whose rights need not be respected; that its inherent worth could only be guessed at. As to what can *I* get out of it?, the answer came in time clear and strong: You can get everything you want from gold and silver to furs and foods, and in any quantity you want, provided only that you are willing to venture and work! And more faintly came the small voice, hardly audible: Something all of you can get as a by-product is some measure of freedom.

The Metropolitans decided to accept the gifts. Instantly the divisions in Europe were projected into the frontier as each little European power that could man a ship seized a section of the frontier bigger than itself and tried to fight all the others off. Each nation wanted it all. The result was a series of wars lasting from 1689 to 1763 and from these wars England, France, and Spain emerged as chief owners of the frontier world. Their success was more apparent than real, for a spirit of freedom had been nurtured in the distant lands, and in less than fifty years England had lost her chief prize while Spain and France had lost practically everything.

But their loss, like their previous gain, was more apparent than real. True, by 1820 the Metropolis had lost title to most of the new land, but it had not lost something more precious than title—namely, the beneficent effects that the frontier exerted on the older countries. The political separation of most of North and South America relieved the Metropolis of responsibility and onerous obligations, but it did not cut off the abundance of profits. Europe continued to share in the riches and the opportunity that the opening of the golden door had made visible.

Relationship Between the Metropolis and the Frontier

What was the essential character of the frontier? Was the direct force it exerted spiritual, intellectual, or was it material? The frontier was basically a vast body of wealth without proprietors. It was an empty land more than five times the size of Western Europe, a land whose resources had not been exploited. Its first impact was mainly economic. Bathed in and invigorated by a flood of wealth, the Metropolis began to seethe with economic excitement. . . .

The factors involved, though of gigantic magnitude, are simple in nature and in their relation one to another. They are the old familiar ones of population, land, and capital. With the opening of the Great Frontier, land and capital rose out of all proportion to population, of those to share it, and therefore conditions were highly favorable to general prosperity and a boom. What we are really concerned with is an *excess* of land and an *excess* of capital for division among a relatively *fixed* number of people. The population did increase, but not until the nineteenth century did the extra population compare with the extra land and capital that had been long available. . . .

Capital may be considered in two forms, as gold and silver and as capital goods or commodities. The Metropolis was short of both forms of wealth throughout the medieval period, and the dearth of coin prior to the discoveries was most critical. It has been estimated that the total amount of gold and silver in Europe in 1492 was less than 200 million dollars, less than two dollars per person. Certainly there was not enough to serve the needs of exchange, which was carried on by barter, or to give rise to erudite theories of money economy. Then very suddenly the whole money situation changed.

By 1500 the Spaniards had cracked the treasure houses of the Great Frontier and set a stream of gold and silver flowing into the Metropolis, a stream that continued without abatement for 150 years, and that still continues. This flood of precious metals changed all the relations existing between man and money, between gold and a bushel of wheat or a *fanega* of barley. That changed relationship wrought the price revolution because temporarily—so fast did the metals come—there was more money than things, and so prices rose to the modern level. This new money was a powerful stimulus to the quest for more, and set the whole Metropolis into the frenzy of daring and adventure which gave character to the modern age. . . .

The boom hypothesis of modern history may be summed up by stating that with the tapping of the resources of the Great Frontier there came into the possession of the Metropolis a body of wealth consisting of land, precious metals, and the commodities out of all proportion to the number of people. . . .

The Individual and the Great Frontier

If the opening of the Great Frontier did precipitate a boom in Western civilization, the effects on human ideas and institutions must have been profound and far-reaching. In general such a boom would hasten the passing away of the ideas and institutions of a static culture and the sure appearance of others adapted to a dynamic and prospering society. There is no doubt that medieval society was breaking up at the time of the discoveries, that men's minds had been sharpened by their intellectual exercises, and that their spirits had been stirred by doubt. The thinkers were restless and inquiring, but what they lacked was room in which to try out their innovations, and a fresh and uncluttered soil in which some of their new ideas could take hold and grow. Their desires had to be matched with opportunity before they could realize on their aspirations, however laudable. The frontier offered them the room and the opportunity. It did not necessarily originate ideas, but it acted as a relentless sifter, letting some pass and rejecting others. Those that the frontier favored prospered, and finally matured into institutions; those it did not favor became recessive, dormant, and many institutions based on these ideas withered away. Feudal tenure, serfdom, barter, primogeniture, and the notion that the world was a no-good place in which to live are examples of things untenable in the presence of the frontier.

Since we are dealing with the modern age, it would be very helpful if we could discover what it emphasized most. Where

Vestiges of Frontier Individualism

Long a supporter of Turner's frontier thesis, historian Ray Allen Billington believed that while the closing of the frontier effected significant changes in the American character, the frontier's influence continues to be seen. In his book America's Frontier Heritage *he comments on the democratic influence of the frontier.*

The social democracy and frontier-type individualism that characterized America's growing period have not persisted unchanged into the twentieth century. Individualism has retreated before the advance of social cohesiveness essential in an urban-industrial society. The nation's folk hero may still be the rugged individualist, but the lone wolves of the past have found that they cannot fight the pack and that in cut-throat competition all throats are cut. At least since the 1890s the economic community had grudgingly accepted the regulation that the pioneer resisted save when it was to his advantage, and today cooperation and reliance on government are almost as commonplace in the United States as in the older countries of Europe. Yet American individualism differs from that of France or England in its continued insistence on a degree of economic freedom that has long since vanished in those countries, and in a glorification of the individual's ability to care for himself despite daily proof that joint effort alone will succeed in a society increasingly enmeshed.

Just as vestiges of frontier individualism remain to distinguish the social attitudes of modern America from those of modern Europe, so do remnants of pioneer democracy. The United States is no longer a country free of class distinctions and so wedded to egalitarianism that manifestations of wealth arouse public resentment. But its social democracy does differ from that of older nations, marked by its relative lack of class awareness, and by the brash assurance of the humble that they are as worthy of respect as the elite. The house painter who addresses a client by his first name, the elevator operator who enters into casual conversation with his passengers, the garage mechanic who condescendingly compares his expensive car with your aging model, could exist only in the United States. Their counterparts are unknown in England or on the Continent partly because America's frontiering experience bred into the people attitudes toward democracy that have persisted down to the present.

was the chief accent of modernity? What has been its focus? *Who* has held the spotlight on the stage of history since 1500? There can be little doubt, though there may be enough to start an argument, that the answer to all these questions is: the Individual. It is he who has been emphasized, accented; it is on him that the spotlight has focused; it is his importance that has been magnified. He is—or was—the common denominator of modern times, and an examination of any strictly modern institution such as democracy or capitalism will reveal an individual at the core, trying to rule himself in one case and make some money in the other. Not God nor the devil nor the state, but the ordinary man has been the favorite child of modern history.

Did the Great Frontier, which was his contemporary, have any part in giving the individual his main chance, the triple opportunity of ruling himself, enriching himself, and saving his own soul on his own hook? These three freedoms were institutionalized in Protestantism, capitalism, and democracy—whose basic assumption is that they exist for the individual, and that the individual must be free in order to make them work. The desire for freedom men surely have always had, but in the old Metropolis conditions prevailed which made freedom impossible. Everywhere in Europe the individual was surrounded by institutions which, whether by design or not, kept him unfree. He was walled in by man-made regulations which controlled him from baptism to extreme unction.

Then the golden door of the Great Frontier opened, and a way of escape lay before him. He moved out from the Metropolis to land on a distant shore, in America, Australia, South Africa. Here in the wild and empty land there was not a single institution; man had left them, albeit temporarily, far behind. Regardless of what befell him later, for an instant he was free of all the restrictions that society had put upon him. In short, he had escaped his human masters only to find himself in the presence of another, a less picayunish one.

Naked in the Presence of Nature

The character of the new master, before whom he stood stripped of his institutions, was so in contrast with that of the old one as to defy comparison. Man stood naked in the presence of nature. On this subject, Alexander von Humboldt said, "In the Old World, nations and the distinction of their civilization form the principal point in the picture; in the New World, man and his production almost disappear amidst the stupendous display of wild and gigantic nature." The outstanding qualities of wild and gigantic nature are its impersonality and impassiveness. Nature broods over man, casts its mysterious spells, but it never intervenes for or against him. It gives no orders, issues no proclamations, has no prisons, no privileges; it knows nothing of vengeance or mercy. Before nature all men are free and equal.

The important point is that the abstract man we have been following did not have to *win* his freedom. It was imposed upon him and he could not escape it. Being caught in the trap of freedom, his task was to adjust himself to it and to devise procedures which would be more convenient for living in such a state. His first task was to govern himself, for self-government is what freedom imposes.

Of course there was not just one man on the frontier. In a short time the woods were full of them, all trained in the same school. As the years went by, they formed the habits of freedom, cherished it; and when a distant government tried to take from them that to which they had grown accustomed, they resisted, and their resistance was called the American Revolution. The American frontiersmen did not fight England to gain freedom, but to preserve it and have it officially recognized by the Metropolis. "Your nation," wrote Herman Melville, "enjoyed no little independence before your declaration declared it." Whence came this independence? Not from parliaments or kings or legislative assemblies, but from the conditions, the room, the space, and the natural wealth amidst which they lived. "The land was ours," writes Robert Frost, "before we were the land's.". . .

There is an unpleasant logic inherent in the frontier boom hypothesis of modern history. We come to it with the reluctance that men always have when they come to the end of a boom. They look back on the grand opportunities they had, they remember the excitement and adventure of it, they tote up their accounts and hope for another chance. Western civilization today stands facing a closed frontier, and in this sense it faces a unique situation in modern times.

Impact of Frontier's End

If we grant the boom, we must concede that the institutions we have, such as democracy and capitalism, were boomborn; we must also admit that the individual, this cherished darling of modern history, attained his glory in an abnormal period when there was enough room to give him freedom and enough wealth to give him independence. The future of the individual, of democracy and capitalism, and of many other modern institutions are deeply involved in this logic, and the lights are burning late in the capitals of the Western world where grave men are trying to determine what that future will be. . . .

I should like to make it clear that mankind is really searching for a new frontier which we once had and did not prize, and the longer we had it, the less we valued it; but now that we have lost it, we have a great pain in the heart, and we are always trying to get it back again. It seems to me that historians and all thoughtful persons are bound by their obligation to say that there is no new frontier in sight comparable in magnitude or importance to the one that is lost. They should point out the diversity and heterogeneity, not to say the absurdity, of so-called new frontiers. They are all fallacies, these new frontiers, and they are pernicious in proportion to their plausibility and respectability. The scientists themselves should join in disabusing the public as to what science can be expected to do. It can do much, but, to paraphrase Isaiah Bowman, it is not likely soon to find a new world or make the one we have much bigger than it is. If the frontier is gone, we should have the courage and honesty to recognize the fact, cease to cry for what we have lost, and devote our energy to finding the solutions to the problems now facing a frontierless society. And when the age we now call modern is modern no longer, and requires a new name, we may appropriately call it the Age of the Frontier, and leave it to its place in history.

Chapter 2

The Frontier and the Native American

Chapter Preface

If, as Walter Prescott Webb suggests, "what happened in America was but a detail of a much larger phenomenon, the interaction between European civilization and the vast raw lands into which it moved," an appropriate beginning point for an examination of the frontier and the native American is in that first recorded contact between European and American people, Columbus's log for October 12, 1492.

This passage is important not only as record of a momentous historical event but also as the first statement of European ambivalence toward residents of the Americas. Columbus's log clearly shows his fascination with the "naked people" who are "well-built . . . with handsome bodies and very fine faces." They are "friendly and well-dispositioned" people, exotically attractive, as some "paint their whole bodies" and others "only the eyes or nose" in red and black and white. But they are naive, he records, lacking iron for weapons and remarkably easily pleased by inexpensive red caps and glass beads. "They have very little and are poor for everything," he writes, already showing his perception that the Indians are inferior. It is only a few days before the idea of taking them back to Spain as slaves is broached and yet a few more before the initial skirmish between peoples of the two old worlds takes place.

For much of the next five centuries, Europeans seemed undecided whether the native American was a noble savage—living close to nature and thus close to God, generous, just, and wise—or a brutish manifestation of savagery—cunning, devious, and vicious. The former position, with roots in the writings of Rousseau and Montaigne, found mid-nineteenth century personification in James Fenimore Cooper's *Leatherstocking Tales*. Cooper's Indian characters Chingachgook and Uncas epitomize the noble savage: they are brave, dignified, and loyal, but they, like their Huron arch-enemies, must be swept aside in the progress of civilization. Cooper's white hero, Leatherstocking, though respecting all good men, recognizes a hierarchy in which whites, and whites' "gifts" or character traits, are superior to others', and, thus, must ultimately triumph.

Significantly, Indians' views of the encroaching whites were also polarized. On the one hand, the whites were seen as fulfillment of prophesy, often as near-reincarnations of the gods. Mexican myth told of the bearded white god Quetzalcoatl who would one day return to claim his kingdom. An Ojibway story tells of "visitors from heaven" wearing what the Indians later learned was woven fabric, unknown to the Ojibway who then wore buckskins. The Sac chief Black Hawk, in his autobiography first published in 1833, tells of his great-grandfather's dream of the coming of the white man who would be the Indians' father. But the visitor was not always seen as so benevolent. A story of the Wintun tribe in California tells of White Rabbit, who will devour the Indians' grass, their seeds, their living. And Archie Fire Lame Deer, a twentieth-century Sioux writer and teacher, remembers that disobedient children were threatened with *chichiye*, a horrible white monster: "Little boy, behave yourself, or the *chichiye* will get you. . . . If you are bad, the white man will come and take you away."

For people in both cultures, personal experience was likely to affect where on the continuum between demon and deity the Others were to be placed. People often see what they have been conditioned to expect. But there was also the need to be pragmatic. Once America became the ever-moving frontier of Europe, whites were not going to go away; the tide of population could not be stopped. Temporary attempts to dam the flood, like the Proclamation of 1763, which established a "firm" boundary between Indian and white lands, were soon breached by land-hungry settlers. Intercultural conflict was exacerbated by the westering movement. As more and more Indians were compressed into less and less space, conflict—intertribal as well as inter-racial—seemed inevitable.

Though Frederick Jackson Turner has often been criticized for ignoring the Indian in his discussion of the frontier, this is not the case. Although he is more interested in the impact of the frontier on American character, he also recognized stresses on Indian culture. In his analysis of Indian preference for the French over the English, he notes that the French emphasis on fur trading was less threatening, less stressful—environmentally and culturally—than the English goal of clearing land for agriculture. But paradoxically, the trader too was an agent for change:

> The trading post left the unarmed tribes at the mercy of those that had purchased firearms—a truth which the Iroquois Indians wrote in blood, and so the remote and unvisited tribes gave eager welcome to the trader. . . . Thus the disintegrating forces of civilization entered the wilderness. Every river valley and Indian trail became a fissure in Indian society . . . . The Indian trade pioneered the way for civilization.

In addition to the inroads into Indian culture that Turner addresses, other factors were at work. European diseases devastated native American populations lacking natural immunity. Measles and smallpox, for example, endemic in Europe, became epidemic in America. The military often accompanied settlement, and forts soon dotted the map farther and farther west. With settlement came other assaults on Indian culture—missionaries and educators, ostensibly more benign than the military but ultimately more revolutionary.

How, then, at the frontier, that "border between civilization and savagery," were two peoples to treat each other? Extermination, seriously suggested by some on both sides, was not only morally reprehensible but practically not feasible. Assimilation seemed a more likely solution. Initially, as Turner points out, it was the European who adapted to the new environment, who "strips off the garments of civilization" and replaces them with "the hunting shirt and the moccasins." Explorers and fur traders demonstrated this adaptation to Indian culture. Mary Jemison, a white woman abducted by a Shawnee raiding party in 1758 and later adopted by the Iroquois, died at the age of ninety as an Iroquois grandmother on the Buffalo Creek Reservation in New York. And even Elaine Goodale Eastman, who, with many Eastern reformers, believed strongly in assimilating the Indian into the dominant white culture, would find love among the Sioux.

Her experiences in the 1880s and 1890s perhaps point to today's resolution of centuries-old issues: an integration of the two cultures, rather than a denial of either. Ben Nighthorse Campbell illustrates such integration. In January 1993, after three terms in the House of Representatives, Campbell, whose great-grandfather, Black Horse, fought at Little Bighorn, took his seat in the U.S. Senate. A year earlier, in full tribal regalia, he had ridden his horse, War Bonnet, in the Quincentennial Year Rose Bowl parade, just ahead of a direct descendant of Christopher Columbus. To outraged critics within the American Indian Movement who believe the explorer's arrival eventually led to the annihilation of the Indian nations, Campbell replied, "You can't keep hate alive."

VIEWPOINT 1

"Nature intended him for a savage state; every instinct, every impulse of his soul inclines him to it. . . . He cannot be himself and be civilized; he fades away and dies."

The Indian Cannot Be Civilized

George Armstrong Custer (1839-1876)

George Armstrong Custer viewed the Indian from the perspective of a military man whose job was to defeat the red man and destroy his ability to impede the advance of white civilization westward. Ultimately—and ironically—Custer was to be defeated by his quarry at the Battle of the Little Big Horn.

In the following viewpoint, Custer's position is clear: others, such as novelists, peace commissioners, and well-meaning philanthropists, can romanticize the Indian; he cannot. And, though he demonstrates grudging admiration for the Indian in a savage state, he argues that the Indian cannot be civilized without destroying his personal and cultural identity.

If the character given to the Indian by Cooper and other novelists, as well as by well-meaning but mistaken philanthropists of a later day, were the true one; if the Indian were the innocent, simple-minded being he is represented, more the creature of ro-

From *My Life on the Plains; or Personal Experiences with Indians* by George A. Custer. New edition © 1962 by the University of Oklahoma Press.

mance than reality, imbued only with a deep veneration for the works of nature, freed from the passions and vices which must accompany a savage nature; if, in other words, he possessed all the virtues which his admirers and works of fiction ascribe to him and were free from all the vices which those best qualified to judge assign to him, he would be just the character to complete the picture which is presented by the country embracing the Wichita Mountains. Cooper, to whose writings more than to those of any other author are the people speaking the English language indebted for a false and ill-judged estimate of the Indian character, might well have laid the scenes of his fictitious stories in this beautiful and romantic country.

It is to be regretted that the character of the Indian as described in Cooper's interesting novels is not the true one. But as, in emerging from childhood into the years of a maturer age, we are often compelled to cast aside many of our earlier illusions and replace them by beliefs less inviting but more real, so we, as a people, with opportunities enlarged and facilities for obtaining knowledge increased, have been forced by a multiplicity of causes to study and endeavor to comprehend thoroughly the character of the red man. So intimately has he become associated with the government as ward of the nation, and so prominent a place among the questions of national policy does the much mooted "Indian question" occupy, that it behooves us no longer to study this problem from works of fiction, but to deal with it as it exists in reality. Stripped of the beautiful romance with which we have been so long willing to envelope him, transferred from the inviting pages of the novelist to the localities where we are compelled to meet with him, in his native village, on the war path, and when raiding upon our frontier settlements and lines of travel, the Indian forfeits his claim to the appellation of the "*noble* red man." We see him as he is, and, so far as all knowledge goes, as he ever has been, a *savage* in every sense of the word; not worse, perhaps, than his white brother would be similarly born and bred, but one whose cruel and ferocious nature far exceeds that of any wild beast of the desert. That this is true no one who had been brought into intimate contact with the wild tribes will deny. Perhaps there are some who, as members of peace commissions or as wandering agents of some benevolent society, may have visited these tribes or attended with them at councils held for some pacific purpose, and who, by passing through the villages of the Indian while *at peace*, may imagine their opportunities for judging of the Indian nature all that could be desired. But the Indian, while he can seldom be accused of indulging in a great variety of wardrobe, can be said to have character capable of adapting itself to almost every occasion. He has one character, perhaps his most serviceable one, which he preserves carefully, and only airs it when making his appeal to the government or its agents for arms, ammunition, and license to employ them. This character is invariably paraded, and often with telling effect, when the motive is a peaceful one. Prominent chiefs invited to visit Washington invariably don this character, and in their "talks" with the "Great Father" and other less prominent personages they successfully contrive to exhibit but this one phase. Seeing them under these or similar circumstances only, it is not surprising that by many the Indian is looked upon as a simpleminded "son of nature," desiring nothing beyond the privilege of roaming and hunting over the vast unsettled wilds of the West, inheriting and asserting but few native rights, and never trespassing upon the rights of others. This view is equally erroneous with that which regards the Indian as a creature possessing the human form but divested of all other attributes of humanity, and whose traits of character, habits, modes of life, disposition, and savage customs disqualify him from the exercise of all rights and privileges, even those pertaining to life itself.

Peter Rindisbacher, a Swiss émigré, depicts the Indian as a savage destroyer of the innocent. In this painting, he shows the frontiersman David Tully (in the background), outnumbered and fighting for his life, using his empty gun as a club, while his wife and children await the inevitable atrocity.

Taking him as we find him, at peace or at war, at home or abroad, waiving all prejudices, and laying aside all partiality, we will discover in the Indian a subject for thoughtful study and investigation. In him we will find the representative of a race whose origin is, and promises to be, a subject forever wrapped in mystery; a race incapable of being judged by the rules or laws applicable to any other known race of men; one between which and civilization there seems to have existed from time immemorial a determined and unceasing warfare—a hostility so deep-seated and inbred with the Indian character that in the exceptional instances where the modes and habits of civilization have been reluctantly adopted, it has been at the sacrifice of power and influence as a tribe and the more serious loss of health, vigor, and courage as individuals. . . .

Why It Is Impossible to Civilize the Indian

Inseparable from the Indian character, wherever he is to be met with, is his remarkable taciturnity, his deep dissimulation, the perseverance with which he follows his plans of revenge or conquest, his concealment and apparent lack of curiosity, his stoical courage when in the power of his enemies, his cunning, his caution, and last, but not least, the wonderful power and subtlety of his senses. Of this last I have had most interesting proof, one instance of which will be noted when describing the Washita campaign. In studying the Indian character, while shocked and disgusted by many of his traits and customs, I find much to be admired and still more of deep and unvarying interest. To me, Indian life, with its attendant ceremonies, mysteries, and forms, is a book of unceasing interest. Grant that some of its pages are frightful and, if possible, to be avoided, yet the attraction is none the weaker. Study him, fight him, civilize him if you can, he remains still the object of your curiosity, a type of man peculiar and undefined, subjecting himself to no known law of civilization, contending determinedly against all efforts to win him from his chosen mode of life. He stands in the group of nations solitary and reserved, seeking alliance with none, mistrusting and opposing the advances of all. Civilization may and should do much for him, but it can never civilize him. A few instances to the contrary may be quoted, but these are susceptible of explanation. No tribe enjoying its accustomed freedom has ever been induced to adopt a civilized mode of life or, as they express it, to follow the white man's road. At various times certain tribes have forsaken the pleasures of the chase and the excitement of the warpath for the more quiet life to be found on the "reservation." Was this course adopted voluntarily and from preference? Was it because the Indian chose the ways of his white brother rather than those in which he had been born and bred?

In no single instance has this been true. What then, it may be asked, have been the reasons which influenced certain tribes to abandon their predatory, nomadic life, and today to influence

We Are Free to Destroy the Indians

As early as 1622, the Indian had become an impediment in some people's minds to the advance of civilization. In "A Declaration of the State of the Colonie and Affaires in Virginia," Edward Waterhouse justifies war against native Americans.

Because our hands which before were tied with gentlenesse and faire usage, are now set at liberty by the treacherous violence of the Savages, not untying the Knot, but cutting it: So that we, who hitherto have had possession of no more ground then their waste, and our purchase at a valuable consideration to their owne contentment, gained; may now by a right of Warre, and law of Nations, invade the Country, and destroy them who sought to destroy us.

others to pursue a similar course? The answer is clear, and as undeniable as it is clear. The gradual and steady decrease in numbers, strength, and influence, occasioned by wars both with other tribes and with the white man, as well as losses brought about by diseases partly attributable to contact with civilization, have so lowered the standing and diminished the available fighting force of the tribe as to render it unable to cope with the more powerful neighboring tribes with any prospect of success. The stronger tribes always assume an overbearing and dominant manner toward their weaker neighbors, forcing them to join in costly and bloody wars or themselves to be considered enemies. When a tribe falls from the position of a leading one, it is at the mercy of every tribe that chooses to make war, being forced to take sides, and at the termination of the war is generally sacrificed to the interests of the more powerful. To avoid these sacrifices, to avail itself of the protection of civilization and its armed forces, to escape from the ruining influences of its more warlike and powerful neighbors, it reluctantly accepts the situation, gives up its accustomed haunts, its wild mode of life, and nestles down under the protecting arm of its former enemy, the white man, and tries, however feebly, to adopt his manner of life. In making this change, the Indian has to sacrifice all that is dear to his heart; he abandons the only mode of life in which he can be a warrior and win triumphs and honors worthy to be sought after; and in taking up the pursuits of the white man, he does that which he has always been taught from his earliest infancy to regard as degrading to his manhood—to labor, to work for his daily bread, an avocation suitable only for squaws.

To those who advocate the application of the laws of civilization to the Indian, it might be a profitable study to investigate the effect which such application produces upon the strength of the tribe as expressed in numbers. Looking at him as the fearless hunter, the matchless horseman and warrior of the Plains, where Nature placed him, and contrasting him with the reservation Indian, who is supposed to be reveling in the delightful comforts and luxuries of an enlightened condition, but who in reality is groveling in beggary, bereft of many of the qualities which in his wild state tended to render him noble, and heir to a combination of vices partly his own, partly bequeathed to him from the paleface, one is forced, even against desire, to conclude that there in unending antagonism between the Indian nature and that with which his well-meaning white brother would endow him. Nature intended him for a savage state; every instinct, every impulse of his soul inclines him to it. The white race might fall into a barbarous state, and afterwards, subjected to the influence of civilization, be reclaimed and prosper. Not so the Indian. He cannot be himself and be civilized; he fades away and dies. Cultivation such as the white man would give him deprives him of his identity.

Education, strange as it may appear, seems to weaken rather than strengthen his intellect.

VIEWPOINT 2

"The commissioner had been guilty of absolute dishonesty . . . and . . . the Indians were actually, as they had claimed, 'starving.'"

The Indian Cannot Be Civilized by Force, Starvation, and Hypocrisy

Helen Hunt Jackson (1830-1885)

Like her friend Emily Dickinson, who was the model for Helen Hunt's anonymous novel *Mercy Philbrick's Choice* (1876), Helen Hunt Jackson was a poet first. Born in Amherst, Massachusetts, she moved to Colorado after her second marriage to William S. Jackson. There she heard native Americans tell of their mistreatment by whites. Her compassion aroused, she did further research, which led to *A Century of Dishonor*, a documented attack on the federal government's treatment of Indians. Following its publication in 1881, she was appointed by the secretary of the interior to a commission examining the needs of California's mission Indians. Though that report was not acted upon, her research in California led to *Ramona* (1884), compared by some in intent to *Uncle Tom's Cabin*. The novel was a popular success, but

From *A Century of Dishonor: A Sketch of the United States Government's Dealings with Some of the Indian Tribes* by Helen Hunt Jackson. New York: Harper & Brothers, 1881.

most readers simply enjoyed the romantic view of the old Spanish aristocracy in Mexican California. Few focused on the plight of the Indians caught between that aristocracy and the Americans pouring into the region. The following selection from *Century of Dishonor* analyzes the failure of government relocation policy.

———————

The winter of 1877 and summer of 1878 were terrible seasons for the Cheyennes. Their fall hunt had proved unsuccessful. Indians from other reservations had hunted the ground over before them, and driven the buffalo off; and the Cheyennes made their way home again in straggling parties, destitute and hungry. Their agent reports that the result of this hunt has clearly proved that "in the future the Indian must rely on tilling the ground as the principal means of support; and if this conviction can be firmly established, the greatest obstacle to advancement in agriculture will be overcome. With the buffalo gone, and their pony herds being constantly decimated by the inroads of horse-thieves, they must soon adopt, in all its varieties, the way of the white man. . . ."

The ration allowed to these Indians is reported as being "reduced and insufficient," and the small sums they have been able to earn by selling buffalo-hides are said to have been "of material assistance" to them in "supplementing" this ration. But in this year there have been sold only $657 worth of skins by the Cheyennes and Arapahoes together. In 1876 they sold $17,600 worth. Here is a falling off enough to cause very great suffering in a little community of five thousand people. But this was only the beginning of their troubles. The summer proved one of unusual heat. Extreme heat, chills and fever, and "a reduced and insufficient ration," all combined, resulted in an amount of sickness heart-rending to read of. "It is no exaggerated estimate," says the agent, "to place the number of sick people on the reservation at two thousand. Many deaths occurred which might have been obviated had there been a proper supply of anti-malarial remedies at hand. . . . Hundreds applying for treatment have been refused medicine."

The Northern Cheyennes grew more and more restless and unhappy. "In council and elsewhere they profess an intense desire to be sent North, where they say they will settle down as the others have done," says the report; adding, with an obtuseness which is inexplicable, that "no difference has been made in the treatment of the Indians," but that the "compliance" of these Northern Cheyennes has been "of an entirely different nature from that of the other Indians," and that it may be "necessary in the future to compel what so far we have been unable to effect by kindness and appeal to their better natures."

If it is "an appeal to men's better natures" to remove them by force from a healthful Northern climate, which they love and thrive in, to a malarial Southern one, where they are struck down by chills and fever—refuse them medicine which can combat chills and fever, and finally starve them—then, indeed, might be said to have been most forcible appeals made to the "better natures" of these Northern Cheyennes. What might have been predicted followed.

Escape and Punishment

Early in the autumn, after this terrible summer, a band of some three hundred of these Northern Cheyennes took the desperate step of running off and attempting to make their way back to Dakota. They were pursued, fought desperately, but were finally overpowered, and surrendered. They surrendered, however, only on the condition that they should be taken to Dakota. They were unanimous in declaring that they would rather die than go back to the Indian Territory. This was nothing more, in fact, than saying that they would rather die by bullets than of chills and fever and starvation.

These Indians were taken to Fort Robinson, Nebraska. Here they were confined as prisoners of war, and held subject to the orders of the Department of the Interior. The department was informed of the Indians' determination never to be taken back alive to Indian Territory. The army officers in charge reiterated these statements, and implored the department to permit them to remain at the North; but it was of no avail. Orders came—explicit, repeated, finally stern—insisting on the return of these Indians to their agency. The commanding officer at Fort Robinson has been censured severely for the course he pursued in his effort to carry out those orders. It is difficult to see what else he could have done, except to have resigned his post. He could not take three hundred Indians by sheer brute force and carry them hundreds of miles, especially when they were so desperate that they had broken up the iron stoves in their quarters, and wrought and twisted them into weapons with which to resist. He thought perhaps he could starve them into submission. He stopped the issue of food; he also stopped the issue of fuel to them. It was midwinter; the mercury froze in that month at Fort Robinson. At the end of two days he asked the Indians to let their women and children come out that he might feed them. Not a woman would come out. On the night of the fourth day—or, according to some accounts, the sixth—these starving, freezing Indians broke prison, overpowered the guards, and fled, carrying their women and children with them. They held the pursuing troops at bay for several days; finally made a last stand in a deep ravine, and were shot down—men, women, and children together. Out of the whole band there were left alive some fifty women and children and seven men, who, having been confined in another part of the fort, had not had the good fortune to share in this outbreak and meet their death in the ravine. These, with their wives and children, were sent to Fort Leavenworth, to be put in prison; the men to be tried for murders committed in their skirmishes in Kansas on their way to the north. Red Cloud, a Sioux chief, came to Fort Robinson immediately after this massacre, and entreated to be allowed to take the Cheyenne widows and orphans into his tribe to be cared for. The Government, therefore, kindly permitted twenty-two Cheyenne widows and thirty-two Cheyenne children—many of them orphans—to be received into the band of the Ogallalla Sioux.

Nature and the Indian

In his journal for April 1841, Henry David Thoreau muses on the contrasts between white and Indian attitudes toward nature and weighs in on the side of the Indian.

The charm of the Indian to me is that he stands free and unconstrained in Nature, is her inhabitant and not her guest, and wears her easily and gracefully. But the civilized man has the habits of the house. His house is a prison, in which he finds himself oppressed and confined, not sheltered and protected. . . .

The white man comes, pale as the dawn, with a load of thought, with a slumbering intelligence as a fire raked up, knowing well what he knows, not guessing but calculating; strong in community, yielding obedience to authority; of experienced race; of wonderful, wonderful common sense; dull but capable, slow but preserving, severe but just, of little humor but genuine; a laboring man, despising game and sport; building a house that endures, a framed house. He buys the Indian's moccasins and baskets, then buys his hunting-grounds, and at length forgets where he is buried and plows up his bones. . . .

It is the spirit of humanity, that which animates both so-called savages and civilized nations, working through a man, and not the man expressing himself, that interests us most. The thought of a so-called savage tribe is generally far more just than that of a single civilized man.

An attempt was made by the Commissioner of Indian Affairs, in his Report for 1879, to show by tables and figures that these Indians were not starving at the time of their flight from Indian Territory. The attempt only redounded to his own disgrace; it being proved, by the testimony given by a former clerk of the Indian Bureau before the Senate committee appointed to investigate the case of the Northern Cheyennes, that the commissioner had been guilty of absolute dishonesty in his estimates, and that the quantity of beef actually issued to the Cheyenne Agency was hundreds of pounds less than he had reported it, and that the Indians were actually, as they had claimed, "starving."

Testimony Before the Senate

The testimony given before this committee by some of the Cheyenne prisoners themselves is heart-rending. One must have a callous heart who can read it unmoved.

When asked by Senator Morgan, "Did you ever really suffer from hunger?" one of the chiefs replied, "We were *always* hungry; we *never* had enough. When they that were sick once in awhile felt as though they could eat something, we had nothing to give them."

"Did you not go out on the plains sometimes and hunt buffalo, with the consent of the agent?"

"We went out on a buffalo-hunt, and nearly starved while out; we could not find any buffalo hardly; we could hardly get back with our ponies; we had to kill a good many of our ponies to eat, to save ourselves from starving."

"How many children got sick and died?"

"Between the fall of 1877 and 1878 we lost fifty children. A great many of our finest young men died, as well as many women."

"Old Crow," a chief who served faithfully as Indian scout and ally under General Crook for years, said: "I did not feel like doing anything for awhile, because I had no heart. I did not want to be in this country. I was all the time wanting to get back to the better country where I was born, and where my children are buried, and where my mother and sister yet live. So I have laid in my lodge most of the time with nothing to think about but that, and the affair up north at Fort Robinson, and my relatives and friends who were killed there. But now I feel as though, if I had a wagon and a horse or two, and some land, I would try to work. If I had something, so that I could do something, I might not think so much about these other things. As it is now, I feel as though I would just as soon be asleep with the rest."

The wife of one of the chiefs confined at Fort Leavenworth testified before the committee as follows: "The main thing I complained of was that we didn't get enough to eat; my children nearly starved to death; then sickness came, and there was nothing good for them to eat; for a long time the most they had to eat was corn-meal and salt. Three or four children died every day for awhile, and that frightened us."

(This testimony was taken at Fort Reno, in Indian Territory.)

Indians Can Become Citizens

Julius Seelye, president of Amherst College, was among those who felt that through education and humane treatment, the Indian could be brought into mainstream America. He saw this to be not only a humane process, but a practical one since he believed whites should not exterminate the Indian and was convinced those same whites would not withdraw from Indian lands.

The great difficulty with the Indian problem is not with the Indian, but with the Government and people of the United States. Instead of a liberal and far-sighted policy looking to the education and civilization and possible citizenship of the Indian tribes, we have suffered these people to remain as savages, for whose future we have had no adequate care, and to the consideration of whose present state the Government has only been moved when pressed by some present danger. . . . We have encroached upon their means of subsistence without furnishing them any proper return; we have shut them up on reservations often notoriously unfit for them, or, if fit, we have not hesitated to drive them off for our profit, without regard to theirs; we have treated them sometimes as foreign nations, with whom we have had treaties; sometimes as wards, who are entitled to no voice in the management of their affairs; and sometimes as subjects, from whom we have required obedience, but to whom we have recognized no obligations. That the Government of the United States, which has often plighted its faith to the Indian, and has broken it as often, and, while punishing him for his crimes, has given him no status in the courts except as a criminal, has been sadly derelict in its duty toward him, and has reaped the whirlwind only because it has sown the wind, is set forth in no exaggerated terms in the following pages, and ought to be acknowledged with shame by every American citizen.

It will be admitted now on every hand that the only solution of the Indian problem involves the entire change of these people from a savage to a civilized life. They are not likely to be exterminated. Unless we ourselves withdraw from all contact with them, and leave them to roam untrammeled over their wilds, or until the power of a Christian civilization shall make them consciously one with us, they will not cease to vex us.

When asked if there were anything she would like to say to the committee, the poor woman replied: "I wish you would do what you can to get my husband released. I am very poor here, and do not know what is to become of me. If he were released he would come down here, and we would live together quietly, and do no harm to anybody, and make no trouble. But I should never get over my desire to get back north; I should always want to get back where my children were born, and died, and were buried. That country is better than this in every respect. . . . There is plenty of good, cool water there—pure water—while here the water is not good. It is not hot there, nor so sickly. Are you going where my husband is? Can you tell when he is likely to be released?"

The Senators were obliged to reply to her that they were not going where her husband was, and they could not tell when he would be released.

Reports of Progress

In view of the accounts of the sickness and suffering of these Indians in 1877 and 1878, the reports made in 1879 of the industry and progress at the Cheyenne and Arapahoe Agency are almost incredible. The school children have, by their earnings, bought one hundred head of cattle; 451,000 pounds of freight have been transported by the Indians during the year; they have also worked at making brick, chopping wood, making hay, hauling wood, and splitting and hauling rails; and have earned thereby $7121.25. Two of the girls of the school have been promoted to the position of assistant teachers; and the United States mail contractor between this agency and Fort Elliott, in Texas—a distance of one hundred and sixty-five miles—has operated almost exclusively with full-blooded Indians: "there has been no report of breach of trust on the part of any Indians connected with this trust, and the contractor expresses his entire approval of their conduct."

It is stated also that there was not sufficient clothing to furnish each Indian with a warm suit of clothing, "as promised by the treaty," and that, "by reference to official correspondence, the fact is established that the Cheyennes and Arapahoes are judged as having no legal rights to any lands, having forfeited their treaty reservation by a failure to settle thereon," and their "present reservation not having been, as yet, confirmed by Congress. Inasmuch as the Indians fully understood, and were assured that this reservation was given to them in lieu of their treaty reservation, and have commenced farming in the belief that there was no uncertainty about the matter, it is but common justice that definite action be had at an early day, securing to them what is their right."

It would seem that there could be found nowhere in the melancholy record of the experiences of our Indians a more glaring instance of confused multiplication of injustices than this. The Cheyennes were pursued and slain for venturing to leave this very reservation, which, it appears, is not their reservation at all, and they have no legal right to it. Are there any words to fitly characterize such treatment as this from a great, powerful, rich nation, to a handful of helpless people?

VIEWPOINT 3

"Volume after volume might be filled in recounting the unprovoked and merciless atrocities committed upon the people of the frontier by their implacable foe, the red man."

The Military Protects Civilization from Savages

George Armstrong Custer (1839-1876)

George Armstrong Custer, born in New Rumley, Ohio, on December 5, 1839, began life as the son of a blacksmith. After attending normal school, he taught for a year in a one-room schoolhouse. Recognizing that the military was a path for upward mobility, he applied to West Point, from which he barely graduated in June 1861. He served in the Union Army, seeing action at Bull Run, Antietam, Gettysburg, and Appomattox. His cavalry tactics were often audacious and full of initiative, successful even though sometimes in violation of orders. By age twenty-three, because of his combat skills, his self-promotion, and his popularity with influential generals, he was made brigadier general. This incredibly young appointment and his flamboyant personality led to his Civil War exploits being reported in *Harper's Weekly* and the *New York Times*. Perhaps because of this journalistic entree, he first pub-

From *My Life on the Plains; or Personal Experiences with Indians* by George A. Custer. New edition © 1962 by the University of Oklahoma Press.

lished *My Life on the Plains*, from which the following excerpt comes, serially in *Galaxy*, a popular magazine of the time. In the following excerpt, Custer argues forcibly for a military policy which would re-open travel across the Plains and punish Indians responsible for outrages against settlers and travelers.

Aided by daylight, and moving nearly due north, [an army scout] soon struck the well-traveled overland route, and from the frightened employees at the nearest station he obtained intelligence which confirmed our worst fears as to the extent of the Indian outbreak. Stage stations at various points along the route had been attacked and burned, and the inmates driven off or murdered. All travel across the Plains was suspended, and an Indian war with all its barbarities had been forced upon the people of the frontier.

As soon as the officer ascertaining these facts had returned to camp and made his report, the entire command was again put in motion and started in the direction of the stage route with the intention of clearing it of straggling bands of Indians, reopening the mainline of travel across the Plains, and establishing if possible upon the proper tribes the responsibility for the numerous outrages recently committed. The stage stations were erected at points along the route distant from each other from ten to fifteen miles, and were used solely for the shelter and accommodation of the relays of drivers and horses employed on the stage route. We found in passing over the route on our eastward march that only about every fourth station was occupied, the occupants of the other three having congregated there for mutual defense against the Indians, the latter having burned the deserted stations.

From the employees of the company at various points we learned that for the few preceding days the Indians had been crossing the line going toward the north in large bodies. In some places we saw the ruins of burned stations, but it was not until we reached Lookout Station, a point about fifteen miles west of Fort Hays, that we came upon the first real evidences of an Indian outbreak. Riding some distance in advance of the command, I reached the station only to find it and the adjacent buildings in ashes, the ruins still smoking. Near by I discovered the bodies of the three station-keepers, so mangled and burned as to be scarcely recognizable as human beings. The Indians had evidently tortured them before putting an end to their sufferings. They were scalped and horribly disfigured. Their bodies were badly burned, but whether before or after death could not be determined. No arrows or other article of Indian manufacture could be found to positively determine what particular tribe was the guilty one. The men at other stations had recognized some of the Indians passing as belonging to the Sioux and Cheyennes, the same we had passed from the village on Pawnee Fork.

General Hancock's Orders

Continuing our march, we reached Fort Hays, from which point I dispatched a report to General Hancock, on the Arkansas, furnishing him all the information I had gained concerning the outrages and movements of the Indians. As it has been a question of considerable dispute between the respective advocates of the Indian peace and war policy, as to which party committed the first overt act of war, the Indians or General Hancock's command, I quote from a letter of inquiry from the latter when commanding the armies of the United States. General Hancock says:

"When I learned from General Custer, who investigated these matters on the spot, that directly after they had abandoned the villages they attacked and burned a mail station on the Smoky Hill, killed the white men at it, disemboweled and burned them, fired into another station, endeavored to gain admittance to a third, fired on my expressmen both on the Smoky Hill and on their way to Larned, I concluded that this must be war, and therefore deemed it my duty to take the first opportunity which presented to resent these hostilities and outrages, and did so by destroying their villages."

The first paragraph of General Hancock's special field order directing the destruction of the Indian village read as follows:

"II. As a punishment for the bad faith practiced by the Cheyennes and Sioux who occupied the Indian village at this place, and as a chastisement for murders and depredations committed since the arrival of the command at this point, by the people of these tribes, the village recently occupied by them which is now in our hands, will be utterly destroyed."

From these extracts the question raised can be readily settled. This act of retribution on the part of General Hancock was the signal for an extensive pen and ink war directed against him and his forces. This was to be expected. The pecuniary loss and deprivation of opportunities to speculate in Indian commodities, as practiced by most Indian agents, were too great to be submitted to without a murmur. The Cheyennes, Arapahoes, and Apaches had been united under one agency; the Kiowas and Comanches under another. As General Hancock's expedition had reference to all of these tribes, he had extended invitations to each of the two agents to accompany him into Indian country and be present at all interviews with the representatives of these respective tribes for the purpose, as the invitation states, of showing the Indians "that the officers of the government are acting in harmony."

Outrages Against Whites

These agents were both present at General Hancock's headquarters. Both admitted to General Hancock in conversation that Indians had been guilty of all the outrages charged against them, but each asserted the innocence of the particular tribes under his charge, and endeavored to lay their crimes at the door of their neighbors. The agent of the Kiowas and Comanches declared to the department commander that "the tribes of his agency had been grossly wronged by having been charged with various offenses which had undoubtedly been committed by the Cheyennes, Arapahoes, and Apaches, and that these tribes deserved severe and summary chastisement for their numerous misdeeds, very many of which had been laid at the doors of his innocent tribes."

George Armstrong Custer believed that native Americans must make way for the encroaching white settlers and that it was his job to assure the Indians' subjugation.

Not to be out done in the profuse use of fair words, however, the agent of the three tribes thus assailed informed General Hancock that his three tribes "were peacefully inclined, and rarely committed offenses against the laws, but that most unfortunately they were charged in many instances with crimes which had been perpetrated by other tribes, and that in this respect they had suffered heavily from the Kiowas, who were the most turbulent Indians of the Plains, and deserved punishment more than any others."

Here was positive evidence from the agents themselves that the Indians against whom we were operating were guilty, and deserving of severe punishment. The only conflicting portion of the testimony was as to which tribe was most guilty. Subsequent events proved, however, that all of the five tribes named, as well as the Sioux, had combined for a general war throughout the Plains and along our frontier. Such a war had been threatened to our post commanders along the Arkansas on many occasions during the winter. The movement of the Sioux and Cheyennes toward the north indicated that the principal theater of military operations during the summer would be between the Smoky Hill and Platte rivers. General Hancock accordingly assembled the principal chiefs of the Kiowas and Arapahoes in council at Fort Dodge, hoping to induce them to remain at peace and observe their treaty obligations.

The Box Massacre

The most prominent chiefs in council were Satanta, Lone Wolf, and Kicking Bird of the Kiowas, and Little Raven and Yellow Bear of the Arapahoes. During the council, extravagant promises of future good conduct were made by these chiefs. So effective and convincing was the oratorical effort of Satanta that at the termination of his address the department commander and staff presented him with the uniform, coat, sash, and hat of a major general. In return for this compliment Satanta, within a few weeks after, attacked the post at which the council was held, arrayed in his new uniform. This same chief had but recently headed an expedition to the frontier of Texas, where, among murders committed by him and his band, was that known as the "Box Massacre." The Box family consisted of the father, mother, and five children, the eldest a girl about eighteen, the youngest a babe. The entire family had been visiting at a neighbor's house, and were returning home in the evening, little dreaming of the terrible fate impending, when Satanta and his warriors dashed upon them, surrounded the wagon in which they were driving, and at the first fire killed the father and one of the children. The horses were hastily taken from the wagon, while the mother was informed by signs that she and her four surviving children must accompany their captors. Mounting their prisoners upon led horses, of which they had a great number stolen from the settlers, the Indians prepared to set out on their return to the village, then located hundreds of miles north. Before departing from the scene of the massacre, the savages scalped the father and child, who had fallen as their first victims. Far better would it have been had the remaining members of the family met their death in the first attack. From the mother, whom I met when released from her captivity, after living as a prisoner in the hands of the Indians for more than a year, I gathered the details of the sufferings of herself and children.

The Indians Must Be Thoroughly Whipped

Albert and Jennie Barnitz were, in many ways, quite like George and Elizabeth Custer: Both were young military couples; both were loving, almost to the point of being adulatory. Albert Barnitz, however, a lieutenant in Custer's 7th Cavalry, in letters to his Jennie was often overtly critical of Custer. In the following passages, nonetheless, he supports Custer's views on Indian policy.

Aug. 13, 1867:

. . . We are to have peace soon it seems!—Genl. Sherman, and the Peace Commissioners have met, and decided upon it, it appears, and the big councils are to be held up on the Platte in the full moon of September and at Larned in the full moon of October, and the presents will be distributed, and the new guns, and everything, and then we will go into winter quarters before Christmas, and in the Spring we will repeat the pleasant little farce of a Big Indian War, and a hand-full of men to carry it on.

Of course the peace won't amount to any thing, except that it will enable the Commissioners to distribute presents!—But may be some more extensive preparations will be made for the next war. The Indians must be thoroughly whipped before they will respect us, or keep any peace, and they haven't been whipped yet very much to speak of.

Fearing pursuit by the Texans and desiring to place as long a distance as possible between themselves and their pursuers, they prepared for a night march. Mrs. Box and the three elder children were placed on separate horses and securely bound. This was to prevent escape in the darkness. The mother was at first permitted to carry the youngest child, a babe of a few months, in her arms; but the latter becoming fretful during the tiresome night ride, began to cry. The Indians, fearing the sound of its voice might be heard by pursuers, snatched it from its mother's arms and dashed its brains out against a tree, then threw the lifeless remains to the ground and continued their flight. No halt was made for twenty-four hours, after which the march was conducted more deliberately. Each night the mother and three children were permitted to occupy one shelter, closely guarded by their watchful enemies.

After traveling for several days this war party arrived at the point where they rejoined their lodges. They were still a long distance from the main village near the Arkansas. Each night the scalp of the father was hung up in the lodge occupied by the mother and children. A long and weary march over a wild and desolate country brought them to the main village. Here the captives found that their most serious troubles were to commence. In accordance with Indian custom, upon the return of a successful war party, a grand assembly of the tribe took place. The prisoners, captured horses, and scalps were brought forth, and the usual ceremonies, terminating in a scalp dance, followed. Then the division of the spoils was made. The captives were apportioned among the various bands composing the tribe, so that when the division was completed the mother fell to the possession of one chief, the eldest daughter to that of another, the second, a little girl of probably ten years, to another, and the youngest, a child of three years, to a fourth. No two members of the family were permitted to remain in the same band, but were each carried to separate villages, distant from each other several days march. This was done partly to prevent escape.

Painful Tortures

No pen can describe the painful tortures of mind and body endured by this unfortunate family. They remained as captives in the hands of the Indians for more than a year, during which time the eldest daughter, a beautiful girl just ripening into womanhood, was exposed to a fate infinitely more dreadful than death itself. She first fell to one of the principal chiefs, who, after robbing her of that which was more precious than life, and forcing her to become the victim of his brutal lust, bartered her in return for two horses to another chief; he again, after wearying of her, traded her to a chief of a neighboring band; and in that way this unfortunate girl was passed from one to another of her savage captors, undergoing a life so horribly brutal that, when meeting her upon her release from captivity, one could only wonder how a young girl, nurtured in civilization and possessed of the natural refinement and delicacy of thought which she exhibited, could have survived such degrading treatment.

The mother and second daughter fared somewhat better. The youngest, however, separated from mother and sisters and thrown among people totally devoid of all kind feeling, spent the time in shedding bitter tears. This so enraged the Indians that, as a punishment as well as preventive, the child was seized and the soles of its naked feet exposed to the flames of the lodge fire until every portion of the cuticle was burned therefrom. When I saw this little girl a year afterward, her feet were from this cause still in a painful and unhealed condition. These poor captives were re-claimed from their bondage through the efforts of officers of the army, and by payment of a ransom amounting to many hundreds of dollars.

The facts relating to their cruel treatment were obtained by me directly from the mother and eldest daughter immediately after their release, which occurred a few months prior to the council held with Satanta and other chiefs. . . .

The treatment of the Box [family] is not given as [an] isolated instance, but is referred to principally to show the character of the enemy with whom we were at war. Volume after volume might be filled in recounting the unprovoked and merciless atrocities committed upon the people of the frontier by their implacable foe, the red man. It will become necessary, however, in making a truthful record of the principal events which transpired under my personal observation, to make mention of Indian outrages sur-passing if possible in savage cruelty any yet referred to.

"The officers told me they killed and butchered all they came to."

The Military Savagely Destroys the Indians

Testimony from U.S. Congressional Investigations

During the gold and silver rushes of the 1850s, thousands of miners and settlers poured into Colorado Territory, dislocating and infuriating the Arapahoe and Cheyenne. Consequently, they escalated raids on wagon trains, stagecoaches, and towns, so that citizens of Denver were terrified of imminent Indian attack. The governor of the territory issued a proclamation in effect giving Colorado citizens carte blanche to kill Indians; however, he failed to inform the Indians that a previous proclamation promising protection to friendly Indians was no longer in effect. Because regular army forces were involved in Civil War actions, the Third Colorado Cavalry, mostly composed of hundred-day volunteers, was sent into the field under Col. John M. Chivington, an ex-minister and aspiring politician. Despite the fact that other officers had promised protection to peaceful Cheyenne led by Black Kettle, Chivington insisted that it was honorable to "use any means under God's heaven to kill Indians who would kill women and children." To his subordinates who protested, Chivington asserted, "Damn any man who is in sympathy with an Indian" and pointedly suggested that such officers should get out of the military.

On the morning of November 19, 1865, the Third Cavalry charged the sleeping Cheyenne village of Sand Creek. Black Ket-

Excerpted from the Appendix to *The Sand Creek Massacre* by Stan Hoig. Copyright © 1962 by the University of Oklahoma Press. Reprinted by permission of the University of Oklahoma Press.

tle, wearing a peace medal, rushed out of his tent and raised an American flag symbolic of his people's loyalty and then a white flag. Nonetheless, over two hundred of the five hundred Indians of all ages died there. Among them was White Antelope, killed chanting his death song: "Nothing lives long/ except the earth and the mountains." Ironically, Black Kettle survived this day, only to be killed by Custer at the Battle of Washita.

People in Denver greeted the returning troopers, many decorated with grisly souvenirs, as conquering heroes. Still, Congress launched several investigations. The following testimony is from three of them, the House of Representatives' "Massacre of Cheyenne Indians" (1865) and the Senate's "Sand Creek Massacre" (1867) and "The Chivington Massacre" (1867). While some of the testimony supports Chivington's actions, most is strongly critical.

Testimony and affidavits concerning the number of Indians killed at Sand Creek, the question of flags, white scalps found in the Indian camp, and atrocities committed by the soldiers.

Samuel G. Colley, Indian Agent

The Chivington Massacre, Testimony, p. 29—I can state according to the received version, that the command marched at 8 o'clock in the evening from Fort Lyon. They attacked the village, which was 30 miles distant, and fired into it about daylight. The Indians, for a while, made some resistance. Some of the chiefs did not lift an arm, but stood there and were shot down. One of them, Black Kettle, raised the American flag, and raised a white flag. He was supposed to be killed, but was not. They retreated right up the creek. They were followed up and pursued and killed and butchered. None denied that they were butchered in a brutal manner and scalped and mutilated as bad as an Indian ever did to a white man. That is admitted by the parties who did it. They were cut to pieces in almost every manner and form. . . .

He [Ed Guerrier] rode with them to the camp and was with them 14 days after they got together on Smoky Hill. He said there were 148 missing when they got in. After that quite a number came in; I cannot tell how many. There were eight who came into Fort Lyon to us, reducing it down to about 130 missing, according to the last information I had. . . .

The officers told me they killed and butchered all they came to. They saw little papooses killed by the soldiers. Colonel Shupe was in command of the regiment; Colonel Chivington in command of the whole force.

The Chivington Massacre, Affidavit, January 27, 1865, p. 52— . . . Colonel Chivington did, on the morning of the 29th of November last, surprise and attack said camp of friendly Indians and massacre a large number of them, (mostly women and children,) and did allow the troops of his command to mangle and mutilate them in the most horrible manner. . . .

Big Foot, frozen in the snow at Wounded Knee. Though at a separate engagement, it is a stark commentary on the army as a destroyer rather than a defender of civilizations.

John S. Smith, Interpreter

The Chivington Massacre, Testimony, p. 42—I think about seventy or eighty, including men, women, and children, were killed; twenty-five or thirty of them were warriors probably, and the rest women, children, boys, and old men.

[The Indian barbarities practiced were] The worst I have ever seen.

All manner of depredations were inflicted on their persons; they were scalped, their brains knocked out; the men used their knives, ripped open women, clubbed little children, knocked them in the head with their guns, beat their brains out, mutilated their bodies in every sense of the word.

It would be hard for me to tell who did these things: I saw some of the first Colorado regiment committing some very bad acts there on the persons of the Indians, and I likewise saw some of the one-hundred-day men in the same kind of business.

The Chivington Massacre, Affidavit, January 15, 1865, p. 51—When the troops began approaching, I saw Black Kettle, the head chief, hoist the American flag, fearing there might be some mistake as to who they were.

Massacre of Cheyenne Indians, Testimony, p. 9—I saw the bodies of those lying there cut all to pieces, worse mutilated than any I ever saw before, the women cut all to pieces.

[They were cut] With knives; scalped; their brains knocked out; children two or three months old; all ages lying there, from sucking infants up to warriors.

I do not think that I saw more than 70 lying dead then, as far as I went.

James D. Cannon, First Lieutenant
First Infantry New Mexico Volunteers

The Chivington Massacre, Affidavit, January 16, 1865, p. 53—The command of Colonel Chivington was composed of about one thousand men; the village of the Indians consisted of from one hundred to one hundred and thirty lodges, and, as far as I am able to judge, of from five hundred to six hundred souls, the majority of which were women and children; in going over the battle-ground the next day I did not see a body of man, woman, or child but was scalped, and in many instances their bodies were mutilated in the most horrible manner—men, women, and children's privates cut out, &c; I heard one man say that he had cut out a woman's private parts and had them for exhibition on a stick; I heard another man say that he had cut the fingers off an Indian to get the rings on the hand; according to the best of my knowledge and belief these atrocities that were committed were with knowledge of J.M. Chivington, and I do not know of his taking any measures to prevent them; I heard of one instance of a child a few months old being thrown in the feed-box of a wagon, and after being carried some distance left on the ground to perish; I also heard of numerous instances in which men had cut out the private parts of females and stretched them over the saddle-bows, and wore them over their hats while riding in the ranks. All these matters were a subject of general conversation, and could not help being known by Colonel J.M. Chivington.

Sand Creek Massacre, Testimony, p. 111—My estimate of the number of Indians killed was about two hundred, all told.

They were scalped and mutilated in various ways.

p. 113—I heard one man say that he had cut a squaw's heart out, and he had it stuck up on a stick.

David Louderback, Private
First Colorado Cavalry

The Chivington Massacre, Affidavit by Louderback and R.W. Clark, citizen, January 27, 1865, pp. 53-54— . . . that according to their best knowledge and belief the entire Indian village was composed of not more than five hundred (500) souls, two-thirds of which were women and children; that the dead bodies of women and children were afterwards mutilated in the most horrible manner; that it was the understanding of the deponents, and the general understanding of the garrison of Fort Lyon, that this village were friendly Indians. . . .

Commentary

The Daily Rocky Mountain News *of August 10, 1864, heartily endorsed Governor John Evans' call to exterminate the Indians.*

Self preservation demands decisive action, and the only way to secure it is to fight them [the Indians] in their own way. A few months of active extermination against the red devils will bring quiet, and nothing else will.

Joseph A. Cramer, Second Lieutenant
First Colorado Cavalry

The Chivington Massacre, Affidavit, p. 73—I estimated the loss of the Indians to be from one hundred and twenty-five to one hundred and seventy-five killed; no wounded fell into our hands, and all the dead were scalped. The Indian who was pointed out as White Antelope had his fingers cut off. . . . It is a mistake that there were any white scalps found in the village. I saw one, but it was very old, the hair being much faded. I was ordered to burn the village. . . .

Lucien Palmer, Sergeant
Co. C. First Colorado Cavalry

The Chivington Massacre, Affidavit, p. 74—I counted 130 bodies, all dead; two squaws and three papooses were captured and brought to Fort Lyon. I think among the dead bodies one-third were women and children. The bodies were horribly cut up, skulls broken in a good many; I judge they were broken in after they were killed, as they were shot besides. I do not think I saw any but what was scalped; saw fingers cut off, saw several bodies with privates cut off, women as well as men. I saw Major Sayre, of the 3d regiment, scalp an Indian for the scalp lock ornamented by silver ornaments; he cut off the skin with it. He stood by and saw his men cutting fingers from dead bodies. . . . All I saw done in mutilating bodies was done by members of the 3d regiment. . . .

Amos C. Miksch, Corporal
Co. E, First Colorado Cavalry

The Chivington Massacre, Affidavit, pp. 74-75—Next morning after the battle I saw a little boy covered up among the Indians in a trench, still alive. I saw a major in the 3d regiment take out his pistol and blow off the top of his head. I saw some men unjointing fingers to get rings off, and cutting off ears to get silver ornaments. I saw a party with the same major take up bodies that had been buried in the night to scalp them and take off ornaments. I saw a squaw with her head smashed in before she was killed. Next morning, after they were dead and stiff, these men pulled out the bodies of the squaws and pulled them open in an indecent manner. I heard men say they had cut out the privates, but did not see it myself. It was the 3d Colorado men who did these things. I counted 123 dead bodies; I think not over twenty-five were full-grown men; the warriors were killed out in the bluff. . . . Next day I saw Lieutenant Richmond scalp two Indians; it was disgusting to me. . . .

Robert Bent, Guide

The Chivington Massacre, Sworn Statement, pp. 95-96—When we came in sight of the camp I saw the American flag waving and heard Black Kettle tell the Indians to stand round the flag, and there they were huddled—men, women, and children. This was when we were within fifty yards of the Indians. I also saw a white flag raised. These flags were in so conspicuous a position that they must have been seen. When the troops fired the Indians ran, some of the men ran into their lodges, probably to get their arms. They had time to get away if they had wanted to. . . . I think there were six hundred Indians in all. I think there were thirty-five braves and some old men, about sixty in all. All fought well. At the time the rest of the men were away from camp, hunting. I visited the battleground one month afterwards; saw the remains of a good many; counted sixty-nine, but a number had been eaten by the wolves and dogs. . . . Everyone I saw dead was scalped.

VIEWPOINT 5

"Little Bull cannot understand why a great and rich nation should invite him into partnership and afterward fall down on its part of the bargain."

Indians Must Submerge Their Identity in the Dominant Culture

Elaine Goodale Eastman (1863-1953)

At age twenty, Elaine Goodale, already a published poet, took a teaching job at Hampton Institute, Virginia, working with Gen. Richard Henry Pratt, then in charge of the Indian Department at that school and later founder of the Carlisle Indian Industrial School in Pennsylvania. At Hampton she absorbed the philosophy of eastern reformers such as Sen. Henry L. Dawes and Herbert Welsh, co-founder in 1882 of the Indian Rights Association. According to Kay Graber, editor of Goodale's memoirs, these reformers believed that the Indians'

> only chance for survival in the face of the overwhelming encroachment of white Americans lay in their adoption of white civilization. They particularly emphasized the need to obtain formal education, espouse Christianity, dissolve tribal bonds, and become private property owners—self-sufficient farmers.

Convinced of her calling, Goodale went to teach at the Lower Brulé agency on the Great Sioux Reservation in South Dakota. Her memoirs describe the Sioux's attempts to adjust to reservation life and to strange customs and religions. Goodale also witnessed the

Reprinted from *Sister to the Sioux: The Memoirs of Elaine Goodale Eastman*, edited by Kay Graber, by permission of the University of Nebraska Press. Copyright © 1978 by the University of Nebraska Press.

emergence of the Ghost Dance religion and helped care for the survivors of the Battle of Wounded Knee. Perhaps ironically, Goodale, who went west to advance the Indians' assimilation into white society, fell in love with and married the agency physician, Dr. Charles Eastman (Ohiyesa), a mixed-blood Sioux.

In the following viewpoint, Goodale describes difficulties the Sioux faced in becoming farmers. Despite, or perhaps because of, her belief, in principle, in assimilation, she is appalled by some of the ignorance and corruption the Indians' white "mentors" exhibit.

"Those lazy, dirty, good-for-nothing Sioux!" Such was the cry of the ambitious speculator in town lots, the western politician, the industrious and land-hungry immigrant. "They don't need all that land. Everybody knows that Injuns won't work!"

In the words of Dr. Fred Riggs, a missionary of the third generation, brought up among these people, the Sioux had, in fact, plenty of energy and initiative—otherwise they could not have survived under the hard conditions of primitive life. Theirs was an incessant, hand-to-hand struggle against hunger and cold, wild beasts, and lurking enemies.

What motive was there for regular, persistent labor under the new dispensation? We exterminated the buffalo which originally furnished them with a livelihood, confined them to a limited range of the least desirable part of their territory (for the purpose of cultivation), and doled out just enough monotonous food and shoddy clothing to keep them alive. It was proposed gradually to transform nomadic hunters into farmers, a difficult but by no means an impossible feat. (Some tribes have long been successful agriculturists.) Money was appropriated by Congress to buy seed, implements, and fence wire, and to employ an instructor in farming at every agency. Let us see just how the plan worked in the Dakota of the eighteen eighties.

The "assistant farmer" of that day, not unlike the average office-holder before civil service reform, was usually a political hench-man or needy favorite of some man higher up. Such posts were poorly paid and regarded as desirable mainly because of opportunities for private pickings. "We're none of us here for our health" was the common and significant jest. Many farmers, to my personal knowledge, devoted most of their time to hauling water, cutting ice, cultivating small vegetable gardens, and doing other chores for the agent. When they did undertake to instruct an Indian, their ignorance was sometimes laughable. I heard of one who directed his neophytes to cut turnips in pieces and plant them in hills!

Plowing in South Dakota may be begun as early as February or March. Let us suppose that one Little Bull, seeing nothing for it but to walk henceforth in the white man's road, has made up his mind to put in a crop. The first step is to join a crude local Grange which meets from time to time during the winter, for the enjoyment of much long-winded debate and a substantial supper.

Having none of his own, he applies to the assistant farmer for the use of a plow. One is assigned to him for a given period—perhaps ten days. When the preordained date arrives (provided it doesn't rain, that Little Bull isn't sick, and that the farmer hasn't forgotten and let another man have the plow, the would-be planter stands before his cabin door and utters a musical halloo which may be heard at a distance of at least half a mile. This is the regular way of issuing a general invitation and in this case is understood to mean that the caller bids his fellow Grangers to a plowing bee.

In the course of the morning several pony teams appear and cut a shallow, uneven furrow around the selected piece of ground. The tough prairie sod and the heavy breaking-plow form a combination that is almost too much for these light, unseasoned ponies, used to "rustling" pasture for themselves and innocent of the taste of grain. The slenderly muscled bodies of the amateur farmers are better suited to spurts of intense effort than to continuous toil. Their bright-hued shirt-tails and long black hair float on the stiff breeze as they run and leap and almost dance behind the plow. The ponies sweat and strain, jerk and tug desperately; the much mended harness often gives way; and Little Bull is fortunate indeed if the plow does not break—perhaps forty miles from a blacksmith shop. At the end of every round, all the men sit down in a ring and the inevitable long red pipe is passed from hand to hand.

By the time the field is plowed—or half plowed more likely—it is time to eat. The wives have been busy, too. They appear on the scene at noon by the sun, laden with steaming coffee pots, kettles of boiled beef, and huge piles of fried bread, each round the size of a dinner plate. Again the circle is formed, this time including many who have been no more than interested spectators at the morning's labor.

The farmer has duly applied for enough grain to plant his field. He may have asked for a few potatoes with seed of melons, squashes, and other vegetables. He is lucky if he gets half as much as he wants of any of these. The agent's estimates, none too liberal to begin with, have been severely pruned in Washington, in the interest of "economy." Little Bull cannot understand why a great and rich nation should invite him into partnership and afterward fall down on its part of the bargain.

The native fertility of our Dakota soil was then untapped, but sufficient rainfall was to be expected no more than one year in three. Careless fencing led to much destruction by horses and cattle. Necessary trips to the agency after supplies and long visits to relatives in other jurisdictions seriously interfered with proper cultivation of corn. Occasionally a fine crop of wheat was lost for lack of timely help in threshing and marketing the grain, with the nearest gristmill fifty to a hundred miles away, on the other side of the great river. At long intervals, separated by miles of crisp buffalo grass or silvery sage, prickly white poppies, and blazing wild sunflowers, cramped cornfields choked with weeds marked the unequal fight.

The caption to the cover illustration of an 1884 issue of Leslie's Illustrated Newspaper *reads: "Educating the Indian—A Female Pupil at the Government School at Carlisle Visits Her Home at Pine Ridge Agency." Unwittingly, the newspaper hints at the difficulties such students, now caught between two worlds, would face returning to their homes.*

It was sometimes urged that the government buy the Indian's surplus produce on the spot for distribution, instead of importing it. This seemed a commonsense plan to all except contractors and others interested in supplying the Indian Service. The Sioux could easily have grown all their own beef and probably their flour or cornmeal as well. Yet even the cash business of freighting supplies from the nearest railroad station was usually given to white men! Agent McGillycuddy at Pine Ridge was one of the first to insist that the Sioux should have it. This reform was inaugurated in 1878, under Secretary [of the Interior Carl] Schurz, and the Oglalas alone were said to have earned forty-five thousand dollars in one year by freighting.

A double error has been made through the years in assuming that red men are incompetents—hardly men at all, in fact—and in building up a vested right among white men to work they might far better have done for themselves. As communities they have been practically without money and so unable to buy the product of one another's labor. In my day, there were among them no blacksmiths, carpenters, or shoemakers whose services could be purchased. Although young men were already being taught these trades in eastern schools, one who attempted to practice them at home must starve for lack of custom. So, probably, would the enterprising "returned student" who managed to open a small store, breaking the monopoly of the licensed trader, whose exorbitant prices were a standing grievance. His technique was to hold his customers by keeping them continuously in debt.

The limited number of salaried positions open to Indians in government employ was no real solution, although ability to secure one of these posts was, and still is, practically the only chance to earn a decent living on the reservation. The man with a regular pay check, however small, was handicapped by incessant demands upon his hospitality, an obligation impossible to evade under tribal custom. That there has been little gain in these respects in the past half century is indicated by the most recent official survey, which states that "no opportunity exists within the home area for wage employment, except of a temporary nature in emergency government agencies."

The Sioux naturally tended to huddle in groups along the creeks and river bottoms, where shade, water, and some fuel might be had, rather than to "scatter out" on the open prairie, as required under the "land in severalty" system. [The 1887 General Allotment Act (commonly called the Dawes Act after its sponsor, Senator Henry L. Dawes) authorized the President to proceed with the allotment of Indian reservation in severalty.] It was hard to give up the prized social life of a small neighborhood for an isolated claim and even harder to travel eighty or a hundred miles once every fortnight after rations, with frequent breakdowns of wagons and harnesses on the road. Whenever a new "count" was ordered or "*wakpamni* week" came around in the dead of winter, it was customary to take the entire family to camp in tents, leaving pigs and poultry, if any, to their fate. Even today, I am told, the home ranch is similarly neglected for a chance of a few week's work on the CCC or for the doubtful amusements of a rodeo!

But (you may ask) wasn't it known fifty years ago that most of the Great Sioux Reservation was fit only for grazing and much of it "bad lands" fit for nothing at all? A glance at the record proves that the well-informed knew then, as well as we know now, that the Sioux could never expect to support themselves by agriculture. Without artificial irrigation, it is still only in exceptional years that a crop can be raised. Indeed, the water table has fallen and droughts are growing more severe, as everyone realizes. Many of the white settlers who followed the Sioux with high hopes and industrious habits have since abandoned their claims. A general depopulation of that part of the country is not at all impossible. Deep tillage, green manuring, and fallowing have all been tried and found, in the main, unprofitable.

In a word, this is and always has been a cattle country. Not isolated quarter-sections of treeless and waterless prairie, but cooperative herds or individually owned cattle pastured on common land, might have solved the problem for those Dakotas who chose to stay where they were. I knew white men married to Sioux women who amassed a competence in this way. The standard excuse for discouraging so natural a trend was that herding, as a way of life, was too much like the old hunting economy! It could, however, have been combined with ownership of a small, well-watered homestead and garden spot, as was done by the better class of "squaw men."

"Visions and Vision Quests are of utmost importance to our people. . . . Through dreams and visions, we receive [personal] power."

Indians Must Assert Their Ethnic Identity

Archie Fire Lame Deer (1935-) and Richard Erdoes

The conventional nineteenth-century assumption was either that Indians had no culture (they were "savages") or, even if they did have their own culture, they must abandon it and assimilate into the dominant culture if they were to survive. Some Indian leaders of the time voiced opposition to policies of the United States government and the philanthropists and reformers. Chief Joseph of the Nez Percé, for example, long before his exhausted "I will fight no more forever" speech, remembered his father's dying words: "Never sell the bones of your father and your mother," and he argued passionately against giving up traditional tribal lands. Ohiyesa, or Charles Eastman, a Sioux who had never seen a white person before he was sixteen, later attended Dartmouth College, graduated from medical school at Boston College, and returned to the Dakotas to provide medical care to his people. He, too, argued for respect for his people and their beliefs: "Every religion has its Holy Book, and ours was a mingling of history, poetry, and prophecy, of precept and folk-lore, even such as the modern reader finds within the covers of his Bible."

Generally speaking, leaders like Chief Joseph and Charles Eastman were ignored. What today might be called WASP (White Anglo-Saxon Protestant) Eurocentrism was the norm. Writers like Helen Hunt Jackson and Elaine Goodale Eastman were the exceptions. In the intervening century, much has changed in American attitudes toward Indians and other minorities.

The changes have been slow in coming, however. The young Archie Fire Lame Deer was raised in the 1930s and 1940s on the Rosebud Reservation in South Dakota by his maternal grandfather. At age twelve, after his grandfather's death, the boy was taken to the Catholic boarding school at St. Francis, ten miles from Rosebud, to begin the process of assimilation. There students were forbidden to speak their own language, were required to wear identical clothes "to make us into little white people," and were introduced to "alien gods." Eventually, Lame Deer ran away from the school, telling his uncles that "the only way they could get me back to St. Francis was as a corpse." Lame Deer spent his next several years "moving in an alcoholic haze from one career to another and compiling a record of 185 arrests for drunken fights." He was "a ranchhand, bartender, paratrooper with the U.S. Army in Korea, the chief rattlesnake catcher of the state of South Dakota, and the best-known Indian stunt man in Hollywood." After this apparently aimless life, he went on the wagon, became a counselor to Indian alcoholics and prison inmates, and finally became a spiritual leader of the Lakota. In the following viewpoint, Lame Deer explains the importance of a Vision Quest to the Lakota—and the importance of giving oneself up to one's own destiny.

---

*H*anblecheya means "crying for a vision." It means going on a Vision Quest, up to the hilltop, maybe crawling into a vision pit, and staying there without eating or drinking for four days and nights, praying for an answer from the Supernaturals. That's a hard thing to do.

A man going to the hilltop for Hanblecheya gives his flesh and bones to Wakan Tanka, the Grandfather Spirit. And if he is accepted, he goes on living, but his spirit somehow works apart from his body. He has been given a power. In order to have a vision, you have to give yourself up completely. It is almost like dying, only you come back. Hanblecheya is one of the toughest things a man can experience.

"Crying for a vision," my father once told me, "that's the beginning of our religion. It is the thirst for a dream from above—a vision which, while it lasts, will make you more than just a man. If you never had a vision, you are nothing. This is what I believe.

"It is like the prophets in the Christian Bible, like Jesus fasting in the desert, or Jacob wrestling with the angel, wrestling for a dream. It means hearing soundless voices, seeing things with your heart and mind, not with your eyes. It means shutting your eyes in order to see.

"White men have forgotten this. Their God no longer talks to them out of a burning bush. If he did, they wouldn't believe it. They'd call it hallucination or science fiction. They'd say, 'A voice from a burning bush? That guy had too much LSD!' Those old Hebrew prophets went into the desert praying for a vision, but the white men of today have made a desert of their beliefs. Inside themselves, they have made a desert where nothing grows, a dead place without dreams. But the spirit water is always there to make the desert bloom again." That my father told me.

Usually, Lakota girls do not go on Vision Quests. My daughter Josephine went on a Vision Quest because my father told me that she would one day become a medicine woman. For her, Hanblecheya was necessary; for most women it is not. In the old days, the staying alone for four days during the moon time was in itself a Vision Quest for the women.

A young boy goes on a Vision Quest searching for his own path, which he will travel to the end of his life. He comes back from the hill a man. But the crying for a dream does not stop there. Men do not go up to the mountaintop just one time. I know of men who have undergone this four-day trial more than a dozen times—even very old men who keep crying for visions until the end of their days.

Preparation for a Hanblecheya

Usually you need the help of a *wichasha wakan*, a spiritual man, to go on Hanblecheya. A man might come to me and say, "Uncle, my mother is sick. Perform a ceremony for her. Pray that she will get well, and a year from now I will go on a Vision Quest for four days and nights." So this man makes a vow to do this. It is a solemn commitment. And when the year is over, I prepare him for his ordeal.

Or someone might say, "Lame Deer, I need help. I have these dreams that don't reveal their meanings. I need understanding. I have to find out. Prepare me for a Vision Quest."

To tell the truth, a man should go to the hilltop whenever he is about to do something of great importance, or whenever there is a great crisis in his life, in order to seek guidance from above.

Before your Hanblecheya, you have a medicine man perform an Inipi with you, and you get instructions on how to conduct your long vigil. You go to the mountain naked, just as you were born, except for your loincloth and a buffalo robe or star blanket around your shoulders. You go up with your Pipe and sacred tobacco; you will need it. If you have a medicine bundle, wear it. Maybe your mother or sister will have made a flesh offering for you by cutting forty small pieces of skin from their arms. Put them into a gourd; they will help you endure your Hanblecheya, your long, lonely watch amid the hooting of owls and the mournful call of the coyotes.

Up on the hill, make yourself a small, holy place in which to settle down. Maybe lean against a rock or tree while praying for your vision. Do not go to dream at a place where nothing grows, where there are no plants or trees. Such a place of no dreams could harm you mentally.

Those who pray for dreams inside a vision pit do it the hardest way. Sometimes a tarp is spread over the pit and strewn with earth and grass. *Canli*—that is, tobacco ties—mark out the space, and Four-Direction flags are planted at the four corners. The one left down in the pit is then truly buried alive. He sees, feels, and hears nothing. To stay like this in a vision pit is a brave thing to do. It demands fearlessness and a complete giving of yourself to the spirits.

When you are up there alone, you should pray as hard as you can. Do not think of anything tying you to the everyday world. Do not think of your joys, your sorrows, your problems, or your pains. Think only about what is holy. Empty your mind. Make it into a receptacle for visions. Listen to the spirits of the winds and the clouds.

You will suffer up there, fasting, praying, wrapped in loneliness. And even this is no guarantee that you will receive a vision. It is easy to fool yourself. I know an old traditional man who went on Hanblecheya twenty-seven times and never had a vision. He prayed and prayed but never got his dream.

A True Vision

And then there is a young man, twenty-two years old, with a beautiful buffalo robe, a gorgeous Pipe with quill-decorated stem, and fully beaded, sparkling moccasins who goes up to the mountain and comes down with seven visions. He goes into the sweatlodge and says, "Lame Deer, let me tell you about these terrific visions." Then he tells me about his heroic, elaborate dreams, and his imagination runs away with him.

He sits up there, and his mind is full of ideas. He thinks up visions, and he comes down and tells of the wonderful things he has thought up—not what he really received on the mountaintop. This young man should have saved himself the trouble and stayed home. He could have more comfortably fantasized while sitting in an easy chair eating a hot dog. He had received no true vision.

I get that way, too. Sometimes when I'm mentally fatigued, I see psychedelic images. I see a tree jumping over another tree. Was that a vision? No! You're tired, sucker. You haven't slept for three days, so your brain is playing tricks on you. A vision is hard to explain. You receive it consciously, when you are wide awake. You see it in front of you, like turning on the TV. You pray hard, and all of a sudden, you see yourself doing something specific, or you see an eagle fly into your vision pit, as happened to my father. These are visions, and they come to you while you're conscious, or at least half awake.

There are also images or scenes you see while you are semiconscious or asleep. These are dreams rather than visions, but they are also important. But both must come *to you*, not *out of you*. We have to weigh what is real and what is just fantasy. That is not always easy.

You could also *hear* a vision rather than see it. Up on the hill, you might hear someone speaking Hanbloglaka, a dream language that only a medicine man could understand. During a Vision Quest, birds spoke to my father, and he could understand what they were saying.

Some medicine men are afraid of going on Hanblecheya. They are afraid their visions might tell them something that would make them come back as a *heyoka* or a *winkte*. A vision could put you on a path you don't want to follow. Those who have a vision receive a great gift that could change their lives. Those who experience this come down singing. The ones who have had no dream descend silently.

After the Quest, the dreamer goes into the sweatlodge again and describes his vision to the medicine man, who will interpret it and lay out a path for him to follow, so there is always an Inipi at the beginning and the end.

Approaching the Spirits

You cannot force the spirits to give you a vision; you have to approach them humbly. This my father taught me. He once told me the story of a big chief—my father called him the "Super Indian." Before going to the mountain, this chief boasted that he would receive the greatest vision ever given to a human being. Well, he was up there, singing and lamenting, praying up a storm, imploring the spirits for a most terrific vision. Suddenly he heard a voice shout, "*Shut up!* You keep me from sleeping, carrying on like that. *Shut up!*"

The chief was scared and stopped his chanting, but after a while he started up again. And once more the voice shouted, "*Shut up!* You're keeping me awake. You're disturbing the trees, the plants, and the animals with that awful racket."

The chief noticed that this voice came from within a great boulder above him. He said, "No lousy rock is telling me what to do. It won't prevent me from getting my vision."

The Super Indian went on chanting and lamenting with such force that his helpers, waiting far below, could hear him. Then the boulder got really angry and rolled down with full force upon the chief, squashing the vision pit and crushing his Pipe and buffalo robe.

That Super Indian barely escaped with his life. He ran down the hill in a panic, as if being pursued by the Great Water Monster. He rushed into the sweatlodge, where three medicine men were waiting for him, and stammered, "That boulder wanted to kill me. It has smashed all my sacred things, flattened the vision pit, uprooted trees!"

The medicine men went up the mountain. They found everything intact. The pit, the Pipe, and the trees were untouched. The boulder rested in its accustomed place. Then the medicine men told that Super Indian, "Be humble. Don't boast. Step lightly. Respect nature. Then maybe you'll have better luck next time."

When I was twelve years old, my grandfather took me to the mountaintop. As I sat there praying, I felt myself flying across the sky, looking down at the Earth, gyrating in a swirl of sparkling rainbow colors. It seemed all very real. I had no other vision but this, and I did not know what it meant. At about the same time, lightning struck a spot near where I was sitting, and the same night I dreamt of horses. When I told this to three of our elders, they said, "You're a *heyoka* now. Do something backward every day!" It was fifteen years before I went on another Hanblecheya, and it changed me completely, from a *heyoka* into what I am now.

I was already past thirty when I went on what I consider my first real Vision Quest. I was keeping company with my father, who was visiting a friend in California. He went there to bless this man's place. Then something urged me to tell my father, "This is a good time for me to go to the mountaintop. Would you take me?"

My father looked at me and smiled. He loaded the Pipe and said, "I can't take you. I don't think anyone can take you. You must take yourself. Go on!"

This was a little sad and puzzling to me, but I waved goodbye to him and climbed up. I stayed on that mountain four days and four nights but did not receive a single vision. Then, on the last day, just as I was about to go down, I suddenly felt my spirit leaving my body.

Before I knew it, I was up in the top of an oak tree looking down on my body, which was lying on its back. As I watched, a strange, indistinct shape came up from the South and talked to me in Lakota. The apparition told me, "We have come after you, and we are going to take you with us."

The apparition was pulling hard at my body, and I started to laugh. My body was in the earthly dimension, and my spirit, up in the tree, was in the spirit dimension. For this reason, the one who was jerking my body around could not see me, and that seemed funny to me up there among the leaves.

Spirits from the North

Then from the North came two more shapes. I knew that the first apparition was Nagi, the Shadow or Ghost. The second was Niyah, the Spirit or Breath of Life. And the third was the Spirit of the Sky and the Clouds. The first one was still tugging at my body, but the two others from the North said, "Leave him alone. He is one of us. His work is only beginning now, but one day his work will be done and then the three of us will come and get him, for that is the way it is." They left singing and laughing, going toward the North.

Next I saw my father sitting below me with his head down and his old cowboy hat pushed way back. And all of a sudden, my spirit reentered my body. I looked again, and my father had vanished, as had the log he had been sitting on. I was very scared, even though it was only five o'clock in the afternoon and the sun was still up. That first apparition, I know, had wanted to take me to the spirit world.

I ran all the way to the foot of the mountain, jumped into my car, and drove as fast as I could to the house where my father and I were staying. I ran into the house. My father was sitting at the fireplace, exactly as I had seen him in my vision.

He looked up and smiled. "I made some coffee for you just now. Here, have some *pejiuta sap*, some 'black medicine.'"

I took the cup of steaming coffee. My father lit a cigarette, and I sat down next to him. I was about to say, "Let me tell you what I experienced on my Vision Quest," but he stopped me as soon as I opened my mouth.

"There's no need to tell me anything," he said. "I was there. My spirit was there. I have seen them, and now I know what you are. You have experienced this spiritual power. It flowed from me to you, and it will flow to your son. It will be passed on from generation to generation as long as there is one Lame Deer left. There's no need to explain. For me it's time to go. I'm ready."

A month and a half later, my father got into that car accident. He was grievously hurt and never recovered. He lingered on, but in the end he heard the owl calling him.

The Gift of Seeing

I came back from that Vision Quest with the gift of being able to see in your face what is in store for you. It does not always work, but most of the time it does. I look at you, but I don't tell you that your woman will leave you or that your family will break up. There may be two among you who won't be around when I come through the next time, but I am not allowed to tell of these things. I have to keep this knowledge within myself. . . .

Visions and Vision Quests are of utmost importance to our people and to myself personally. Through dreams and visions, we receive power and the gift of "seeing ahead," of getting glimpses of the future. A young man's first Vision Quest often determines what kind of life he will lead. Visions are not imaginings; they are messages from the Supernaturals. True visions have a reality distinct from what the white man usually calls "reality." A man who never had a vision is impoverished, indeed.

Always in my mind and heart will remain the words of Crazy Horse's song, which Iron Hail taught me on that memorable day many years ago. The way I translated it may not be the best way, but it was the best I could do:

> My friend,
> They will return again.
> All over the Earth,
> They are returning again.
> Ancient teachings of the Earth,
> Ancient songs of the Earth,
> They are returning again.
>
> My friend, they are returning.
> I give them to you,
> And through them
> You will understand,
> You will see.
> They are returning again
> Upon the Earth.

CHAPTER 3

The Wilderness Versus the Pioneer

Chapter Preface

Major Robert Rogers could scarcely contain his enthusiasm:

> You should have been with me. General Amherst sent me West, out to the Great Lakes, to take over our magnificent new territory and accept the surrender of the French posts. Fifteen whaleboats flying the English colors—two hundred Rangers—Toronto, Niagara Falls, Presque Isle, Pittsburgh, Detroit—Indians by the hundreds: Indians by the thousands! Hurons, Ottawas, Mississaugas, Mingos, Chippeways—deer in droves, and lakes full of the finest fish in the world.

His audience, the comfortable merchants and minor British officials of Portsmouth, Maine, eyed him with astonishment between bites of broiled lobster washed down with glasses of hot cider. Irrepressibly, Rogers continued:

> You don't know what this country is till you go to the westward. You live here on a little strip of seacoast that's like—that's like the braid on my weskit. You don't know what's beyond the braid! Why, you see lakes like oceans: tremendous mountains rolling off for a thousand miles into a golden haze. There's cliffs of solid copper along the lakes . . . there's springs that gush three rods in the air: oil lying on top of the ground so you can touch a coal to it and put your meat to broil; rivers so long you can travel for months on 'em! . . . You can't even dream what it's like!

Thus in the historical novel *Northwest Passage* Kenneth Roberts introduces themes which many writers on the American West—no matter what their genre—find important. There is, first of all, a sense of the almost incredible scope of the country, stretching thousands of miles beyond ordinary imaginations, a country epic in its dimensions, calling out for epic action from those who hope to settle it. It is, moreover, a land rich in resources, a land literally fabulous, challenging belief but offering to believers limitless opportunities. It is a territory to experience and exploit.

Because of its scope, the land offers repeated chances to start anew, to break out of old molds. Colonial Maine, once part of England's western frontier, by the time of the novel's setting—the mid-eighteenth century—is settled, urban, mercantile, conservative, safe. People there have mastered their environment and most doubt whether they want to repeat the process. But opportunity lies west for those who dare. Finally there is, in Roberts' passage, the germ of inevitable Anglo-American expansion westward, the string of captured French forts a manifestation that it is not other

The epitome of the rugged individualist, the mountain man abandoned the secure but boring "civilized" life back East in search of furs and freedom in the West.

nations' destiny to control this continent. Rogers, committed as he is to search for the Northwest Passage, personifies for his time the dream of westering. Because he not only dares to go beyond civilization but also exults in the process, he becomes an early real-life model for the Western hero. Though a servant of the Crown, Rogers is far different from his British superiors. As Frederick Jackson Turner wrote, "The frontier is the line of most rapid and effective Americanization," and Rogers was, indeed, becoming Americanized.

Initially, as Turner wrote, "the wilderness masters the colonist."

The very force, the size, the power of the country demanded adaptation to nature if people were to survive; only later could exploitation become possible. The frontiersmen of this chapter, the fur traders and forty-niners, had to acquire survival skills. The fur trapper, because his frontier was the first, had no teacher but nature and those who lived with nature—the Indians, mentors and partners before becoming antagonists with the advent of agriculture and the army.

Historian Bernard DeVoto suggests that the survival skills of the mountain men—the trappers—were as "intricate . . . as any developed by any way of working and living anywhere," a "total behavior" with "specific crafts, technologies . . . and . . . codes of behavior." The mountain man had to *know* what he was doing. DeVoto writes in *Across the Wide Missouri:*

> Why do you follow the ridges into or out of unfamiliar country? What do you do for a companion who has collapsed for want of water while crossing a desert? How do you get meat when you find yourself without gunpowder in a country barren of game? What tribe of Indians made this trail, how many were in the band, what errand were they on, were they going to or coming back from it, how far from home were they, were their horses laden, how many horses did they have and why, how many squaws accompanied them, what mood were they in?. . . The mountain man had mastered his conditions—how well is apparent as soon as soldiers, goldseekers, or emigrants come into his country and suffer where he has lived comfortably and die where he has been in no danger.

DeVoto's passage clearly suggests that the successful mountain man not only had to know nature but also had to understand Indian cultures. The German prince, Maximilian of Wied, who traveled through the fur country in 1832-34 with the painter Karl Bodmer, reinforced the necessity for cultural adaptation. He tells of a trader utilizing a strange Blackfoot custom to cement friendship and secure trade with a recalcitrant chief. Knowing that the chief wanted some of his brandy and having been told of this highest demonstration of friendship, the trader Miller sipped a mouthful of brandy, embraced the chief, and "discharged" the liquor into his mouth. (It is perhaps worth noting that *both* cultures had adapted to the other. The trader acted according to the Blackfoot's social expectations: the Blackfoot custom, however, is predicated on the introduction of alcohol into Indian society as an item of trade.)

Turner notes that the fur traders brought with them into the wilderness "the disintegrating forces of civilization. . . . Every river valley and Indian trail became a fissure in Indian society, and so that society became honeycombed." As the disintegration of Indian culture had begun, so, too, had the depletion of natural resources. In many locations, beaver were trapped out to fulfill the fashion fads of Easterners and Europeans. The demand for buffalo hides or "coarse hair" inaugurated the buffalo's demise, later exacerbated by sport hunting and military policy. And, as we turn to the California gold fields, we see rivers turned from their banks and entire hillsides blasted away.

At first glance, the forty-niners should have had an easier time of it than did the mountain men. Passes had been discovered by those fur seekers and mapped by army topographers. But no matter which route the emigrants to the gold fields took, physical hardships accompanied them: too little grass for their animals if they started too early, and the threat of becoming snowbound in the passes if they started too late; seasickness, cholera, or Chagres fever; bad water, moldy food, uncomfortable wagons; the threat of attack by Indians or bandits or old hands lying in wait for the greenhorns. The gold seekers, like their predecessors of the fur frontier, also made cultural adaptations. But instead of adapting Indian mores, they established new codes to fit new situations. Rules of the road were enunciated: a person delaying the start in the morning would have to take his place at the end of the line and eat dust all day; land claimed by miners had to be worked rather than held for speculation; conventional law might define crime, but punishment was often immediate, allowing judge and jury a quick return to their claims.

The fur frontier and the gold frontier had points of similarity. Both provided a fresh start—for renegade or bored farmer or out-of-work craftsman or ambitious businessman. Both were dominantly male environments, requiring adjustments in expectations about social interactions. The mountain man, trapper, or trader often took an Indian wife, however temporarily. The forty-niner wrote voluminous letters to the woman he had left behind and attended dances where half the participants wore handkerchiefs on their sleeve designating them the "females" for the evening. All welcomed even the homeliest woman swelling the distaff population. Finally, on both the mining and fur trapping frontiers, we can note a transition from individual to collective action: The most independent trapper looked forward to rendezvous, prospective miners formed companies for safety on the overland journey, and the introduction of capital and technology sparked radical change in both livelihoods.

People were no longer mastered by the environment; humans began to dominate, even to exploit it.

VIEWPOINT 1

"One Single word lonesome—would suffice to express our feelings any day throughout the Year."

Physical Hardships Challenge the Fur Trader

Francis Chardon (?-1848)

From 1834 to 1839 Francis Chardon was agent for the American Fur Company at Fort Clark, the company's Mandan post on the Upper Missouri, roughly sixty miles above Bismarck, North Dakota. Though not an admirer of the Indians, Chardon negotiated business matters with them and generally managed to intercede to maintain intertribal peace. Bernard DeVoto calls the journals of Francis Chardon and Charles Larpenteur the best accounts illuminating daily life at a trading post. Chardon's day-by-day account gives a realistic picture of the hardships fur trappers and traders had to face—disease, frostbite, Indian skirmishes, and the threat of starvation. Chardon's journal is also the best contemporary account of the smallpox epidemic of 1837.

September [1835]
Tuesday 1—Morning cloudy and windy—hard wind last night—The war party which left on the 23ᵈ. returned this evening done nothing—The Soldiers made a large feast for the entertainment of the Sioux. The Sioux were well recᵈ. by the *Mandans*, the peace concluded, and ratified between them, I have no doubt will

From *Chardon's Journal at Fort Clark, 1834-1839* edited by Annie Heloise Abel. Pierre: State of South Dakota, Department of History, 1932.

last at least, as long as the Mandans corn lasts—The day has been cloudy, and threatened rain all day but had none a little misty about 10 Oclock—The Agent, made the 2 bravs, the *Fool* Chief & Little Sioux a present of a Blanket each, & some powder, lead & tobacco, for their exertions in concluding the peace between them & the Sioux

Wednesday 2—Morning fine—The Sioux left this, in company with the Agent, myself, and several of the principal Chiefs and soldiers of the *Mandans*, for the Gros Ventres, to ratify the treaty concluded between them—they were well rec^d. by the Gros Ventres and Saluted by a couple of fires from their Cannon, the treaty was ratified and we called on as witnesses—left there about 5 OClock P.M. and returned to the Fort—arrived to day from Fort Union two *free trapers* on their way to St Louis brought a letter from Mr. Hamilton—Met *Pecot* with the Boats just above the mouth of white River, all was well, they Report there are about 300 Assinneboins and Crees, on their way to attact the Gros Ventres—The day has been fine— . . .

Wednesday 9—Another fine morning—The Yanktonas danced the *bull* dance in the fort Yesterday—& gave us a dance again to day, the Agent and myself each made them small present of Tobacco—I diffeering a little by giving a fieu Knives, but not so much tobacco—

Thursday 10—The weather changed last night, morning cloudy and windy—wind from the west—made a feast for the Chiefs and Soldiers of the Sioux Camp—the Agent made them a small present of Powder, Balls and Tobacco—They talked very fine, always taking care however to praise themselves much—love the whites dearly—(at least, till they are refused something)—

—A difficulty took place to day between the Mandan Soldiers, and some Young men of the Yanktonas; which had nearly been a serious thing; as the Y's armed themselves with Guns and their Bows and arrows, and came to the fort to attact them; but fortunately, the One they wanted [to] see had gone to the Village—they went in quest of him, about 8 in number; nothing however was done; I anticipate, the matter is not yet settled—They threatened to shoot any one, which I apprehend they will do if they cannot get revenge out of the Mandans—

Friday 11—the morning cloudy but calm—Breakfasted by candle light—Had three dances by the Sioux Squaws, had to make them all small presents, the Agent had to do like wise—Some lads danced also, the Agent gave them a fieu knives and a little Tobacco, I gave nothing—I wish to God dancing is over—Reported the Assinnaboins had attacted the Gros Ventres, it was handsome to see the Sioux and Mandans start to their assistance; but greatly to their mortification, before they had proceeded far, it was ascertained the report was false; . . .

Saturday 12—Morning cloudy and calm—last night, it lightened, Thunder'd, raind and the wind blew, every appearance of rain to day—Yesterday the Yanktonas stole 4 of the best horses belonging to the Mandan Village and crossed the River with them, I anticipate h—l among them Yet before they leave this—Shot at one of the Sioux dogs for chasing my chickens, but unfortunately missed him in consequence of my pistol being too hard in triger—had a little rain at (10)-O.C., fine day from that to (4) O.C. rained again—M' *Charboneau* was taken sick yesterday, with something like the Cholic,—the 4 Bear, and two or three others of the Mandans have pursued the Yanktonas who stole the horses—

Elizabeth Lochrie's painting of fur traders negotiating with some Plains Indians hints at the ever-present possibility of danger in the fur traders' business; here, armed guards keep watch during the bargaining.

Sunday 13—Morning cloudy—Saw a flock of wild Geese—The Sioux danced the bear dance in the fort, we made them a small present; they also danced at the Village: there to imitate the *bear* more thoroughly, they killed a dog and devoured him raw—In the afternoon, another company of the big dog band danced also in the fort—had to make them a small present, Oh! God, but I am tired of dancing–The Mandan Squaws danced at the Sioux Camp, received some pretty good presents,—a horse or two, worth dancing for—The day partially cleared off—The Ree Squaws, married to the *Saons*, have disappeared 7 or 8 in number, there will be the DEVIL to pay about it before they leave this I expect, as they must be secreted at the Mandan Village—The Yanktonas returned to the Mandans two horses in part pay for the 4 they pillaged a fieu days Since—everything appears almost like the Yanktonas were trying to pick a quarrel with the Mandans, I hardly think it possible they can leave without a fight—

Monday 14—Morning Clear—killed 38 *rats*, 5 last Knight and 33 this morning—The 4 Bear and his companions returned Yesterday having lost the track—7 OClock A.M. Sioux Camp commenced moving, lodges all down—8 OClock, all off except a fieu, beggars,—bought a horse from the Yanktonas—Cleared out the Store, and found I had traded from the Sioux 360 Robes, 102 Calf Skins, 74[lb] Beaver, 200 pieces of Meat, 12 Sacks of Cords,—They carried off with them, 1½ pack of Beaver to buy horses with—Contrary to all expectations the Sioux have gone without a fight with the Mandans, & I believe have Stole no more horses,—to day has been Tolerable windy— . . .

Wednesday 16—Morning Cloudy, inclined to be windy—looks cold but cant say it is overly so—7 OClo'k Peacot with Mackanaw Boats arrived from Fort Union, for S[t] Louis—Making preperations to go down in with them—rained a little in the afternoon— Shipped on them 70 packs of Robes, and 2 packs of Beaver— Pecot Brot 2 Bottle of wine and we fergot to drink it—The Agent distributed the bal. of his presents among the Mandans—powder lead and Tobacco—

Killed 98 Rats this Month . . .

Fort Clark—1st January 1836

I commence the dull, irksome task of recording the petty incidents of this post, on New Years day and if the weather may be considered as emblematic of the Year—It will be calm and pleasant as heart could wish.

2nd—Rode up to the Gros Ventre Village in company with old Charboneau—Indians all absent making Meat, returned in the evening, pleasant day.

3rd—The Sioux all moveing up from below—complain of being in a Starving condition.

4th—Weather continues fine as usual, no news—

5th—Walked over to where the men were choping wood—found them idle.

6th—Started out our Hunters in quest of Meat our larder being completely empty. D. Ewing commenced cuting Steam Boat wood in the Point below—Many of the Yanctonas passed the Fort on their way out in search of Buffalo—they are all Sta(r)ving. . . .

Indian Battles

Sunday 10th—Cold Stormy day—The turbulent passions of the Indians seems to have been in accordance with the waring of the elements. The Camp of Yanctonas that passed up Yesterday camped near the Gros Ventre Village where they were attacked this Morning at daylight by the whole force of the Gros Ventres—The only inteligence we have received of the Battle was from a few stragling Sioux who had escaped the general Slaughter—they State that the Sioux Camp consisting of about 40 Lodges—was taken by surprise—and that the Sioux Men,

Women, and children were indiscriminately butchered, they istimated their loss at upward of a 100.—

The Sioux who were camped near the Mandans distrusting the friendly talk of their allies, fled during the night, A Young Sioux—who had lost all his relations in the Morning—attempted to Kill a Gros Ventre Boy in the Fort. . . .

Tuesday 12th—No tidings of our Hunters—I am becoming Seriously alarmed for their Safety, The unsetled State of the country Justifies the worst anticipations . . .

Wednesday 13th—No News of our Hunters. One of Premeau's Men came up from below—he States that the Sioux who were retreating from this Place robed him on his way up. (it is supposed of whiskey), weather calm—cold, & Clear (we are all starving.)

Thursday 14th—We still remain in a state of anxious suspense respecting the Hunters. Old Charboneau went up to the Gros Ventre Village, weather intensely cold—I purpose going out tomorrow in search of my Men, Provided the weather Moderates.

Friday 15th—We were highly gratified this morning by the arrival of the Hunters—whom we had given up for lost. After ten days hard traveling they returned without seeing a Single cow. This is truly a gloomy prospect. Old Charboneau returned from the Gros Ventres bringing down 30 Robes—the proceeds of 2 Months Trade. . . .

Saturday 16th—Weather continues unsettled—Heavy fall of Snow in the Evening, Sent down the Men to Haul Hay—But they returned with the distressing report of its all being burnt for this neighbourly act I suppose we thank our Sioux friends—Our prospect for the winter is now gloomy in the extreme. I have concluded to send off all my horses & Hunters to make a liveing in the Prairies—or starve as fate May direct, no news from any quarter. . . .

Thursday 21st—We have all been confined to the House by the cold, which seems to have increased at least 10 degrees since Yesterday, it is with great dificulty the Men can prevent themselves from freezing while Hauling a load of wood,

Old Charboneau Started to the Gros Ventres to aid in Moveing the goods to the Summer Village, this being the day appointed by the Indians for that purpose. . . .

Sunday 24th—Wrote letters & prepared to start the Men to Fort Union in the morning—gave a Dinner to our Opponants which must have been very welcome as they were in a Straving [*sic*] State. Cold as usual—. . .

Lonesome Life

Wednesday 27th—Weather moderated very much since Yesterday—Made preparations to go out in search of cattle tomorrow.

No news from any quarter—*lonesome*

One Single word *lonesome*—would suffice to express our feelings any day throughout the Year—We might add—discontented—but this would include the fate of all Mankind. It is a Melancholy reflection when we look forward into futurity—and know that the remnant of our days *must* be spent in toilsome and unavailing pursuits of happiness. And that sooner or later we must sink into the grave without ever being able to attain the object for which we have toiled and suffered so much. If we turn with discontent from this ideal picture, and take a retrospective glance at the past, the scene is no less gloomy. It is like a dreary expansive waste—without one green verdant spot on which Memmory loves to linger. The day dreams in which we used to indulge during our halcyon days of Youth have long since proved as baseless as Visions ever are. The little experience that time has given only teaches us to Know,   ,That Man was Made to Mourn, . . .

Saturday 30th—Two Young Mandans came down from the Camp, they bring the cheering inteligence of Buffalo being very plenty—cold day.

Sunday 31st—Last day of a long gloomy Month. God send the next may be more agreeable. Heard from our Hunters Cattle plenty, beginning to look out anxiously for the Express from St. Louis.

[February, 1836]

Monday 1st—One of the Men belonging to Premeau & Co came up this Evening who brings the melancholy inteligence of Premeau's death. He was Killed by the Yanctonas a few Miles below Apple River. The Indians pillaged all their goods—and my informant thinks it highly probabley that Old Bijou and the other Men who remained behind has been murdered also. But as he recived a blow with a tomahawk on the side of his head—which seems to have unsettled his wits, besides being thoroughly frightened, I am in hopes his Story is Somewhat exagerated. He also States that he found a [man] lieing dead in the road a few miles below this place, he was entirely naked and appears to have been recently Killed. I think it highly probable it may be Baptist Dufond who left this place a few days since for Beaver River.

Tuesday 2nd—Rode down below in search of the Man who was found murdered Yesterday, met two of Campbells Men comeing up for corn who satisifed me it was an Indian and not Dufond—as I had supposed—they confirm the report of Premeau's death and State more over that the Yanctonas are behaveing in a most outragious Manner—and that there is no security for either life or property amongst them. Both Indians & whites are Starving below.

Wednesday 3rd—The Express from St Louis arrived late this evening—lots of news—busy making preparations to Send to Ft. Union in the morning. . . .

Killing for Tongues

The hard life of the mountain men often included near-starvation, and plenty sometimes led to epicurean excess, as Peter Skene Ogden's Snake Country Journal *from the 1820s records.*

Saturday, 2nd. We had a most stormy night. This day cold and fair. Our hunters arrived late last night and report they killed fifteen buffalo, but all so poor that not one did they skin. The tongues alone were taken, and the meat allowed to remain in the plains. This is a sinful waste of meat and they richly deserve to be punished for it; how many hundreds in the Columbia, and even we ourselves, last two years, would willingly have paid dear for food. I severely reprimanded the hunters for wasting ammunition as they do, and the only reply they made was, we want fat meat, we have been living too long on lean.

Sunday 14th—Mild Beautiful Weather. The Indians went across the River in search of Cattle—but returned late in the Evening without haveing seen any—Extremely lonesome and low Spirited—I hardly know how to account for it, but I have always found Sunday to be the dullest and longest day in the week—that is—the Sundays spent in the Indian Country—I suppose it is because we are apt to contrast the scene with that of civilized life—when Kin and acquaintances all assemble at the sound of the *church going bell*—Although the solemn tolling of a church bell—never possessed much attraction for me, (only so far as Served to announce the time and place - where bright eyes were to be seen.) But I could not help feeling this evening—(Whilst gazing round on this dreary, Savage waste,) That could I at this moment hear even the tinkling of a sheep bell—much less the solemn toll of the church going bell, that the joyful Sound would repay Me for whole Months of privation. Alas, how little do we suspect during our halcyon days of Youth—Surrounded by all that can cheer our gloomy path through life, what Years of Sorrow are Yet in Store, But I will not repine for joys that is past and gone.

'For joys that is past let us never repine,
Nor grieve for the days of auld lang syne. . . .
Saturday 20th—The Hunters returned—brought in three cows—report Buffalo plenty on on the North Side of the River. Weather continues remarkably warm.

114

Sunday 21ˢᵗ—Fine Weather continues Same as Yesterday—No news from any quarter—Beaver Hunters preparing to Start out on the spring hunt.

A Glass of Grog

Monday 22ⁿᵈ—Rode up to the Gros Ventre Village found the Indians all in the summer Village—the Ice having become too rotten for them to remain longer on the N. Side. Drank a glass of grog to the health of our glorious old Washington, this being his birth day, . . .

Wednesday 24ᵗʰ—Can find nothing to record worthy the attention of Posterity—unless the fact of an Indian horse falling down the bank and breaking his neck - may be so considered—This however I leave to be decided by the learned. . . .

Monday 29ᵗʰ—The last day of a long gloomy winter, I have Spent many a winter in the Indian Country—and the Monotonous dulness of preciding Seasons have possibly been erased from the tablets of my Memory—But I am certain I never spent a more unpleasant one, take it all in all, than the last. God send better times for the future,

[March, 1836]

Tuesday 1ˢᵗ—Hail gentle Spring, I greet thee with feelings of the most heartfelt delight, Although in this dreary region there are no green flowery Meads—or sweet singing birds, no balmy breezes loaded with the fragrant odour of regenerated nature, No romantic or love sick swains, no lovely wood nymphs, or in short anything else to Beautify this favourite Season, But though art no less welcome,

Wednesday 2ⁿᵈ—Rode up to the Gros Ventre Village for the purpose of giveing a feast. Met the greater part of them coming down to dance at the Mandans, the feast was consequently postponed. . . .

Wednesday 9ᵗʰ—Our cow had a fine calf—An event that was celebrated with much rejoicing, cold as usual—Boulie came down from the Gros Ventres with news that the whole Village had gone out to make Meat—. . .

Monday 14ᵗʰ—Collected Several eggs to day—the first this Season, weather continues cold and windy. . . .

Wednesday 16ᵗʰ—Tremendious Snow Storm during the day, Engaged Delorm till the arrival of the S. Boat

Thursday 17ᵗʰ—Stormy windy day—one of our horses perished with cold and poverty—had a glass of Milk for supper—and great luxury in this country . . .

Friday 25ᵗʰ—Great change in the weather—a warm South wind has prevailed during the day—the Snow has disappeared from the prairies as if by Magic, each ravine or gully has become a roaring torrent. Several flocks of ducks passed over in the morning. The Sure harbingers of Spring—we are all delighted with the change. . . .

Saturday 26th—Our Hunters returned unsuccessful—haveing found no Buffalo in the S Side of the River—they Saw great quantities on the opposite Side but found the ice too weak to cross the Horses—fine weather. . . .

One Cause of Indigestion

Mountain men learned to eat unusual foods. Boiled puppy, for instance, was often served ceremonially by some Indian tribes. But the incident described here, from Charles Larpenteur's fur-trading accounts, stretched even the most adventurous stomach.

When breakfast was served by the wife of Mr. Broken Arm, the great chief of the Crees, who had been to Washington, Pitcher would not partake. "What is the matter, Pitcher," said I, "are you sick? Why not have some of this good fat buffalo meat?" "Not much the matter," he replied; "I will tell after a while"—fearing perhaps that the story he had to tell would not agree with my digestive organs. Some time after that, when the things were removed, dishes washed up, and the cook had gone out, my Pitcher poured out his story. "Mr. Larpenteur," he said, "if you please, after this I will do our cooking." "Why so," said I. "Why, sir, because that enfant de garce—that old squaw is too dirty. Sacré! She scrape the cloths of that baby of hers with her knife, give it a wipe, cut up the meat with it, and throw into the kettle. This morning I see same old crust on the knife—that what the matter—too much for me." After this explanation I was no longer surprised at poor Pitcher's looking so broken; and if my digestive powers had not been strong, as they have always proven to be, I am afraid my own breakfast would have returned the way it went; but with me, whenever the meat-trap was once shut down it was not easily opened again, and things had to take their natural course.

April, 1836

Friday 1st—Calm beautiful day. Ice runing very thick in the River—The Indians had great Sport in catching buffalo that was floating down on the ice—a few were still living having taken their Station on large masses of ice—traveled very quickly down Stream. But the greater part that was hauled on Shore had been previously drowned. It is astonishing the feats of hardy dexterity that was performed by some of the Young Men in pursuit of the loathsome Meat. They would boldly embark on the first piece of floating ice that approached the Shore, and Springing from piece to piece - or swiming when the distance was too great to leap, would generally succeed in fastning a cord round the horns—and towing the carcase to shore. Sent out my hunters and horses in search of cattle. . . .

Monday 4th—May Started below in a cannoe intending to trap Beaver between this and St. Louis. The Hunters returned well loaded having found plenty of Cattle. Our warehouses having become very leaky - I commenced re-covering them with dirt and straw. The Indians Killed a great number of Cattle only a few miles below the Fort, . . .

Wednesday 6th—Rain in the forenoon—the wolves eat one of our Mules—cold north wind—finished covering the warehouses.

Thursday 7th—Tremendious Snow Storm during the whole day. My chimny smoked so bad that it was impossible to have fire in my room - so that I have been shivering with cold since morning, to complete the unlucky day all of our horses are missing—supposed to be Stolen by the Sioux, this is truly a day of *Malheur*. . . .

Thursday 14th—commenced pressing packs—B. Lebrun Started Hunting—The Mandans danced the Bull dance in the fort. fine day—

Friday 15th—Finished making up our packs—136 packs of Robes and 4 of Beaver traded up to this date, had a repetition of the Bull dance this Evening.

Saturday 16th—Commenced raining about noon - Strong E. wind and has continued till the present time with unabated violence—broke our press—so that we were unable to finish pressing our packs,

Sunday 17th—I mark this day with a cross—it being one of the longest and most lonely I ever spent. The rain continued last evening till 10 oclock when it changed to a Snow Storm which lasted till 2 oclock P.M. to day The Snow is now lieing near a foot deep and but little more appearance of Spring than there was three months since, I am out of all patience though it is said all things are for the best and I must try to comfort myself in this Christian belief. no news from above—Thy will be done *Amen*

VIEWPOINT 2

"Two leading objects of commercial gain have given birth to wide and daring enterprise in the early history of the Americas: the precious metals of the south, and the rich peltries of the north."

Fiscal and Organizational Problems Challenge the Fur Entrepreneur

Washington Irving (1783-1859)

Washington Irving, author of such familiar tales as "Rip Van Winkle" and "The Legend of Sleepy Hollow," was fascinated by history and by people who changed the world. His *History of the Life and Voyages of Christopher Columbus* (1828) reflected this interest. He viewed John Jacob Astor as another mover and shaker.

In 1811 Astor had sent one party by ship and another overland to the mouth of the Columbia River. They were to found a trading post, Astoria, on the site of Fort Clatsop, which Lewis and Clark had built for the winter of 1805-1806. Astor allowed Irving access to all his New York business records. The resulting *Astoria* (1836) is an enthusiastic and admiring history of Astor's fur empire. Another volume, *The Adventures of Captain Bonneville* (1837), demonstrated Irving's continued interest in the fur trade of the American West. Unlike the experiences of Francis Chardon, who had to face the physical hardships of the fur frontier, John Jacob Astor's adventures were financial ones; his weapons of choice were business contracts, skillful manipulation of government officials, and an intricate, multi-layered organization that included investors, ship captains, trappers, and traders.

From *Astoria; or, Anecdotes of an Enterprise Beyond the Rocky Mountains* by Washington Irving. New York: G.P. Putnam and Son, 1869.

Two leading objects of commercial gain have given birth to wide and daring enterprise in the early history of the Americas; the precious metals of the south, and the rich peltries of the north. . . .

These two pursuits have thus in a manner been the pioneers and precursors of civilization. Without pausing on the borders, they have penetrated at once, in defiance of difficulties and dangers, to the heart of savage countries: laying open the hidden secrets of the wilderness; leading the way to remote regions of beauty and fertility that might have remained unexplored for ages, and beckoning after them the slow and pausing steps of agriculture and civilization.

It was the fur trade, in fact, which gave early sustenance and vitality to the great Canadian provinces. Being destitute of the precious metals, at that time the leading objects of American enterprise, they were long neglected by the parent country. The French adventurers, however, who had settled on the banks of the St. Lawrence, soon found that in the rich peltries of the interior, they had sources of wealth that might almost rival the mines of Mexico and Peru. The Indians, as yet unacquainted with the artificial value given to some descriptions of furs, in civilized life, brought quantities of the most precious kinds and bartered them away for European trinkets and cheap commodities. Immense profits were thus made by the early traders, and the traffic was pursued with avidity.

The French Fur Trade

As the valuable furs soon became scarce in the neighborhood of the settlements, the Indians of the vicinity were stimulated to take a wider range in their hunting expeditions; they were generally accompanied on these expeditions by some of the traders or their dependents, who shared in the toils and perils of the chase, and at the same time made themselves acquainted with the best hunting and trapping grounds, and with the remote tribes, whom they encouraged to bring their peltries to the settlements. In this way the trade augmented, and was drawn from remote quarters to Montreal. . . .

Now would ensue a brisk traffic with the merchants, and all Montreal would be alive with naked Indians running from shop to shop, bargaining for arms, kettles, knives, axes, blankets, bright-colored cloths, and other articles of use or fancy; upon all which, says an old French writer, the merchants were sure to clear at least two hundred per cent. There was no money used in this traffic, and, after a time, all payment in spirituous liquors was prohibited, in consequence of the frantic and frightful excesses and bloody brawls which they were apt to occasion. . . .

To check these abuses, and to protect the fur trade from various irregularities practised by these loose adventurers, an order was issued by the French government prohibiting all persons, on pain of death, from trading into the interior of the country without a license.

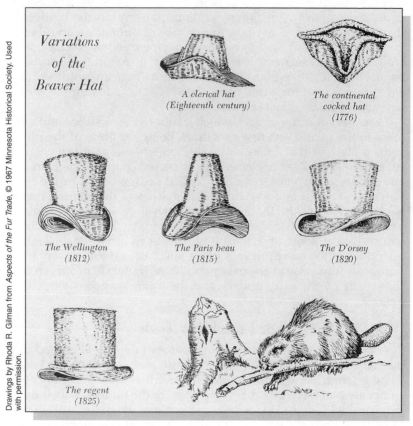

Variations of the Beaver Hat

A clerical hat (Eighteenth century)

The continental cocked hat (1776)

The Wellington (1812)

The Paris beau (1815)

The D'orsay (1820)

The regent (1825)

As is often the case, the fads of fashion create demand for raw materials. When the beaver hat became fashionable, beaver pelts became increasingly valuable. This led to great corporate profits but eventually to a near extermination of the beaver.

These licenses were granted in writing by the governor general, and at first were given only to persons of respectability; to gentlemen of broken fortunes; to old officers of the army who had families to provide for; or to their widows. Each license permitted the fitting out of two large canoes with merchandise for the lakes, and no more than twenty-five licenses were to be issued in one year. By degrees, however, private licenses were also granted, and the number rapidly increased. . . .

At length it was found necessary to establish fortified posts at the confluence of the rivers and the lakes for the protection of the trade, and the restraint of these profligates of the wilderness. The most important of these was at Michilimackinac, situated at the strait of the same name, which connects Lakes Huron and Michigan. It became the great interior mart and place of deposit, and some of the regular merchants who prosecuted the trade in person, under their licenses, formed establishments here. This, too, was a rendezvous for the rangers of the woods, as well those who came up with goods from Montreal as those who returned with peltries from the interior. Here new expeditions were fitted out and took their departure for Lake Michigan and the Mississippi; Lake Superior and the northwest; and here the peltries brought in return were embarked for Montreal.

The French merchant at his trading post, in these primitive days of Canada, was a kind of commercial patriarch. With the lax habits and easy familiarity of his race, he had a little world of self-indulgence and misrule around him. He had his clerks, canoe-men, and retainers of all kinds, who lived with him on terms of perfect sociability, always calling him by his Christian name; he had his harem of Indian beauties, and his troop of half-breed children; nor was there ever wanting a louting train of Indians, hanging about the establishment, eating and drinking at his expense in the intervals of their hunting expeditions. . . .

In 1762, the French lost possession of Canada, and the trade fell principally into the hands of British subjects. . . .

Funding of the Northwest Company

It was not until the year 1766, that the trade regained its old channels; but it was then pursued with much avidity and emulation by individual merchants, and soon transcended its former bounds. Expeditions were fitted out by various persons from Montreal and Michilimackinac, and rivalships and jealousies of course ensued. The trade was injured by their artifices to outbid and undermine each other; the Indians were debauched by the sale of spirituous liquors, which had been prohibited under the French rule. Scenes of drunkenness, brutality, and brawl were the consequence, in the Indian villages and around the trading houses; while bloody feuds took place between rival trading parties when they happened to encounter each other in the lawless depths of the wilderness.

To put an end to these sordid and ruinous contentions, several of the principal merchants of Montreal entered into a partnership in the winter of 1783, which was augmented by amalgamation with a rival company in 1787. Thus was created the famous "Northwest Company," which for a time held a lordly sway over the wintry lakes and boundless forests of the Canadas, almost equal to that of the East India Company over the voluptuous climes and magnificent realms of the Orient.

The company consisted of twenty-three shareholders, or partners, but held in its employ about two thousand persons as clerks, guides, interpreters, and "voyageurs," or boatmen. These were distributed at various trading posts, established far and wide on the interior lakes and rivers, at immense distances from each other, and in the heart of trackless countries and savage tribes. . . .

The company, as we have shown, was at first a spontaneous association of merchants; but after it had been regularly organized, admission into it became extremely difficult. A candidate had to enter, as it were, "before the mast," to undergo a long probation, and to rise slowly by his merits and services. He began, at an early age, as a clerk, and served an apprenticeship of seven years, for which he received one hundred pounds sterling, was maintained at the expense of the company, and furnished with suitable clothing and equipments. His probation was generally passed at the interior trading posts; removed for years from civilized society, leading a life almost as wild and precarious as the savages around him; exposed to the severities of a northern winter, often suffering from a scarcity of food, and sometimes destitute for a long time of both bread and salt. When his apprenticeship had expired, he received a salary according to his deserts, varying from eighty to one hundred and sixty pounds sterling, and was now eligible to the great object of his ambition, a partnership in the company; though years might yet elapse before he attained to that enviable station. . . .

Astor Enters the Fur Trade

The success of the Northwest Company stimulated further enterprise in this opening and apparently boundless field of profit. The traffic of that company lay principally in the high northern latitudes, while there were immense regions to the south and west, known to abound with valuable peltries; but which, as yet, had been but little explored by the fur trader. A new association of British merchants was therefore formed, to prosecute the trade in this direction. The chief factory was established at the old emporium of Michilimackinac, from which place the association took its name, and was commonly called the Mackinaw Company. . . .

The Mackinaw Company sent forth their light perogues, and barks, by Green Bay, Fox River, and the Wisconsin, to that great artery of the west, the Mississippi; and down that stream to all its tributary rivers. In this way they hoped soon to monopolize the trade with all the tribes on the southern and western waters, and of those vast tracts comprised in ancient Louisiana.

A Free Hunter's Contract

This copy of a contract between a free hunter and an agent of the American Fur Company clearly reveals the formal business practices of the far-flung fur trading enterprises.

Articles of agreement made and entered into at Fort Union, Upper Missouri, on the fifth day of July, one thousand eight hundred and thirty-two, by and between Kenneth Mackenzie, agent of the American Fur Company, and Johnson Gardner, citizen of the United States and free hunter in the Indian country—

The said Johnson Gardner hereby agrees to sell, and the said Kenneth Mackenzie agrees to purchase, all his stock of beaver skins now *en cache* on the Yellowstone river, at and for the price per pound net weight of four dollars twelve and a half cents, to be delivered by the said Johnson Gardner to the agent or servants of the said Kenneth Mackenzie on the spot where it is cached, the weight thereof to be regulated and adjusted by Francis A. Chardon and James A. Hamilton on its arrival at Fort Union, the number of skins being . . . and the weight now considered to be. . . . The said Johnson Gardner further agrees to sell, and the said Kenneth Mackenzie agrees to purchase, all his stock of castorum at and for the price per pound of three dollars, the weight thereof to be adjusted by the parties aforesaid. The said Kenneth Mackenzie hereby further agrees to and with the said Johnson Gardner to furnish and supply and equip two men to hunt and trap beaver for the fall and spring seasons next ensuing, at the entire charge and cost of the said Kenneth Mackenzie, to hunt and trap under the direction of the said Johnson Gardner; and the said Kenneth Mackenzie further agrees to furnish a third man, and at his cost and charge to supply a moiety or one-half of the requisite, necessary and usual equipment for a beaver hunter, and the said Johnson Gardner hereby agrees to supply the said third man with the other moiety or half part of the needful equipment usual for a beaver hunter, and it is hereby agreed by and between the said Kenneth Mackenzie and the said Johnson Gardner that an entire moiety or half part of the beaver skins and castorum killed, taken and secured by the united skill and exertions of the said Johnson Gardner and the said three men to be furnished as aforesaid shall be the just and lawful share of the said Kenneth Mackenzie, the other moiety or half part to be the just and lawful share of the said Johnson Gardner, and it is further agreed that the said moiety or half part which shall become the property of the said Johnson Gardner shall be purchased of him by the said Kenneth Mackenzie at and for the price of three dollars fifty cents per pound for beaver skins taken and secured in the fall approaching, and four dollars per pound for beaver skins taken and secured in the spring following, and three dollars per pound for castorum.

The government of the United States began to view with a wary eye the growing influence thus acquired by combinations of foreigners, over the aboriginal tribes inhabiting its territories, and endeavored to counteract it. For this purpose, as early as 1796, the government sent out agents to establish rival trading houses on the frontier, so as to supply the wants of the Indians, to link their interests and feelings with those of the people of the United States, and to divert this important branch of trade into national channels.

The expedient, however, was unsuccessful, as most commercial expedients are prone to be, where the dull patronage of government is counted upon to outvie the keen activity of private enterprise. What government failed to effect, however, with all its patronage and all its agents, was at length brought about by the enterprise and perseverance of a single merchant, one of its adopted citizens; and this brings us to speak of the individual whose enterprise is the especial subject of the following pages; a man whose name and character are worthy of being enrolled in the history of commerce, as illustrating its noblest aims and soundest maxims. . . .

John Jacob Astor, the individual in question, was born in the honest little German village of Waldorf, near Heidelberg, on the banks of the Rhine. He was brought up in the simplicity of rural life, but, while yet a mere stripling, left his home, and launched himself amid the busy scenes of London, having had, from his very boyhood, a singular presentiment that he would ultimately arrive at great fortune.

At the close of the American Revolution he was still in London, and scarce on the threshold of active life. An elder brother had been for some few years resident in the United States, and Mr. Astor determined to follow him, and to seek his fortunes in the rising country. Investing a small sum which he had amassed since leaving his native village, in merchandise suited to the American market, he embarked, in the month of November, 1783, in a ship bound to Baltimore, and arrived in Hampton Roads in the month of January. The winter was extremely severe, and the ship, with many others, was detained by the ice in and about Chesapeake Bay for nearly three months.

During this period, the passengers of the various ships used occasionally to go on shore, and mingle sociably together. In this way Mr. Astor became acquainted with a countryman of his, a furrier by trade. Having had a previous impression that this might be a lucrative trade in the New World, he made many inquiries of his new acquaintance on the subject, who cheerfully gave him all the information in his power as to the quality and value of different furs, and the mode of carrying on the traffic. He subsequently accompanied him to New-York, and, by his advice,

Mr. Astor was induced to invest the proceeds of his merchandise in furs. With these he sailed from New-York to London in 1784, disposed of them advantageously, made himself further acquainted with the course of the trade, and returned the same year to New-York, with a view to settle in the United States.

He now devoted himself to the branch of commerce with which he had thus casually been made acquainted. He began his career, of course, on the narrowest scale; but he brought to the task a persevering industry, rigid economy, and strict integrity. To these were added an aspiring spirit that always looked upward; a genius bold, fertile, and expansive; a sagacity quick to grasp and convert every circumstance to its advantage, and a singular and never wavering confidence of signal success.

As yet, trade in peltries was not organized in the United States, and could not be said to form a regular line of business. Furs and skins were casually collected by the country traders in their dealings with the Indians or the white hunters, but the main supply was derived from Canada. As Mr. Astor's means increased he made annual visits to Montreal, where he purchased furs from the houses at that place engaged in the trade. These he shipped from Canada to London, no direct trade being allowed from that colony to any but the mother country.

In 1794 or '95, a treaty with Great Britain removed the restrictions imposed upon the trade with the colonies, and opened a direct commercial intercourse between Canada and the United States. Mr. Astor was in London at the time, and immediately made a contract with the agents of the Northwest Company for furs. He was now enabled to import them from Montreal into the United States for the home supply, and to be shipped thence to different parts of Europe, as well as to China, which has ever been the best market for the richest and finest kinds of peltry. . . .

After an interval of some years, about 1807, Mr. Astor embarked in this trade on his own account. His capital and resources had by this time greatly augmented, and he had risen from small beginnings to take his place among the first merchants and financiers of the country. His genius had ever been in advance of his circumstances, prompting him to new and wide fields of enterprise beyond the scope of ordinary merchants. . . .

A plan had to be devised to enable him to enter into successful competition. He was aware of the wish of the American government, already stated, that the fur trade within its boundaries should be in the hands of American citizens, and of the ineffectual measures it had taken to accomplish that object. He now offered, if aided and protected by government, to turn the whole of that trade into American channels. He was invited to unfold his plans to government, and they were warmly approved, though the executive could give no direct aid.

Thus countenanced, however, he obtained, in 1809, a charter from the legislature of the state of New-York, incorporating a company under the name of "The American Fur Company," with a capital of one million of dollars, with the privilege of increasing it to two millions. The capital was furnished by himself—he, in fact, constituted the company; for, though he had a board of directors, they were merely nominal; the whole business was conducted on his plans, and with his resources, but he preferred to do so under the imposing and formidable aspect of a corporation, rather than in his individual name, and his policy was sagacious and effective. . . .

Extending Trade Across the Continent

In the meantime the attention of the American government was attracted to the subject, and the memorable expedition under Messrs. Lewis and Clarke, fitted out. . . . They ascended the Missouri, passed through the stupendous gates of the Rocky Mountains, hitherto unknown to white men; discovered and explored the upper waters of the Columbia, and followed that river down to its mouth. . . . Here they passed the winter, and returned across the mountains in the following spring. The reports published by them of their expedition demonstrated the practicability of establishing a line of communication across the continent, from the Atlantic to the Pacific Ocean.

It was then that the idea presented itself to the mind of Mr. Astor, of grasping with his individual hand this great enterprise, which for years had been dubiously yet desirously contemplated by powerful associations and maternal governments. For some time he revolved the idea in his mind, gradually extending and maturing his plans as his means of executing them augmented. The main feature of his scheme was to establish a line of trading posts along the Missouri and the Columbia, to the mouth of the latter, where was to be founded the chief trading house or mart. Inferior posts would be established in the interior, and on all the tributary streams of the Columbia, to trade with the Indians; these posts would draw their supplies from the main establishment, and bring to its the peltries they collected. Coasting craft would be built and fitted out, also, at the mouth of the Columbia, to trade, at favorable seasons, all along the northwest coast, and return, with the proceeds of their voyages, to this place of deposit. Thus all the Indian trade, both of the interior and the coast, would converge to this point, and thence derive its sustenance.

A ship was to be sent annually from New-York to this main establishment with reinforcements and supplies, and with merchandise suited to the trade. It would take on board the furs collected during the preceding year, carry them to Canton, invest the proceeds in the rich merchandise of China, and return thus freighted to New-York.

As, in extending the American trade along the coast to the northward, it might be brought into the vicinity of the Russian Fur Company, and produce a hostile rivalry, it was part of the plan of Mr. Astor to conciliate the good will of that company by the most amicable and beneficial arrangements. The Russian establishment was chiefly dependent for its supplies upon transient trading vessels from the United States. These vessels, however, were often of more harm than advantage. Being owned by private adventurers, or casual voyagers, who cared only for present profit, and had no interest in the permanent prosperity of the trade, they were reckless in their dealings with the natives, and made no scruple of supplying them with firearms. In this way several fierce tribes in the vicinity of the Russian posts, or within the range of their trading excursions, were furnished with deadly means of warfare, and rendered troublesome and dangerous neighbors.

The Russian government had made representations to that of the United States of these malpractices on the part of its citizens, and urged to have this traffic in arms prohibited; but, as it did not infringe any municipal law, our government could not interfere. Yet still it regarded, with solicitude, a traffic which, if persisted in, might give offence to Russia, at that time almost the only power friendly to us. In this dilemma the government had applied to Mr. Astor, as one conversant in this branch of trade, for information that might point out a way to remedy the evil. This circumstance had suggested to him the idea of supplying the Russian establishment regularly by means of the annual ship that should visit the settlement at the mouth of the Columbia (or Oregon); by this means the casual trading vessels would be excluded from those parts of the coast where their malpractices were so injurious to the Russians.

Such is a brief outline of the enterprise projected by Mr. Astor, but which continually expanded in his mind. Indeed it is due to him to say that he was not actuated by mere motives of individual profit. He was already wealthy beyond the ordinary desires of man, but he now aspired to that honorable fame which is awarded to men of similar scope of mind, who by their great commercial enterprises have enriched nations, peopled wildernesses, and extended the bounds of empire. He considered his projected establishment at the mouth of the Columbia as the emporium to an immense commerce; as a colony that would form the germ of a wide civilization; that would, in fact, carry the American population across the Rocky Mountains and spread it along the shores of the Pacific, as it already animated the shores of the Atlantic.

VIEWPOINT 3

"This life of severe hardship and exposure has affected my health. ... Our feet are wet all day, while a hot sun shines down upon our heads, and the very air parches the skin like the hot air of an oven."

Nature Severely Challenges the Miner

Daniel B. Woods

Daniel B. Woods, a member of the Amity and Enterprise Association, arrived on the South Fork of the American River on July 4, 1949. He spent sixteen months in the mines before returning to Philadelphia. During that time he learned firsthand the hardships miners endured. He reported on the miner's life in his 1851 book *Sixteen Months at the Gold Diggings*. In other sections of the book he discusses the need for improvements such as dams and aqueducts to make the mining process more efficient and somewhat less arduous. In his concluding chapter, he offers advice to prospective miners, including taking care of one's health, leaving all heavy machinery in the East, and, perhaps not surprising for one soon to be ordained, eschewing readily available vices: gambling, drinking, profanity, and licentiousness.

In the following selection, Woods convincingly argues that gold mining is hard work, rarely rewarding, and occasionally so discouraging as to provoke suicide. Failure was far more common

From *Sixteen Months at the Gold Diggings* by Daniel B. Woods. New York: Harper & Brothers, 1851.

than success for those seeking their fortunes in the mines. Some returned east with only experience to show for their efforts; others achieved success by establishing service industries such as boarding houses and mail delivery, or, like Levi Strauss, by supplying miners' necessities such as tough canvas pants.

July 6th [1849]. We have to-day removed to the opposite side of the river. This, with pitching our tent, has occupied most of the day. Still, we have made $4 each. I have been seated for several hours by the river side, rocking a heavy cradle filled with dirt and stones. The working of a cradle requires from three to five persons, according to the character of the diggings. If there is much of the auriferous dirt, and it is easily obtained, three are sufficient; but if there is little soil, and this found in crevices, so as only to be obtained with the knife, five or more can be employed in keeping the cradle in operation. One of these gives his whole attention to working the cradle, and another takes the dirt to be washed, in pans or buckets, from the hole to the cradle, while one or two others supply the buckets. The cradle, so called from its general resemblance to that article of furniture, has two rockers, which move easily back and forth in two grooves of a frame, which is laid down firmly on the edge of or over the water, so that the person working it may at the same time dip up the water. It must be inclined a few degrees forward, that the dirt may be washed gradually out, and must be so placed that the mud may be carried off with the stream. Cleets are nailed across the bottom of the body, over which the loose dirt passes with the water, and behind which the magnetic sand and gold settle. An apron is placed beneath the hopper, and conducts the water, dirt, &C., from that to the body below—a construction similar to that of the common fanning-mill. The hopper, which is placed at the top of the cradle behind, is a box, the bottom of which is a sheet of tin, zinc, or sheet iron, perforated with holes from the size of a gold dollar up to that of a quarter eagle. Through these the dirt, gravel, and gold are all carried by the water upon the apron and into the body below, leaving only the pebbles, too large to be passed through, in the hopper, which are thrown out by raising it in the hands, and by a sudden forward, then backward motion, depositing them on one side in a heap. To facilitate this operation, the hopper is sometimes made with hinges, by which means, by raising the forward end, the dirt falls over behind. There is generally a handle, so placed on one side that the cradle may be rocked with the left hand, leaving it to the choice of the person rocking whether to stand or sit while at work. The dirt taken from the hole is turned into the hopper at the top. The person, rocking the cradle with his left hand, at the same time uses his right in dipping up continually ladles of water, which he dashes upon the dirt in the hopper. Twenty-five buckets of dirt are generally washed through, the mass in the body of the cradle being occasionally stirred up to prevent its hardening, and thus causing the gold to slide over it and be lost. It is then drawn off into a pan through holes at the bottom of the cradle, and "panned out," or washed, in the same way as in prospecting. While this is being done by one of the company, it is common for the others to spend the ten minutes' interval in resting themselves. Seated upon the rocks about their companion, they watch the ridge of gold as it dimples brightly up amid the black sand, seeming to me always *the smile of hope*, while many enlivening remarks and the cheering laugh go round. At length, the washing completed, the pan passes from one to another, while each one gives his opinion as to the quantity. The holes in the bottom of the cradle are stopped, more dirt is thrown into the hopper, and against the grating, scraping sounds are heard which are peculiar to the rocking of the cradle, and which, years hence, will accompany our dreams of the mines. . . .

Mining Harms Health

July 10. We made $3 each to-day. This life of severe hardship and exposure has affected my health. Our diet consists of hard bread, flour, which we eat half cooked, and salt pork, with occasionally a salmon which we purchase of the Indians. Vegetables are not to be procured. Our feet are wet all day, while a hot sun shines down upon our heads, and the very air parches the skin like the hot air of an oven. Our drinking water comes down to us thoroughly impregnated with the mineral substances washed through the thousand cradles above us. After our days of labor, exhausted and faint, we *retire*—if this word may be applied to the simple act of lying down in our clothes—robbing our feet of their boots to make a pillow of them, and wrapping our blankets about us, on a bed of pine boughs, or on the ground, beneath the clear, bright stars of night. Near morning there is always a change in the temperature of the air, and several blankets become necessary. Then the feet and the hands of the novice in this business become blistered and lame, and the limbs are stiff. Besides all these causes of sickness, the anxieties and cares which wear away the life of so many men who leave their families to come to this land of gold, contribute, in no small degree, to this same result. It may with truth be said, "the whole head is sick, and the whole heart faint."

I have to-day removed to the top of the hill above the encampment, and beneath a large oak-tree, for the benefit of a cooler air and shade during the intense heat of noon. . . .

The basics of placering: in the foreground, panning and feeding a Long Tom; center, winching up ore from a coyote hole and, to the left, washing in a cradle; in the rear, tunneling; and in the distance, flume-sluicing.

At [a] religious meeting . . . , held beneath the ten chapel of the Presbyterian church, it was stated that there had been lately twelve cases of suicide in San Francisco. Yesterday a young man from New England left his tent in "Happy Valley," and went to a retired place, untied his cravat and hung it upon the bushes, took a razor from its case, and put the case upon his cravat, and then deliberately cut his own throat. Pecuniary losses, it is supposed, was the cause. . . .

Work or Perish!

Jan. 14. In company with Captain W. and Dr. R., selected a spot where a mountain ravine opens into the river, and a few yards below the place where a company of Frenchmen took out, a few months since, a large amount of gold. Our best prospect was in the channel of this mountain stream. We spent some hours in diverting the stream from its course by a dam and a canal on a small scale. Then, by bailing, we succeeded in opening the channel. Most of the upper soil, with the stones, must be removed, nearly to the primitive rock below, often a distance of some feet, always ankle or knee deep in the mud. We were greatly encouraged, in the present instance, by an indication of gold rarely presented. About four inches from the surface of the ground, and in

131

the loose upper soil, I found a lump of gold weighing nearly three pennyweights. Greatly cheered by this circumstance, we worked away with spade and pick, with cradle and pan, hour after hour, and were rewarded by finding in our treasury at night a few bright scales of gold, amounting to 25 cents.

Jan. 15th. This morning, notwithstanding the rain, we were again at our work. We *must* work. In sunshine and rain, in warm and cold, in sickness and health, successful or not successful, early and late, it is work, *work*, WORK! *Work or perish!* All around us, above and below, on mountain side and stream, the rain falling fast upon them, are the miners at work—not for *gold*, but for *bread*. Lawyers, doctors, clergymen, farmers, soldiers, deserters, good and bad, from England, from America, from China, from the Islands, from every country but Russia and Japan—all, all at work at their cradles. From morning to night is heard the incessant rock, rock, rock! Over the whole mines, in streamlet, in creek, and in river, down torrent and through the valley, ever rushes on the muddy sediment from ten thousand busy rockers. Cheerful words are seldom heard, more seldom the boisterous shout and laugh which indicate success, and which, when heard, sink to a lower ebb the spirits of the unsuccessful. We have made 50 cents each.

Jan. 16th. A friend put into my hands to-day a copy of the Boston Journal. We laid it aside to read in the evening. But how was this to be accomplished? The luxury of a candle we could not afford. Our method was this: we cut and piled up a quantity of dry brush in a corner near the fire, and after supper, while one put on the brush and kept up the blaze, the other would read; and as the blaze died away, so would the voice of the reader. Our work to-day has amounted to 80 cents each.

Jan. 17th. A very rainy, cold day. As Captain W. is sorely afflicted with an eruption, which covers his whole body, probably the effects of having handled the "poison oak," which grows over the whole. . . .

Our Aqueduct: Only Ephemeral Success

The work before us is truly an arduous one, made doubly so by the limited means we have of prosecuting it. The clay for the construction of our canal must be carried in hand-barrows, borne between two persons, from the side of the hill down a steep bank, then along over a stony path to the canal, a distance varying from one eighth to one sixth of a mile; and this must be done day after day for weeks. Then the lumber for the aqueduct is to be sawed by hand, from logs cut and rolled from the tops and sides of the mountains, with whip-saws. This part of the business is under the direction of a master architect from London.

Almost All ... Seem to Have Lost

The Shirley Letters from the California Mines, 1851-1852, *were a series of succinct and often vividly descriptive eye-witness accounts of life in the mining camps written by "Dame Shirley," pseudonym for Louise Amelia Knapp Smith Clappe a writer and school teacher. In this excerpt she notes that financial success is next to impossible for miners to achieve.*

If a person "work his claim" himself, is economical and industrious, keeps his health, and is satisfied with small gains, he is "bound" to make money. And yet, I cannot help remarking, that almost all with whom we are acquainted seem to have lost. Some have had their "claims" jumped; many holes which had been excavated, and prepared for working at a great expense, caved in during the heavy rains of the fall and winter. Often after a company has spent an immense deal of time and money in "sinking a shaft," the water from the springs, (the greatest obstacle which the miner has to contend with in this vicinity) rushes in so fast, that it is impossible to work in them, or to contrive any machinery to keep it out, and for that reason only, men have been compelled to abandon places where they were at the very time "taking out" hundreds of dollars a day. If a fortunate or an unfortunate (which shall I call him?) does happen to make a "big strike," he is almost sure to fall into the hands of the professed gamblers, who soon relieve him of all care of it. They have not troubled the Bar much during the winter, but as the spring opens, they flock in like ominous birds of prey. Last week one left here, after a stay of four days, with over a thousand dollars of the hard-earned gold of the miners.

Sept. 24th [1850]. We prosecuted both parts of our work at the same time. A part were employed in carrying the clay to the canal. An account was kept one day, and it was ascertained that each barrow was carried, during the day, fourteen miles. Since my last date I have carried such a barrow four hundred and twenty miles. The clay was put in large heaps, where we could easily obtain it when it should be wanted in the making of the canal. This was a most arduous undertaking. Sometimes it must pass through a solid ledge of hard asbestos rock, and then through deep holes in the river, where it has washed into the banks. In such a case, a heavy wall, filled with clay, must be made. When completed, the canal was six hundred and thirty-eight feet in length, and sixteen in width. Making the aqueduct to convey the water from the canal, which passed through Paine's Bar, above us, was the most difficult task. The logs, which were cut upon the mountain, were rolled to the pits, and then sawed by hand. Piers were constructed by making crates of logs, which were firmly pinned together, then sunk in their places by being filled with large stones. Another large pier was made by rolling and carrying stones into the river a distance of thirty feet. The sleepers of the aqueduct were laid upon this and the laden crates. When it was finished, it was a handsome piece of workmanship, of which we were justly proud. It was one hundred and two feet in length, and twelve wide. This kind of labor—yielding no renumeration, only being preparatory to the more exciting, though laborious process of gold-digging—was prosecuted from July the 30th to this date, Sept. 24. . . .

This morning—Sept. 24th—the water was rising in its might. Notwithstanding our aqueduct and canal, the bed of the river was nearly full. We hastened to remove all our mining implements. Slowly, but surely, the freshet came, till the destruction of all our works seemed inevitable. . . .

We perceived at once that the existence of all our works depended upon the Paine's Bar dam above us. Would that stand the torrent? Should that maintain its position, we were safe; let that go, *all* would be swept away! As we kept our eyes fixed upon this—it was a quarter of a mile above us—the black line of wall was suddenly broken, and the torrent poured through a small opening forced in the dam, and in a few seconds the river ran foaming over the entire length of the wall, which bowed and sank before the irresistible force. Then and there was heard a sound new and strangely startling to me. It was caused by large stones *rushing* and *grinding* under water, borne on by the tremendous power of the current. It might be imagined that the thousand submerged chariots and cars of Pharaoh's host were driving impetuously over that river channel. As soon as the dam above us gave way, the water rose with great rapidity—two, three, four, six, eight feet—till it poured over the top of the aqueduct. Still it nobly stood, held in its place by the immense weight of the water which poured through it from the canal above. It was indeed surprising to see a thing so light resisting that mad and mighty force. It was but a moment! Gently and gracefully it yielded, swayed forward, and moved away with the ease and rapidity of a thing of life. Thus, in one moment, we saw the work of *one thousand and twenty-nine days* done by the company swept away and rendered useless. Within five minutes of the time when the aqueduct disappeared around the bend of the river, a meeting of the company was called, and a resolution presented to proceed with our work by means of wing-dams. . . .

More Back-Breaking Labor

To appreciate the difficulties of our arduous and dangerous task, and to understand the kind of work which was to be done, let my reader imagine himself standing by me, and looking at what is going on below us, while I describe the scene to him. The whole force of the company, aided by some thirty Mexicans we have employed to work for us, is concentrated upon the wall which is to be the head of the dam. This is to run from the shore out to the middle of the river, or about forty feet. Two walls are thrown up parallel to each other, and about two feet apart. The difficulty of this is almost inconceivable. We must roll the stones and adjust them where there is a rapid current four feet in depth. Sometimes a whole section of this will be swept off at once, and must be done all over again. After the walls are completed, strong cloth is spread down against the lower wall, and over its whole surface. The space is then filled up with small twigs, sand, and clay. After the wall is carried thus to the middle of the river, it must turn, forming a right angle, and run down through the middle of the river, parallel to the shore, a distance of two hundred and fifty feet, till it passes over some falls, by which means the water is partially drained from a portion of the channel. This portion so drained is then divided off into pens, which are surrounded by small walls, so made as to exclude the water, which is then bailed out, and all the space within the walls of the pens is thus worked. The cradles are set just over the walls, on the outer side, and some six or eight of them are sometimes being rocked at the same time, supplied with dirt by the dozen or twenty miners in the pens. It is a busy scene. It will be seen that this work is not only laborious, but in an extreme degree exposing. At times nearly all the company may be seen working together, waist deep, in the water, which, coming from the sierra Nevada, is very cold. This we must endure, while a burning sun is shining hotly down upon the head.

VIEWPOINT 4

"Never in the history of the world was there such a favourable opportunity as now presents itself in the gold region of California for a profitable investment of capital."

Capital and Technology Foster Victory over Nature

Edward Gould Buffum (1820-1867)

A member of the Seventh Regiment of the New York State Volunteers, Edward Gould Buffum arrived in Yerba Buena (San Francisco) on March 6, 1847. In his book *Six Months in the Gold Mines* he provides a clear description of the area's transition from a recently sleepy Mexican province to a region bustling with hopeful forty-niners from around the world and promising great opportunities for future investment and development. He includes an account of his own experiences in the gold fields during the fall, winter, and spring of 1848-49, experiences which led him to advocate increased use of capital and technology to extract gold.

From *Six Months in the Gold Mines* by Edward Gould Buffum. Philadelphia: Lea and Blanchard, 1850.

I do not believe, as was first supposed, that the gold-washings of northern California are "inexhaustible." Experience has proved, in the workings of other placers, that the rich deposits of pure gold found near the surface of the earth have been speedily displaced, and that with an immense influx of labouring population, they have totally disappeared. Thus, in Sonora, where many years ago fifteen and twenty, and even fifty dollars per day, were the rewards of labour, it is found difficult at present with the common implements to dig and wash from the soil more than from fifty cents to two dollars per day to a man. So has it been partially in the richer and more extensive placers of California. When first discovered, ere the soil was molested by the pick and the shovel, every little rock crevice, and every river bank was blooming with golden fruits, and those who first struck them, without any severe labour, extracted the deposits. As the tide of emigration began to flow into the mining region, the lucky hits upon rich deposits, of course, began to grow scarcer, until, when an immense population was scattered throughout the whole golden country, the success of the mining operations began to depend more upon the amount of labour performed than upon the good fortune to strike into an unfurrowed soil, rich in gold. When I first saw the mines, only six months after they were worked, and when not more than three thousand people were scattered over the immense territory, many ravines extending for miles along the mountains were turned completely upside down, and portions of the river's banks resembled huge canals that had been excavated. And now, when two years have elapsed, and a population of one hundred thousand, daily increasing, have expended so great an amount of manual labour, the old ravines and river banks, which were abandoned when there were new and unwrought places to go to, have been wrought and re-wrought, and some of them with good success. Two years have entirely changed the character of the whole mining region at present discovered. Over this immense territory, where the smiling earth covered and concealed her vast treasures, the pick and the shovel have created canals, gorges, and pits, that resemble the labours of giants. . . .

Great Financial Opportunities

The starving millions of Europe will find in the mountain gorges of California a home with profitable labour at their very door-sills, and the labouring-men of our own country will find it to their interest to settle among the auriferous hills. The miserably suicidal policy, which some of our military officers in California have attempted to introduce, has already proved not only its worthlessness, but the absolute impossibility of carrying it into effect. Never in the world's history was there a better opportunity for a great, free, and republican nation like ours to offer to the oppressed and down-trodden of the whole world an asylum, and a place whereby honest industry, which will contribute as much to our wealth as their prosperity, they can build themselves happy homes and live like freemen.

Long after the present localities, where the washing of gold is prosecuted, are entirely abandoned, gold-washing will be continued by manual labour upon the plains and hills where the gold

Although the site is in Idaho, the painting illustrates the process of hydraulic mining.

lies at a much greater depth beneath the soil than it does in the ravines and river banks, and where of course more severe labour is required. The era which follows the present successful gold-washing operations will be one, when, by a union of capital, manual labour, and machinery, joint-stock companies will perform what individuals now do. While gold can be found lying within a few inches of the earth's surface, and the only capital required to extract it consists in the capability to purchase a pick and a shovel, there is no need of combination; but when the hills are to be torn to their very bases, the plains completely uprooted, and the streams, which flow down from the Sierra Nevada to be turned from their channels, individuals must retire from the field, and make room for combined efforts.

Never in the history of the world was there such a favourable opportunity as now presents itself in the gold region of California for a profitable investment of capital; and the following are some of the modes in which it may be applied. I have before shown, and experience and observation have demonstrated it to me, that the beds of the tributaries to the two great rivers that flow from the Sierra Nevada are richer in gold than their banks have yet proved to be. There are many points, at each one of which the river can easily be turned from its channel by a proper application of machinery. Dams are then to be erected and pumps employed in keeping the beds dry. Powerful steam machines are to be set in operation for the purpose of tearing up the rocks, and separating the gold from them. The hills and plains are also to be wrought. Shafts are to be sunk in the mountain sides, and huge excavators are to bring to the surface the golden earth, and immense machines, worked by steam power, made to wash it. The earth, which had been previously washed in the common rockers, is to be re-washed in a more scientifically constructed apparatus, and the minute particles of gold, which escape in the common mode of washing, and which are invisible to the naked eye, are to be separated by a chemical process.

As yet no actual mining operations have been commenced in the gold region of California, for the two reasons, that they require a combination of labour and capital, and that the gold-washings have thus far proved so profitable as to make them the most desirable. But there is a greater field for actual mining operations in California than was ever presented in the richest districts of Peru or Mexico. The gold-washings, which have thus far enriched thousands, are but the scum that has been washed from the beds of the ore. I would not wish to say one word to increase the gold mania, which has gone out from California, and has attracted from the whole world thousands upon thousands of men who were not at all fitted to endure the hardships consequent upon a life in her mountainous regions, or the severe labour which was necessary to extract gold from the earth. It is to be hoped that this mania, however, has now given way to the "sober second thought," and that men have learned to listen to facts, and take the means to profit by them in the most proper manner. I should not consider myself as acting in accordance with duty, were I to assume the responsibility of publishing to the world an account of the gold mines of California, did I not, like the witness upon the stand, "tell the truth, the whole truth, and nothing but the truth."

The Cream Has Been Skimmed

California's leading newspaper, the Weekly Alta California, *made this assessment of the gold economy on February 15, 1851.*

The real truth is, by far the largest part of the gold . . . [mined hitherto] was taken from the river banks, with comparatively little labour. There is gold still in those banks, but they will never yield as they have yielded. The cream of the gulches, wherever water could be got, has also been taken off. We have now the river bottoms and the quartz veins; but to get the gold from them, we must employ gold. The man who lives upon his labor from day to day, must hereafter be employed by the man who has in his possession accumulated labor, or money, the representative of labor.

Throughout the range on the western slope of the Sierra Nevada, and in every little hill that branches from it, runs a formation of quartz rock, found sometimes at a few feet below the earth's surface, and sometimes rising above it in huge solid masses. This rock throughout the whole mining region has been proved by actual experiment to be richly impregnated with gold. Some of it exhibits the gold to the naked eye, while in other cases a powerful microscope is requisite to discern the minute particles that run in little veins through it. Experiments have been made in the working of this rock, which establish beyond a doubt its great richness. Hon. George W. Wright, one of the present representatives elected to Congress from California, has employed nearly the whole of the past summer in exploring the gold region, with a view of ascertaining the richness and extent of the quartz rock, and his experiments have proved so wonderful, as almost to challenge credulity even among those who have seen the progress of the mining operations in California from their commencement to the present period.

In pulverizing and extracting the gold from about one hundred pounds of this rock, Mr. Wright found that the first four pounds yielded twelve dollars worth of gold, which was the largest yield made, while throughout the whole the smallest yield was one dollar to the pound of rock, and this in many cases where not a particle of gold could be discerned with the naked eye. Mr. Wright has now in his possession a specimen of this quartz weighing twelve pounds, which contains six hundred dollars, or more than one quarter of its weight in pure gold; and one dollar to the pound of rock is the lowest amount which he has ever extracted.

In the gold mines of Georgia, where at present nearly all the profits result from the extraction of gold from the quartz rock, a fifteen horse power machine, working twelve "stamps," will "stamp" or pulverize a thousand bushels of the rock per day. The pulverization is the most important item in the extraction of the gold, as after the rock is reduced to powder, the gold can be very easily secured either by washing or making an amalgam of quicksilver, or by a combination of both processes. Now, in Georgia, if each bushel of rock should produce twelve and a half cents, the profits would be good. If twenty-five cents, greater; and if fifty, enormous. A bushel of the quartz rock weighs about seventy-five pounds, and we thus find that instead of, as in Georgia, yielding from ten to twenty-five *cents* to the bushel, the gold rock of California at its lowest estimate will yield seventy-five *dollars*, and in many cases much more. Let us pursue this subject a little farther. If a fifteen horse power engine will pulverize a thousand bushels, or seventy-five thousand pounds per day, at the estimate which has here been made, from seventy-five to one hundred thousand dollars would be the result of a day's labour, the whole performance of which suitable machinery would not require one hundred men. Even lowering this estimate one-half, profits are exhibited that are indeed as startling as they are true. Here is an immense field for the investment of capital throughout the world, and for the employment of a large portion of its labouring population.

CHAPTER 4

Gender and Race on the Frontier

Chapter Preface

With Natty Bumppo, alias Deerslayer, alias Hawkeye, alias Leatherstocking, James Fenimore Cooper created the literary archetype of the frontiersman: a white man conscious of the superiority of his race but living closely and amicably with "good" Indians, a woodsman and pathfinder who practices strict conservation and kills only what he needs to live, a man uncomfortable living in civilized society and thus on the move farther and farther west, ironically blazing the trail for the very society he wants to escape. Leatherstocking is a paragon of virtue and of strength. He is also an exemplar of male dominance on the frontier. For although Cooper includes women in his plots who, like Judith and Hetty in *The Deerslayer*, are able to paddle canoes and practice rudimentary woodcraft, they cannot function independently of their men. After Tom Hutter, the ostensible father of Judith and Hetty, is scalped, Cooper kills Hetty off and sends Judith back to the fort, eventually to become the mistress of one of the British officers. Natty Bumppo, frontiersman, begins the "men without women" tradition in American literature.

Patricia Nelson Limerick in *The Legacy of Conquest* charges that Frederick Jackson Turner, too, in constructing his frontier thesis, devised "arbitrary limits that excluded more than they contained." Turner, Limerick continues, was, "to put it mildly, ethnocentric and nationalistic. English-speaking white men were the stars of his story; Indians, Hispanics, French Canadians, and Asians were at best supporting actors and at worst invisible. Nearly as invisible were women, of all ethnicities." Today we know that minorities and women were well represented on the frontier even though, prior to the work of revisionist historians, their experiences had not been explored as fully as those of the white male.

It has sometimes been suggested that women were unwilling victims of their men's westering drive. Cooper's own mother may illustrate this type. The story, perhaps apocryphal, is told of his mother's balking at leaving the comparative comforts of her home in Burlington, New Jersey, when her husband acquired a land claim for a settlement later known as Cooperstown, New York. On the day for removal west, when the wagons were all loaded, Mrs. Cooper sat on her front porch in her accustomed rocking chair, adamantly refusing to leave; her husband, according to the story, marched up the steps, hefted his wife, rocking

Bryant Baker's 1927 bronze statue Pioneer Woman *depicts the strength and determination of many women on the frontier.*

chair and all, loaded her into the lead wagon, and set out.

This view of women as impotent and unwilling victims, however, tells only part of the story. On some frontiers—those of the fur trade and the gold rush, for example—women were at least initially peripheral. These were essentially male societies. With varying degrees of skill, men accomplished "feminine" chores. Mountain men could construct moccasins or repair leggings if they must, though they preferred to utilize the skills of Indian women available at trading rendezvous. The forty-niners learned to bake their own bread; these early Californians, however, drew the line at washing clothes, often sending shirts to Hawaii to be laundered! And, in many mining camps, dances were held with the "female" designated by a handkerchief tied around the sleeve

of a bearded man. The few women present on the early fur trapping and mining frontiers were generally native women and
prostitutes, both playing subservient roles in the lives of the trappers and miners.

In sharp contrast, on some frontiers, specifically those of the
homesteader and farmer, women were far more integral. For one
thing, the homesteader was not a sojourner who had left his family behind, but a settler, reestablishing agrarian society in a new
locale. The homestead was almost inevitably a family affair, with
clearly defined divisions of work by sex. In only a few areas did
the work of men and women overlap. John Mack Faragher writes
in *Women and Men on the Overland Trail* that men performed the
heaviest work: clearing the land; logrolling; constructing homes,
outbuildings, and fences; repairing tools, implements, and wagons; caring for the draft animals; and hunting. Women provided
subsistence for the farm family—growing, picking, butchering,
and preserving food; caring for the henhouse and dairy; housekeeping; child rearing; and preparing surplus products for sale.
Life for both sexes was hard, but a frontier aphorism conveys one
slant on reality: "This country is all right for men and dogs, but
it's hell on women and horses."

That the sexes did not always interpret the reality identically is
evident in two sources Faragher cites. John Ludlum McConnel, in
a book published in 1853, describes the frontier wife, contrasting
her with the pampered woman back east:

> There is no coyness, no blushing, no pretense of fright or ner-
> vousness—if you will, no romance—for which the husband has
> reason to be thankful! The wife knows what her duties are and
> resolutely goes about performing them. She never dreamed, nor
> twaddled, about "love in a cottage,". . . and she is, therefore, not
> disappointed on discovering that life is actually a serious thing.
> She never whines about "making her husband happy"—but
> sets firmly and sensibly about making him *comfortable*. She
> cooks his dinner, nurses his children, and encourages his indus-
> try. She never complains of having too much work to do, she
> does not desert her home to make endless visits—she borrows
> no misfortunes, has no imaginary ailings. . . . She never forgets
> whose wife she is,—there is no "sweet confidante" without
> whom "she can not live"—she never writes endless letters
> about nothing. She is, in short, a faithful, honest wife: and in
> "due time" the husband must make *more* "three-legged
> stools"—for the "tow-heads" have now covered them all!

But Abigail Scott Duniway, an Oregon immigrant of 1853, has
quite a different view of a farm woman's life:

> It was a hospitable neighborhood composed chiefly of bachelors,
> who found comfort in mobilizing at meal time at the homes of
> the few married men of the township, and seemed especially

fond of congregating at the hospitable cabin home of my good husband, who was never quite so much in his glory as when entertaining men at his fireside, while I, if not washing, scrubbing, churning, or nursing the baby, was preparing their meals in our lean-to kitchen. To bear two children in two and a half years from my marriage day, to make thousands of pounds of butter every year for market, not including what was used in our free hotel at home; to sew and cook, and wash and iron; to bake and clean and stew and fry; to be, in short, a general pioneer drudge, with never a penny of my own, was not a pleasant business.

Just as the farming frontier was only one of many frontiers, so the farm wife exemplified only one role of the woman on the frontier. Possibly because the mining frontier was more rapidly urbanized, women there played a greater variety of roles. For example, in *Gold Diggers and Silver Miners*, Marion S. Goldman classifies the female occupational structure of Virginia City and Gold Hill in 1875. Of the total of 3,572 women (there were 10,016 men) by far the greatest number, approximately three quarters, were "dependent," that is, married women, adult daughters living at home, and widows with no occupation. Great variety, however, is demonstrated by the other 25 percent of the women. "Working class employment" included servants, laundresses, and seamstresses. "Petit-bourgeois employment" included boardinghouse owners or managers, saloon owners, merchants, milliners, hairdressers, and telegraph operators. Among "professionals" were twenty schoolteachers and thirteen nuns. The rest of the women fall in the "disreputable" category. Of these, 180 were classified as "dependent" but not married; they were listed in the census as having no occupation other than "housekeeper," the official circumlocution for more common euphemisms, such as "soiled dove," for a fallen woman. In addition there were 9 madams and 298 prostitutes. Clearly Virginia City was no longer a raw frontier town: It had service industries, specialization of labor, and dependent families. However, in an environment where men were often killed in mining accidents but before there were safety-net social programs, women, even if initially dependent, often had to devise ways of supporting themselves and their families.

Whether frontier women were wives or madams, hurdy-gurdy dancers, schoolteachers, or doctors, women's increasingly prominent roles on the frontier confirmed the truth of the Chinese proverb "Women hold up half the sky." Nonetheless, many lacked political clout. Wyoming entered the Union in 1890 as the first state to give the franchise to women, and universal female suffrage was not granted until 1919.

In a similar way, many ethnic minorities were disenfranchised and discriminated against. Although one could examine the plight of the Irish, the Bohemians, the Armenians, the Mexicans, or any number of other immigrant groups, this chapter will take a brief look at the Chinese immigrant to America.

Although the date of the first Chinese arrival to the United States is not precisely known, by 1850 forty-six natives of the Celestial Kingdom lived in California. Like other forty-niners from around the world, ever-increasing numbers of Chinese began to travel to Gum Sahn—"Gold Mountain." By 1852 the number of Chinese in California was over 20,000. Initially relations with whites were relatively positive. A California newspaper described the Chinese as "good citizens, deserving of the respect of all"; "China Boys" participated in memorial services for President Taylor; and in 1859, blue-coated Chinese, throwing firecrackers and pinwheels, marched in parades celebrating California's admission to the Union. An orator during that Admission Day celebration commented on the ethnic mix gold had brought to California and optimistically predicted: "We . . . meet here today as brothers. Henceforth we have one country, one hope, one destiny."

However, with increasing population, competition grew for mine claims that were progressively less productive. Chinese were relegated to extracting gold from the tailings of claims others had already worked over and abandoned. In addition, alien miners acts were passed, levying taxes on all miners who were not U.S. citizens. These laws were directed initially against miners from Chile, Mexico, and Australia, but as more Chinese arrived, they were increasingly targeted by the tax collector.

By 1865 when the Central Pacific was laying railroad track eastward through the Sierra Nevada, thousands of Chinese were employed on work crews. At first the railroad had not wanted to employ them, but a shortage of white laborers and the urgency of the race against the Union Pacific necessitated it. The engineering difficulties facing the Central Pacific were notorious; instead of laying track across flat plains, they had to blast and tunnel through the mountains. In one instance, in order to gouge a roadbed out of a sheer granite cliff, Chinese laborers were lowered down the rock face in baskets to drill holes, set dynamite charges, and light the fuses; if they were not pulled up quickly enough, they took the full force of the blast. Over a thousand died from explosions, disease, avalanches, or overwork while they were building the roadbed. From this episode in our history comes the phrase "not worth a Chinaman's chance."

By the 1870s public attitudes toward the Chinese had worsened. One reason was the "credit-ticket system" that had enabled most Chinese to pay for their passage: A broker advanced passage money, to be repaid out of future wages. In the years following the Civil War, some people equated this system with slavery and objected to it, not so much on moral grounds as on economic ones. Laborers, especially, objected to competing against what they perceived as virtually slave labor. Moreover, the very fact that most Chinese came as sojourners rather than settlers, leaving wives and families behind them in China and fully intending to return home as soon as they could afford to, aroused ire. This was exacerbated by the support systems developed by the Chinese: associations based on home districts in China, Chinese-language newspapers, and *de facto* merchant banks to which members contributed and from which they could borrow.

Through the 1870s worsening economic conditions and increasing unemployment convinced white laborers that they were being squeezed from above by the capitalists and from below by the Chinese who provided cheap labor for those capitalists. While it was difficult for workingpeople to joust with financiers, they could create scapegoats for their problems: the Chinese. Antichinese labor demonstrations became frequent. At one such rally, workers carried placards with inflammatory slogans. One of the most extraordinary of these read: "Women's Rights! No More Chinese Chambermaids!" During the summer of 1877 these protests came to a head with the formation of the Workingmen's Party of California, led by Denis Kearney. Opposition to Chinese labor dominated most of the party's resolutions, one of which read: "The Chinese laborer is a curse to our land, is degrading to our morals, is a menace to our liberties, and should be restricted or forever abolished and 'The Chinese must go.'" Such political protest often boiled over into violence. Indeed, a Chinese-English phrasebook of the time includes such helpful phrases as "He took it from me by violence" and "They were lying in ambush."

Almost simultaneously began a process of what may be called legal persecution. Municipal ordinances, apparently innocuous but actually discriminatory, were passed. For example transportation taxes were levied on laundries. For a business using one horse-drawn delivery vehicle, the quarterly tax was $2; for one with two such vehicles, $4; and for those using no vehicles (i.e., the Chinese who usually transported clean laundry through the streets by foot, suspending bundles from poles over their shoulders), the tax was $15. The crowded conditions of Chinatowns were attacked by the cubic air ordinances, stipulating punishment for landlords or renters of any residence of less than five hundred cubic feet of air space per lodger. The legal harassment and the white attitudes toward the Chinese are both evident in the report of the San Francisco health officer in 1869-1870:

> There is no disguising the fact, that [the Chinese] are not only a moral leper in our community, but their habits and manner of life are of such character as to breed and engender disease wherever they reside. . . . Dwelling as they do in the very center of the

city, any contagious disease would necessarily spread with frightful rapidity. . . . As a class, their mode of life is the most abject in which it is possible for human beings to exist. The great majority of them live crowded together in rickety, filthy, and dilapidated tenement houses like so many cattle and hogs. . . . Vice in all its hideousness is on every hand. Apartments that would be deemed small for the accommodation of a single American, are occupied by six, eight, or ten Mongolians, with seeming indifference to all comforts. Nothing short of ocular demonstration can convey an idea of Chinese poverty and depravity.

What began as a local conflict spread across the nation as Chinese were used as strikebreakers in some eastern communities. It was in this atmosphere, during which national debates to limit immigration waxed hot, that the Lee and Phelan articles of this chapter were written. In the midst of this debate, the official San Francisco spokesman, Frank M. Pixley, presented to Congress his case for Chinese exclusion:

The Divine Wisdom has said that He would divide this country and the world as a heritage of five great families: that to the Blacks he would give Africa; to the Red Man He would give America; and Asia He would give to the Yellow race. He inspired us with the determination, not only to have prepared our own inheritance, but to have stolen from the Red Man, America; and it is now settled that the Saxon, American or European groups of families, the White Race, is to have the inheritance of Europe and America and that the Yellow races are to be confined to what the Almighty originally gave them; and as they are not a favored people, they are not to be permitted to steal from us what we have robbed the American savage of.

His irony was unintentional.

The culmination of the debate was the Exclusion Act of 1882, forbidding immigration of Chinese laborers, but leaving open a loophole for merchants and students. Instantly there was an increase of "merchants" applying for visas. Often officials turned a blind eye to passport irregularities. An editorial in the Sacramento *Union Record* noted that

the Chinaman is here because his presence pays, and he will remain and continue to increase so long as there is money in him. When the time comes that he is no longer profitable *that* generation will take care of him and will send him back. We will not do it so long as the pockets into which the profit of his labor flows continue to be those [of] our pantaloons. . . . In this matter, private interest dominates public interest.

For many Chinese immigrants with questionable documentation, the San Francisco earthquake and fire of 1906 was a boon, destroying records and making it impossible to prove that a given laborer was here illegally.

Lest we condemn out of hand the anti-Chinese agitation of the late nineteenth century, based in part on race and in part on perceived economic threat, we should examine the situation of the late spring of 1993. The running aground in New York harbor of the *Golden Venture* crammed with illegals resurrected discussion of Chinese immigration. Like their nineteenth-century predecessors indebted to the Six Companies for their passage money, these erstwhile immigrants had sacrificed thousands of dollars to pay those transporting them. Like those earlier Celestials, these Chinese came not so much for freedom as for survival. But in this post-frontier society, their arrival poses new questions. Is the "West"—from whatever direction one reaches it—any longer a place of opportunity? Once again American labor and American policymakers must ask whether America can continue to be a haven for the world, especially when troublesome related debates—over the North American Free Trade Agreement (NAFTA), over U.S. companies' moving offshore to gain cheap labor, over U.S. insistence that Japan provide a "level playing field" in trade—continue to rage.

Though possibly anachronistic, the myth still lives: America, a land of opportunity. Today's problems demand a rethinking of who we are and what values we hold or can afford to hold. As in the past, when their livelihoods are threatened, people may turn violent; but people threatened, perhaps by violence, may grow strong and endure. The women and Chinese of this chapter, on the whole, demonstrated strength, fortitude, and endurance. They survived, but unlike the figures of the next chapter, they did not become the subject of myth. The bandit captured the public imagination more than did the doctor; the army officer was mythologized by, among others, his wife who remained content in his shadow. Many helped shape this nation on the frontier; few became legends doing so.

VIEWPOINT 1

"All the sad-faced wives of the officers who had forced themselves to their doors to try to wave a courageous farewell and smile bravely to keep the ones they loved from knowing the anguish of their breaking hearts gave up the struggle at the sound of the music."

The Frontier Woman Supports Her Husband and His Career

Elizabeth Custer (1842-1933)

Elizabeth Clift Bacon married George Armstrong Custer in February 1864 at the Presbyterian church in Monroe, Michigan, thus becoming an army wife. From 1864 to 1873, the couple was stationed in Texas, Kansas, and Kentucky. When the Seventh Cavalry was ordered to Dakota Territory in 1873, General Custer was delighted; Elizabeth (Libbie) thought it "seemed as if we were going to Lapland." Fort Abraham Lincoln, a few miles south of what is now Mandan, South Dakota, was one of a chain of forts built "to keep Indians in order, to protect settlers, and to serve as bases for railroad survey and construction parties."

Although the women present were cherished and spoiled by their men, army regulations made no provision for wives. Libbie Custer was indignant:

> It enters into such minute detail in its instructions, even giving the number of hours that bean-soup should boil, that it would

From *"Boots and Saddles"; or, Life in Dakota with General Custer* by Elizabeth Custer. New edition © 1961 by the University of Oklahoma Press.

be natural to suppose that a paragraph or two might be wasted on an officer's wife! The servants and the company laundresses are mentioned as being entitled to quarters and rations and the services of the surgeon. If an officer's wife falls ill she cannot claim the attention of the doctor, though it is almost unnecessary to say that she has it through his most urgent courtesy.

The Custers were almost inseparable when the Seventh was not in the field, riding, hunting, fishing, and camping together. It was not unusual for her to ride off on the first day of a campaign with him or to hope that, if there was no trouble, he would send for her. Yet she did not aspire to heroics herself. She writes:

When I watched the scouts starting off on their mission, I invariably thanked Heaven that I was born a woman, and consequently no deed of valor would ever be expected from me.

For Elizabeth Custer, a woman's role was to support her man and wait for his return from battle.

In the following selection she describes, with some foreshadowing, the regiment marching out of Fort Lincoln. Although there may be a hint of classism between officers' wives and those of enlisted men and Crow scouts, she evokes a universal sense of the helplessness of a warrior's woman as he marches into harm's way. After the fateful news of Little Big Horn reached the fort, the women had to deal with their loss and devise plans for the rest of their lives. Elizabeth Custer turned to writing; in *Boots and Saddles*, *Tenting on the Plain*, and *Following the Guidon* she described military life on the Plains and, most important to her, countered her husband's critics and projected the heroic image of Custer that she wanted the American people to accept.

Our women's hearts fell when the fiat went forth that there was to be a summer campaign, with probably actual fighting with Indians.

Sitting Bull refused to make a treaty with the government and would not come in to live on a reservation. Besides his constant attacks on the white settlers, driving back even the most adventurous, he was incessantly invading and stealing from the land assigned to the peaceable Crows. They appealed for help to the government that had promised to shield them.

The preparations for the expedition were completed before my husband returned from the East, wither he had been ordered. The troops had been sent out of barracks into a camp that was established a short distance down the valley. As soon as the general returned we left home and went into camp.

The morning for the start came only too soon. My husband was to take Sister Margaret and me out for the first day's march, so I rode beside him out of camp. The column that followed seemed unending. The grass was not then suitable for grazing, and as the route of travel was through a barren country, immense quantities of forage had to be transported. The wagons themselves seemed to stretch out interminably. There were pack mules, the ponies already laden, and cavalry, artillery, and infantry followed, the cavalry being in advance of all. The number of men, citizens, employees, Indian scouts, and soldiers was about twelve hundred. There were nearly seventeen hundred animals in all.

As we rode at the head of the column, we were the first to enter the confines of the garrison. About the Indian quarters, which we were obliged to pass, stood the squaws, the old men, and the children, singing, or rather moaning, a minor tune that has been uttered on the going out of Indian warriors since time immemorial. Some of the squaws crouched on the ground, too burdened with their trouble to hold up their heads; others restrained the restless children who, discerning their fathers, sought to follow them.

The Indian scouts themselves beat their drums and kept up their peculiar monotonous tune, which is weird and melancholy beyond description. Their warsong is misnamed when called music. It is more of a lament or a dirge than an inspiration to activity. This intoning they kept up for miles along the road. After we had passed the Indian quarters we came near Laundress Row, and there my heart entirely failed me. The wives and children of the soldiers lined the road. Mothers, with streaming eyes, held their little ones out at arm's length for one last look at the departing father. The toddlers among the children, unnoticed by their elders, had made a mimic column of their own. With their handkerchiefs tied to sticks in lieu of flags, and beating old tin pans for drums, they strode lustily back and forth in imitation of the advancing soldiers. They were fortunately too young to realize why the mothers wailed out their farewells.

Unfettered by conventional restrictions, and indifferent to the opinion of others, the grief of these women was audible and was accompanied by desponding gestures, dictated by their bursting hearts and expressions of their abandoned grief.

It was a relief to escape from them and enter the garrison, and yet, when our band struck up "The Girl I Left Behind Me," the most despairing hour seemed to have come. All the sad-faced wives of the officers who had forced themselves to their doors to try to wave a courageous farewell and smile bravely to keep the ones they loved from knowing the anguish of their breaking hearts gave up the struggle at the sound of the music. The first notes made them disappear to fight out alone their trouble and seek to place their hands in that of their Heavenly Father, who, at such supreme hours, was their never failing solace.

A Premonition

From the hour of breaking camp, before the sun was up, a mist had enveloped everything. Soon the bright sun began to penetrate this veil and dispel the haze, and a scene of wonder and beauty appeared. The cavalry and infantry in the order named, the scouts, pack mules, and artillery, all behind the long line of white-covered wagons, made a column altogether some two miles in length. As the sun broke through the mist a mirage appeared, which took up about half of the line of cavalry, and thenceforth for a little distance it marched, equally plain to the sight on the earth and in the sky.

The future of the heroic band, whose days were even then numbered, seemed to be revealed, and already there seemed a premonition in the supernatural translation as their forms were reflected from the opaque mist of the early dawn.

The sun, mounting higher and higher as we advanced, took every little bit of burnished steel on the arms and equipments along the line of horsemen, and turned them into glittering flashes of radiating light. The yellow, indicative of cavalry, outlined the accouterments, the trappings of the saddle, and sometimes a narrow thread of that effective tint followed the outlines even up to the headstall of the bridle. At every bend of the road, as the column wound its way round and round the low hills, my husband glanced back to admire his men and could not refrain from constantly calling my attention to their grand appearance.

The soldiers, inured to many years of hardship, were the perfection of physical manhood. Their brawny limbs and lithe, well-poised bodies gave proof of the training their outdoor life had given. Their resolute faces, brave and confident, inspired one with a feeling that they were going out aware of the momentous hours awaiting them, but inwardly assured of their capability to meet them.

The general could scarcely restrain his recurring joy at being detained on other duty. His buoyant spirits at the prospect of the activity and field life that he so loved made him like a boy. He had made every plan to have me join him later on, when they should have reached the Yellowstone.

The steamers with supplies would be obliged to leave our post and follow the Missouri up to the mouth of the Yellowstone, and from thence on to the point on that river where the regiment was to make its first halt to renew the rations and forage. He was sanguine that but a few weeks would elapse before we would be reunited, and used this argument to animate me with courage to meet our separation.

As usual we rode a little in advance and selected camp, and watched the approach of the regiment with real pride. They were so accustomed to the march the line hardly diverged from the trail. There was a unity of movement about them that made the column at a distance seem like a broad dark ribbon stretched smoothly over the plains.

Entertaining General Sherman

Today—and on the 1866-1867 frontier—one of the roles of the ambitious army wife is to be a good hostess for her husband. In this insert, Evy Alexander describes entertaining General Sherman for her husband, Col. Andrew J. Alexander, then stationed at Fort Stevens, Colorado. That this is a frontier post is evident in that everyone still lives in tents; the menu is, therefore, all the more amazing.

There were two or three hospital tents pitched at the right of our tent with large fires blazing before them. These were the quarters we offered our guests. I had a larger table made the day before that would just seat eight comfortably. Soon after their arrival we had lunch in the mess tent. General Sherman occupied the seat of honor at my left, on the end of a trunk. . . .

I spent nearly all the afternoon tete-a-tete with him. He took great interest in pointing out to me the boundaries of the different departments in his command, showed me the new lines of railroads, and talked at length and most interestingly about this frontier land. . . .

We had dinner about six o'clock. I had the table brought in this tent, where it was warm and cheerful. It is the fashion after entertaining great men to publish your bill of fare, so I will note mine here. First course, beef vegetable soup; second, saddle of mutton with jelly, green peas, kirshaw squash, cabbage, and beets; third, soft custard, blanc mange with cream and sugar, and coffee. Everything was cooked to perfection, and the general declared he had not tasted so fine a saddle of mutton since he left Saint Louis and said it was the king of dishes. I must say they all ate with a good appetite, and our chief honored the mutton so far as to return to it a third time.

Our dinner was seasoned with a great deal of spicy conversation, stories of camp and field which always abound when old soldiers get together.

We made our camp the first night on a small river a few miles beyond the post. There the paymaster made his disbursements, in order that the debts of the soldiers might be liquidated with the sutler.

In the morning the farewell was said, and the paymaster took sister and me back to the post.

With my husband's departure my last happy days in garrison were ended, as a premonition of disaster that I had never known before weighed me down. I could not shake off the baleful influence of depressing thoughts. This presentiment and suspense, such as I had never known, made me selfish, and I shut into my heart the most uncontrollable anxiety and could lighten no one else's burden. The occupations of other summers could not even give temporary interest.

Word of Indian Troubles

We heard constantly at the Fort of the disaffection of the young Indians of the reservation, and of their joining the hostiles. We knew, for we had seen for ourselves, how admirably they were equipped. We even saw on a steamer touching at our landing its freight of Springfield rifles piled up on the decks en route for the Indians up the river. There was unquestionable proof that they came into the trading posts far above us and bought them, while our own brave 7th Cavalry troopers were sent out with only the short-range carbines that grew foul after the second firing.

While we waited in untold suspense for some hopeful news, the garrison was suddenly thrown into a state of excitement by important dispatches that were sent from division headquarters in the East. We women knew that eventful news had come and could hardly restrain our curiosity, for it was of vital import to us. Indian scouts were fitted out at the Fort with the greatest dispatch and given instructions to make the utmost speed they could in reaching the expedition on the Yellowstone. After their departure, when there was no longer any need for secrecy, we were told that the expedition which had started from the Department of the Platte, and encountered the hostile Indians on the headwaters of the Rosebud, had been compelled to retreat.

All those victorious Indians had gone to join Sitting Bull, and it was to warn our regiment that this news was sent to our post, which was the extreme telegraphic communication in the Northwest, and the orders given to transmit the information, that precautions might be taken against encountering so large a number of the enemy. The news of the failure of the campaign in the other department was a death knell to our hopes. We felt that we had nothing to expect but that our troops would be overwhelmed with numbers, for it seemed to us an impossibility, as it really proved to be, that our Indian scouts should cross that vast extent of country in time to make the warning of use.

The first steamer that returned from the Yellowstone brought letters from my husband, with the permission, for which I had longed unutterably, to join him by the next boat. The Indians had fired into the steamer when it had passed under the high bluffs in the gorges of the river. I counted the hours until the second steamer was ready. They were obliged, after loading, to cover the pilot house and other vulnerable portions of the upper deck with sheet iron to repel attacks. Then sandbags were placed around the guards as protection, and other precautions were taken for the safety of those on board. All these delays and preparations made me inexpressibly impatient, and it seemed as if the time would never come for the steamer to depart.

Meanwhile our own post was constantly surrounded by hostiles, and the outer pickets were continually subjected to attacks. It was no unusual sound to hear the long roll calling out the infantry before dawn to defend the garrison. We saw the faces of the officers blanch, brave as they were, when the savages grew so bold as to make a daytime sortie upon our outer guards.

A picture of one day of our life in those disconsolate times is fixed indelibly in my memory.

On Sunday afternoon, June 25, our little group of saddened women, borne down with one common weight of anxiety, sought solace in gathering together in our house. We tried to find some slight surcease from trouble in the old hymns; some of them dated back to our childhood's days, when our mothers rocked us to sleep to their soothing strains. I remember the grief with which one fair young wife threw herself on the carpet and pillowed her head in the lap of a tender friend. Another sat dejected at the piano and struck soft chords that melted into the notes of the voices. All were absorbed in the same thoughts, and their eyes were filled with faraway visions and longings. Indescribable yearning for the absent, and untold terror for their safety, engrossed each heart. The words of the hymn,

E'en though a cross it be
Nearer, my God, to Thee,

came forth with almost a sob from every throat.

At that very hour the fears that our tortured minds had portrayed in imagination were realities, and the souls of those we thought upon were ascending to meet their Maker.

On July 5—for it took that time for the news to come—the sun rose on a beautiful world, but with its earliest beams came the first knell of disaster. A steamer came down the river bearing the wounded from the battle of the Little Big Horn, of Sunday, June 25. This battle wrecked the lives of twenty-six women at Fort Lincoln, and orphaned children of officers and soldiers joined the cry to that of their bereaved mothers.

From that time the life went out of the hearts of the "women who weep," and God asked them to walk on alone and in the shadow.

VIEWPOINT 2

"Here I was a stranger in a strange land without a friend or acquaintance who might assist me in a dire emergency."

The Frontier Woman Develops Strength and Independence

Bessie Efner Rehwinkel

Despite her father's warning, "You are headed for disaster, and you will come to want in that God-forsaken wilderness," Dr. Bessie Efner started her life over again in Wyoming the week before Christmas, 1907. She had pioneering in her blood; her grandfather and great-grandfather had been pioneers, starting in New York and ending in Iowa, and her brother, also a physician and also restless, had settled in Washington.

Bessie Efner had lost her home in the Panic of 1907. When, in addition to free federal lands available for homesteading, the railroads began to sell lands received as construction subsidies, her future beckoned. The railroad land companies wanted settlers and, to make the new Wyoming communities more attractive, they were anxious to provide essential social services: schools, churches, and medical care. Thus Efner was approached by Carpenter, Wyoming, on a branch of the Burlington Railroad, and was promised a homestead adjoining the town if she would come as their doctor. Efner headed West as a single mother, having adopted three nieces, ages eight, seven, and two and a half, before she set out.

When the train deposited her at a ranch house two miles west of town because there was as yet no station or depot, she surveyed the endless prairie and said to herself, "So this is Wyoming, my new home, the glamorous west of cowboys and cattle about which I have heard and dreamed so much." She soon traded glamour for gutsiness and myth for reality. She owned 160 acres, a four-room house (two rooms of which had to serve as office and examining room), and no indoor plumbing. Here she learned that

> pioneering in a new country is not a glamorous experience, as so often depicted in movie and novel, but a hard day-by-day struggle, and a most unglamorous struggle for one's very existence. And it is not a struggle with gun and rifle and beautiful horses and cowgirls against Indians and wicked gangsters, but a life-and-death struggle with the most primitive enemies of man, namely, against hunger and drought and dust storms and grasshoppers and hail and blizzards and cold, and against failure and frustration, loneliness and despondency. The people that survived in this struggle were not the 40-hours-a-week type, nor had they heard of the slogan that the world owed them a living. If this philosophy had prevailed in those days, America would still be a savage wilderness. If we are to erect national monuments to honor our nation's heroes and heroines, who made America, we ought to erect such monuments to the heroic men and women who with their sweat and brawn and an indomitable determination laid the foundation of the rich and wonderful heritage we now enjoy so bountifully in this our beautiful America.

The following passage, which like the excerpt above, is taken from her autobiography, describes some of Efner's initial difficulties in the triple role of mother, homesteader, and doctor. Her experiences exemplify those of many women who had to develop strength and independence to survive on the frontier.

Several years after settling in Wyoming, Bessie Efner met and married Alfred M. Rehwinkel. Their life together was a happy one, but first Dr. Bessie, as she came to be known, learned what it was to be a single professional woman on the frontier.

The cost of moving my little family and household goods from Moville to Carpenter had completely exhausted my financial resources. I had only enough money left to buy the most essential supplies necessary to start housekeeping in my new home. When I had paid for them, I had exactly 75 cents left. That was my total cash possession to begin life with in this new country. There was no chance to borrow from the bank if the need should arise, because there was no bank. Nor was there any possibility to buy groceries on credit, because the operator of the little store was just beginning himself and could not afford to sell on time to others. And here I was a stranger in a strange land without a friend or acquaintance who might assist me in a dire emergency. And besides that, winter was upon us. It was only one week before Christmas. And so it was not a very pleasant thought to contemplate as to what might happen to us if there would not be an early demand for my professional services. And the prospects for that didn't seem too promising at this time, partly because of the sparseness of the population. Newcomers were steadily arriving, but the number of those who were already established was still comparatively small, and they were scattered over a very large area. There were still miles and miles of open grazing land in all directions without a single occupant in sight.

To this must be added the fact that the people who were there did not know that a doctor had located in their community. I had no way to make my presence known. There was no telephone, no newspaper, no school or church, and not even a post office. But sometimes strange things happen which help to solve our problems in the most unexpected manner.

Early in the morning of the very next day after my arrival, even before I had hung out my shingle to advertise my presence, there was an urgent knock at my door. When I opened it, I was confronted by a man with an anguished look on his face, and he said: "Are you the new doctor? I was told by some workman at the tent that one had located here, and I was directed to this house. I have a very urgent case. One of my horses is very sick, and I might lose him if I am not able to get immediate help. I have only one team, and if I lose this horse I am ruined."

When he stopped for a moment, presumably to await my response, I explained to him that I was a doctor indeed, but not a horse doctor. "I am a doctor for people," I said, "and not for animals. And I know nothing about horses."

"But," he interrupted impatiently, "if you can cure people, you can also cure horses, because horses are very much like people. I will tell you how my horse has been acting, and you can tell me what you would do for a man under similar circumstances. I am sure you can help my horse."

Before I could say any more, he began to describe the symptoms of his sick horse. As I listened to the vivid account he gave, it occurred to me that it might possibly be suffering from an acute case of colic, and I told him what might have caused it.

And he continued, "What would you do for a man under such circumstances?" I told him. Then he urged that I give him the same,

but to make the medicine dose four times as strong as I would pre-
scribe for a man. "Well," I said, "I will do as you wish, but only
with the understanding that you are administering this medicine at
your own risk. I have not seen your horse, and what is more, I
know nothing about sick horses. And I don't pretend to be a horse
doctor. If you are agreed to that, I will give you the medicine."

He was more than ready to assume full responsibility. I filled
out the prescription for him and gave him directions how to use
it. With that he hurried back to his sick horse.

My charge for the consultation and the medicine was 75 cents,
and I felt uneasy to take even that.

That horse was my first patient in Wyoming, and the 75 cents
the first professional fee I earned on the Western frontier.

But that was not the end of the story.

The next day the man returned to tell me that my medicine had
been effective and that his horse was saved. This man was my
friend ever after and my best publicity agent when I needed one
most. He told everybody how this new lady doctor had cured his
horse even without seeing it, and he was sure that if she could cure
sick horses, she would also be able to do something for sick people.

The 75 cents I received for my services doubled my financial
holding, and I now had a total of $1.50 in my treasury. . . .

My practice was slow, in fact, very slow in getting started. Either
people were not getting sick in this healthful climate, or they
lacked confidence in me as a doctor because I was a woman. And
I had already learned before that it required time and patience to
overcome old and deep-seated prejudice against women doctors.

But even babies seemed to have postponed their arrival, which
was more serious for me, because for baby cases women generally preferred a lady doctor to a man, and these cases gave me an
opportunity to gain the confidence of the people for other cases.
As a result of this situation our daily fare for a considerable time
was rather Spartan in character, with very little variations. One
day it was potatoes, pork and beans, and prunes, and the next
day it was prunes, turnips, and pork and beans. Salt pork provided seasoning and the necessary fats, and the homemade bread
spread with molasses was our dessert. We didn't count calories,
nor were we much concerned about vitamins and about a balanced diet. It was a matter of satisfying elementary hunger, the
most urgent drive in human life. But I was surprised how quickly
we learned to adjust to this rather rugged Indian mode of living.
Nor did we suffer any adverse consequence as a result. . . .

Life as a Homesteader

As a whole, my experience on the frontier was about the same
as that of every other homesteader, with the only exception that I

had my profession, and therefore a potential cash income, which gave me a certain advantage.

The life of a homesteader and that of his family was a hard life, especially during the first three or four years.

It is true, the Government gave him a most generous start by giving him a free grant of 160 acres of good farm land, on which he received an absolute title of ownership after five years of occupancy, having fulfilled all other very reasonable requirements prescribed by the Homestead Act.

One hundred sixty acres of land is a princely gift indeed, and it made it possible for people who could never have hoped to own their own farm in the older communities to become independent owners of a very substantial tract of land and to establish their own home for themselves and their families. This had been the great lure which brought thousands of people from all over the United States and from Europe to the West to try their fortune on this new land.

But 160 acres of the best land in a wilderness is not yet a home or a farm.

To make it that required years of hard labor, sacrifice, resourcefulness, courage, vision, determination, and a high degree of pluck and perseverance in the face of reverses and failure. And many who lacked these qualities suffered defeat in this struggle and failed in their homesteading enterprise.

The average homesteader came here with limited means. People well established and in comfortable circumstances in the older parts of the country are usually not inclined to leave what they have and to risk their security and comfort for an uncertain future in a wilderness.

The small capital the homesteader brought with him was generally used up for building a shack or a modest house for his family and some shelter for his farm animals, for drilling a well and providing such other essentials necessary for the minimum of human existence. Whatever capital remained had to tide him over until he had harvested his first crop. Very much therefore depended upon that first harvest.

If he was lucky and struck a good year, he was fortunate and secure for another season. But if it happened to be a dry year without sufficient rain necessary for a crop, he harvested nothing or only enough to recover the seed he had planted. The average rainfall in these parts of Wyoming is so marginal that a small variation of four or five inches in one or the other direction may mean either a bumper crop or a complete failure for the farmer.

But even if the weather conditions were favorable and he had the promise of a good crop, his worries were not yet over.

A hailstorm, so frequent on the prairie, may wipe out in one

162

hour all his hopes and the fruits of his labors for another year and convert the most promising wheat, corn, or bean crop into a field of dismal desolation.

Elaine Goodale's Work Among the Sioux

Elaine Goodale is another example of a professional woman facing the challenges of the frontier alone until her later marriage to the physician Charles Eastman. Here a contemporary New York Evening Post *article analyzes Goodale's role as a supervisor of education for the Indian Bureau.*

Miss Elaine Goodale's work among the Sioux Indians of the two Dakotas in the exercise of her office as supervisor of education is attracting much attention at the Indian Bureau, her communications from the field being wonderfully business-like, candid, and specific in detail. Commissioner Morgan has supplied her with a wagon and camping outfit, as there are no railroads or regular stage conveyances in the country through which her labors carry her, and has hired an Indian man to drive and his wife to do the cooking for the party. This makes her entirely independent, and she is busily engaged in inspecting and reporting upon the condition of the schools.

Her territory is large, embracing a greater number of these institutions than any other state or territory. . . . Of sixty schools, forty-nine are wholly supported by the government, nine by religious societies under contracts by which the government pays annual sums ranging from $108 to $175 per annum for the care of each pupil and his tuition, and two by the government and a religious society combined.

Considerable criticism was provoked by the choice of a young, unmarried woman for the work in this wild Dakota country, but the Commissioner reasoned that . . . one who had already proved her mettle as Miss Goodale has, and whose training was so thorough in all directions, would make a more striking impression upon the Indians than a man. He is very desirous, now that the Sioux—an especially strong and vigorous nation—are coming gradually out of the tribal relation and into recognition of the rights and responsibilities of the individual, to turn their thoughts as much as possible toward education, as the key to the problems that confront them in their new estate.

If he escaped both drought and hail, there was still the possibility of an unseasonable frost, a grasshopper plague, a devastating dust storm, or the ravages of the blight and rust in grain and corn, of cutworms and countless insects, to deprive him of the means of livelihood for himself and his family.

When such calamities struck—and they were by no means uncommon—there was only one thing the poor homesteader could do to keep from actual starvation and that was to seek employment elsewhere to provide the barest living for his family. But opportunities for employment in a new country are scarce. Homesteaders cannot afford to hire other homesteaders. They are all in the same boat. This often meant that the husband and the father had to leave home for a longer period of time and seek employment wherever work was to be found. Sometimes be was able to secure a job with railroad construction gangs, others for a season on the large cattle ranches, still others on irrigation farms in Colorado or in coal mines in Western Wyoming. A few might find jobs in cities like Cheyenne, Greeley, or Denver. But this meant a long separation from the family, the husband and the father at work at an unknown faraway place, leaving the wife and children alone on an isolated homestead, trying to carry on as best they could. Means of communication were very inadequate or nonexistent. There were no telephones or telegraph offices in the country, and even the mail service was poor for the outlying places. No one knows what pain and anguish of soul these early settlers suffered in those trying years. Many did not survive, the physical and mental strain was too much for them, especially the homesteader's wife, forcing him to abandon their hopeful enterprise.

But starting life in a new country is more than building one's home and developing one's own homestead into a productive farm. It means building a whole new community and a new way of life where there was nothing but wilderness before. People who have always lived in an old, well-established community are apt to take the products of civilization, such as the social institutions, the public services, and the countless conveniences provided in modern society, for granted, never asking how they got them or where they came from. But for every institution, every convenience, and every service in human society someone and some previous generations have labored and sacrificed before us; what they have achieved was the capital they passed on to those who followed after them.

In a new community emerging out of a wilderness there are none of these things. They must be created out of nothing, starting from zero.

There were no roads, no bridges, no telephones, no wells, no markets, no merchants, no stores, no schools, no churches, no hospitals, no post office, no community consciousness, no local government.

There was nothing but land and sky, coyotes and prairie dogs and rattlesnakes. All improvements had to be created by those who came here first. This required leadership, cooperation, faith in the future, and a willingness to sacrifice for the future. That is the meaning of pioneering on the new frontier. Humble and courageous pioneers like that laid the foundation for the prosperity and the greatness of our country.

The above description of a homesteader's life, though lacking in many details, will be sufficient to show that a grant of 160 acres of free land by the Government was by no means an unqualified bonanza or a shortcut to economic independence and wealth. It was a long and persistent struggle with the forces of nature, and the continuing variations between success and near disaster required years of perseverance and sacrifice before a degree of economic stability was secured and the normal comforts of home life were made possible.

But if the lot of the average homesteader on the frontier was a life of hardships, the life of a doctor on the same frontier was no better. On the one hand, the general conditions under which he had to live were not different from those of the other homesteaders. His life was essentially the same as theirs, and their failure ultimately had to be shared by him. If they had nothing, he could collect nothing for his services. You cannot squeeze blood from a dry turnip.

Life as a Frontier Doctor

More than that, because of his profession he was exposed much more frequently and more dangerously to the rigors of the prairie weather and to the hazards of night driving over an uncharted wilderness.

To that must be added the great physical hardship to which the frontier doctor was exposed on his long and hazardous rides by day and night in rainstorm and blizzard in an open buggy or in a saddle to serve his patients. Traveling in an enclosed automobile of today in the worst possible weather is sheer luxury compared with the mode of travel by which I had to make my professional calls.

My medical parish, if I may call it that, comprised a territory of about 30 miles by 30. I was the only doctor between Cheyenne and the Nebraska state line to the east. To the south my field extended a considerable distance into Colorado, and northwest I served people beyond Burns and the Union Pacific Railway to the border of the open grazing land in the northern part of Laramie County of that day. To drive 15, 20, or even 30 miles in an automobile over well-marked highways today is no hardship and doesn't involve more than a matter of minutes and not hours. But there were no automobiles or marked roads on the prairie in those days. Road allowances had been provided when the land was surveyed and laid out in sections, but there were no roads and sometimes not even trails, nor were there any bridges over the gullies and creeks, and no fences to mark off roads. What people called a road was a mere trail winding like a cow path without plan or design across the prairie in various directions. If they were well traveled, it was not too difficult to follow them; but often they were so faint that they were lost in the prairie grass. It required the instinct of an Indian to find one's way over such trails.

Of course, there were no road markers to give the directions, no trees or shrubbery or other variations in the scenery to serve as landmarks.

When you came to a fork in the road and had to decide which of the trails to follow, you often had to go by guess and take a chance if you were not well acquainted with the territory in which you happened to be driving. If you chose the wrong trail, it meant a loss of hours of time, a waste of your team's energy, and might prove disastrous for the patient to whose bedside you had been called. Even during the day it was not always easy to find your way over the wide prairie, but it became a nightmare in the darkness of a rainy night or when overtaken by a snowstorm or blizzard. Once the trail was lost, one was hopelessly adrift like a man in an open boat in the wide-open sea without a compass or rudder, battered by wind and waves on all sides. I once had such an experience, and I know of what I am speaking. I was once caught in such a fearful prairie blizzard, and I shall never be able to erase that horrible experience from my memory.

I had been called to a farmhouse some distance from home to the bedside of the wife of a young homesteader. After I had done for her what was possible, I left medicine with instructions how to care for the patient until I would return in a day or so, and made ready to return home.

Becoming a Human Icicle

It was already late, but the sky was clear, the weather was calm and mild, and a beautiful starry heaven above gave the prairie a most peaceful appearance. All of nature lay, as it seemed, in a restful slumber. I was well acquainted with the road from Carpenter to the place where I was at this time, and so I had no misgivings about the drive home, even though it was dark and the hour was late. But before getting into my buggy I looked up once more to scan the sky and make sure about any possible change in the weather. This was standard procedure in the winter months before anyone would start on a long drive over the prairie.

And as I looked around, I noticed a large, dark bank of clouds hovering over the distant northwestern horizon, but it seemed very far away, and even if it were a storm cloud, it would require hours before it could possibly arrive here. That would give me ample time to reach home. And so I started on my homeward drive.

All was going well. My horses were trotting along at their usual pace while my thoughts were still with the patient I had just left. But presently I noticed a change in the atmosphere. The serene calm was abruptly broken by a sudden gust of wind, followed again by a calm and then another gust which was increased in velocity. This was followed by some sporadic snow flurries, not serious yet, but an indication that a storm was on its way. Realizing that these changes were the forebodings of something worse to follow, I urged my horses on to a faster pace, because I was still a considerable distance from home.

But then suddenly the storm broke, and broke with all its fury, as though 10,000 demons had been unleashed from their chains in the lower regions. Snow began to fall in shovelfuls, driven over the prairie by a 70-mile gale and roaring past and around me with the thunderous noise of a fast-traveling freight train. It was a cloudburst of snow combined with the elemental forces of an icy tornado, one of the most deadly weapons nature has in her destructive arsenal. It seemed as though the forces of the universe had conspired together to destroy every living thing that happened to be in their path. Neither man nor beast could long endure this frightful icy bombardment. The swirling snow blotted out everything around me. The road had vanished. I could no longer see the horses before me. I lost all my sense of direction. My eyes became blurred, my hands numb, and my face burned from the frozen pellets to which it was exposed. There was no escape either from this unmerciful blast of snow or the piercing pain of the cold. The pace of my horses had become a creeping walk. I was completely bewildered and no longer able to guide them, and so I relaxed the reins and let them choose their own course, hoping that their native instinct might lead them back to their own stall. Time seemed to have come to a standstill. This was the longest night in all my life that I can remember. As the moments passed, the storm grew in ferocity and the cold increased in intensity. My whole body was becoming numb, and I began to feel an almost irresistible drowsiness creeping upon me, which I recognized as the first stage in the process of freezing to death. My horses were beginning to show signs of fatigue, moving at a very slow walk or even coming to a stop. I urged them on with all the energy I could muster, knowing only too well that if I would be left stranded here, I could not possibly survive until morning.

How long my horses and I had been battered and buffeted by cold and storm I knew not, but hope was beginning to fade. Both my team and I were growing weaker, and I was becoming aware that we were fighting a losing battle. And then I thought of my little orphan nieces at home all alone, and what would become of them if I would perish here in this blizzard.

Then suddenly something happened that gave me a new gleam of hope. I thought I had seen a very faint glimmer of light ahead of me. My horses were heading directly for it, and presently they came to a stop. Yes, it really was a light and not a phantom like a desert mirage created by a crazed imagination. But though safety and rescue were now within reach, I could hardly move. My body was rigid from the cold that had penetrated to the very marrow of my bones. My hands and joints were so stiff that only with the greatest difficulties could I climb out of the buggy. I was covered from head to foot with an icy sheet of snow, which had frozen into a crust so that I had become a human icicle.

I managed to get out of the buggy and reach the house before me. I knocked on the window from which the light came, and called for help. A man opened the door and assisted me into the house. But as I staggered to safety through that open door, I suddenly discovered to my great astonishment that this was the very place I had left sometime before. For more than two or three hours we had wandered over the prairie, but in some miraculous way the remarkable instinct of my faithful prairie broncos had led them back to the place from which we had started and thus had saved my life and also their own.

My team and I found a safe shelter in this homesteader's shack for the rest of the night, but it required hours before I was completely thawed out and warm again in all my body.

I was able to return home and to my frightened little girls the next day. The storm had subsided, and the Wyoming sun shone brighter than ever before. The snow that had been so frightful and deadly only a few hours before now lay like a downy blanket over the prairie, glittering in the brightness of the sun like myriads of brilliant diamond crystals scattered over the landscape like manna that had fallen from heaven. My soul was filled with a song of thanksgiving for this wonderful deliverance. Daniel's escape from the lions' mouths was not more miraculous than my escape from the roaring lion of the prairie blizzard.

VIEWPOINT 3

"How far this Republic has departed from its high ideal and reversed its traditionary policy may be seen in the laws passed against the Chinese."

The Chinese Must Stay

Yan Phou Lee

The first Chinese Exclusion Act was passed in 1882, but it did not satisfy those who opposed the Chinese on the basis of race and economics. Debate and mutual castigation continued as each side jockeyed to win votes in Congress. On the Chinese side, consular officers were active in presenting their case not only to the politicians but also directly to the American public. In the following article from the *North American Review*, Yan Phou Lee refutes the charges made against the Chinese, charges used as a pretext for banning immigration. Equally important, he challenges Americans to live up to their high national ideals.

No nation can afford to let go its high ideals. The founders of the American Republic asserted the principle that all men are created equal, and made this fair land a refuge for the whole world. Its manifest destiny, therefore, is to be the teacher and leader of nations in liberty. Its supremacy should be maintained by good faith and righteous dealing, and not by the display of selfishness

Yan Phou Lee, "The Chinese Must Stay," *North American Review* 148 (April 1889): 476-83.
Courtesy of the University of Northern Iowa, Cedar Falls.

and greed. But now, looking at the actions of this generation of Americans in their treatment of other races, who can get rid of the idea that that Nation, which Abraham Lincoln said was conceived in liberty, waxed great through oppression, and was really dedicated to the proposition that all men are created to prey on one another?

How far this Republic has departed from its high ideal and reversed its traditionary policy may be seen in the laws passed against the Chinese.

Chinese immigrants never claimed to be any better than farmers, traders, and artisans. If, on the one hand, they are not princes and nobles, on the other hand, they are not coolies and slaves. They all came voluntarily, as their consular papers certified, and their purpose in leaving their home and friends was to get honest work. They were told that they could obtain higher wages in America than elsewhere, and that Americans were friendly to the Chinese and invited them to come. In this they were confirmed by certain provisions in the treaties made between China and the United States, by which rights and privileges were mutually guaranteed to the citizens of either country residing in the other. No one can deny that the United States made all the advances, and that China came forth from her seclusion because she trusted in American honor and good faith.

So long as the Chinese served their purposes and did not come into collision with the hoodlum element afterwards imported to California, the people of that State had nothing to complain of regarding them. Why should they, when, at one time, half the revenue of the State was raised out of the Chinese miners? But the time came when wages fell with the cost of living. The loafers became strong enough to have their votes sought after. Their wants were attended to. Their complaints became the motive power of political activity. So many took up the cry against the Chinese that it was declared that no party could succeed on the Pacific coast which did not adopt the hoodlums' cause as its own. Supposing that no party could succeed, would the Union have gone to ruin?

Precedents for Anti-Chinese Feeling

Those who remember events of some thirty-five years ago will see nothing strange in the antagonism of one class of laborers to another. Opposition to the Chinese is identical with the opposition to the free immigration of Europeans, and especially of the Irish; for it was once urged against the trans-Atlantic immigrants that their cheap labor "would degrade, demoralize, and pauperize American labor, and displace intelligent Americans in many branches of employment." There was a bitter conflict, but the sensible view prevailed. For it was found that a greater supply of unskilled labor made it possible for skilled laborers to command higher wages and more regular employment.

Why is it that the American laborer was soon raised to a higher social and industrial plane, and ceased to fear Irish competition, while the Irish still dread the competition of the Chinese? It is simply because the Irish are industrially inferior to their competitors. They have not the ability to get above competition, like the Americans, and so, perforce, they must dispute with the Chinese for the chance to be hewers of wood and drawers of water.

Such industrial conflicts occur every day, as, for instance, between trade-unionists and scabs, Irish and Germans, Italians who came yesterday and Italians who come to-day. Let them fight it out by lawful means, and let the fittest survive; but you do not take the side of one against the other,—least of all, the side of the strong against the weak. Why, then, take the side of the European immigrants against the Chinese? But you say there are many objections against the latter which cannot be made against the former, and the Chinese stand charged with too many things to make them desirable. Ah, yes! I see. But it is only fair to look into these charges before we pass our judgment. It has been urged:

I. *That the influx of Chinese is a standing menace to Republican institutions upon the Pacific coast and the existence there of Christian civilization.*

That is what I call a severe reflection on Republican institutions and Christian civilization. Republican institutions have withstood the strain of 13,000,000 of the lower classes of Europe, among whom may be found Anarchists, Socialists, Communists, Nihilists, political assassins, and cut-throats; but they cannot endure the assaults of a few hundred thousands of the most peaceable and most easily-governed people in the world!

Christianity must have lost its pristine power, for, having subdued and civilized one-half the world, it is now powerless before the resistance of a handful of Chinese! Surely the Chinese must be angels or devils! If angels, they would go without your bidding. If devils, you would not be able to drive them out.

The argument advanced against Chinese immigration by some members of Congress is substantially this: "China has a starving (!) population of 400,000,000; she can spare 10,000,000 easily. It costs only $60—a mere trifle—to come over here. Therefore, as Senator Sargent declared, 'the Pacific Coast must in time become either American or Mongolian.'" The beauty of this argument will strike you at once, if you reflect that the Chinese are not a migratory people; that hardly 1,000,000 have left the country by sea in 100 years; that even to adjacent provinces their migrations have been limited; and that the disposition to lead a life of adventure is peculiar to the people of Canton and its outlying districts.

Moreover, the ten cents per day earned by a *starving* population, though sufficient to buy all the necessaries of life, will not warrant a saving of more than $3 per year. At that rate, how many years will a man require to enable him to save enough for his passage?

This remarkable picture, taken in 1877, when the high Secrettown trestle in the Sierra Nevada Mountains of California was being filled in with dirt by Chinese "coolies" working with pick and shovel, one-horse dumpcarts, wheelbarrows and black powder, shows the meager tools with which the builders of the Central Pacific (now the Southern Pacific) had to work in blasting a trail over and through the rugged mountains for the rails of the first transcontinental railroad. In those days there were none of the power implements that are now so common to modern construction. Scrapers were not even used in the grading. Dynamite had been invented but was not in general use during the years in which the railroad was being built, 1863-1869.

II. *That the Chinese have a quasi-government among themselves.*

If I deny this, perhaps you will not believe me. Allow me to quote the testimony of a man of irreproachable character, the Rev. Dr. William Speer, who wrote to the New York *Tribune* that the Six Companies, credited with the government of the Chinese colony, were purely benevolent associations, and that he had frequently attended their meetings, and could, moreover, speak from many years' experience as a missionary in China. It is a significant fact that the minister of the Gospel, who knew all about the subject, was not believed before howling, ignorant demagogues. It was laying a premium on ignorance.

III. *That the Chinese race seems to have no desire for progress.*

In the last fifteen years the Chinese Government has educated upwards of two hundred students in Europe and America, has built arsenals and navy-yards, established schools and colleges on Western models, disciplined an army that whipped the Russians, created a navy that would put the American navy to shame, put up thousands of miles of telegraph wires; and it is now busily opening up mines, building railroads, and availing itself of American capital and experience to put up telephones and establish a national bank. The Chinese are not ashamed to own that they appreciate the Americans.

No Displacement of White Workers

IV. *That the Chinese have displaced white laborers by low wages and cheap living, and that their presence discourages and retards white immigration to the Pacific States.*

This charge displays so little regard for truth and the principles of political economy that it seems like folly to attempt an answer. But please to remember that it was by the application of Chinese "cheap labor" to the building of railroads, the reclamation of swamp-lands, to mining, fruit-culture, and manufacturing, that an immense vista of employment was opened up for Caucasians, and that millions now are enabled to live in comfort and luxury where formerly adventurers and desperadoes disputed with wild beasts and wilder men for the possession of the land. Even when the Chinaman's work is menial (and he does it because he must live, and is too honest to steal and too proud to go to the almshouse), he is employed because of the scarcity of such laborers. It is proved that his work enables many to turn their whole attention to something else, so that even the hoodlum may don a clean shirt at least once a month. You may as well run down machinery as to sneer at Chinese cheap labor. Machines live on nothing at all; they have displaced millions of laborers; why not do away with machines?

Besides, are you sure that Chinese laborers would not ask more if they dared, or take more if they could get it?

It is the Chinese who are constantly displaced by Caucasians. As soon as an industry gets on its feet by the help of Chinese "cheap labor," Chinese workmen are discharged to make room for others.

V. *That the Chinese do not desire to become citizens of this country.*

Why should they? Where is the inducement? Let me recite briefly a few of the laws and ordinances which, though couched in general terms, were made for their special benefit.

The Foreign-Miners' License Law, which forced every Chinese miner, during a period of twenty years, to pay from $4 to $20 per month for the privilege of working claims which others had abandoned.

An act of the California Legislature, 1855, laid a tax of $55 on each Chinese immigrant.

Another, 1862, provided (with a few exceptions) that every Chinaman over eighteen years of age should pay a capitation-tax of $2.50.

A San Francisco city ordinance, passed March 15, 1876, provided that all laundries should pay licenses as follows: those using a one-horse vehicle, $2 per quarter; two horses, $4; no vehicle, $15. This is discrimination with a vengeance!

I maintain that a sober, industrious, and peaceable people, like the Chinese, who mind their own business and let others do the same, are as fit to be voters as the quarrelsome, ignorant, besotted, and priest-ridden hordes of Europe. Are you sure the Chinese have no desire for the franchise? Some years ago, a number of those living in California, thinking that the reason why they were persecuted was because it was believed they cared nothing about American citizenship, made application for papers of naturalization. Their persecutors were alarmed and applied to Congress for assistance, and the California Constitution was amended so as to exclude them.

In view of the above-mentioned evidences of the fostering care of the State of California, you will not be surprised that very few ventured to bring their families to America. Many would have brought their families over, if they could have been assured of protection.

VI. *That the Chinese live in filthy dwellings, upon poor food, crowded together in narrow quarters, disregarding health- and fire-ordinances.*

The Chinaman does not object to dainty food and luxurious lodgings. But the paternal government of California taxed him as soon as he came ashore; permitted its agents to blackmail him at intervals; made him pay $15 a month for carrying his customers' washing in his hand; levied a progressive poll-tax, without providing a school for him; a road-tax before he began to travel, and, when he went to the mines, collected a water-rent of thirty cents a day, and a progressive license-tax from $4 to $20 per month. Even if he earned five dollars a day, he could not have fifteen cents left to live on.

Sensible people will, perhaps, ask, Why do you permit the Chinese in your city to disregard health- and fire-ordinances? Is it not the business of the municipal authorities to punish such infractions of the law? Must the Nation compromise its honor and disregard its treaty obligations because the officials of your city neglect their duty?

VII. *The Chinese neither have intercourse with the Caucasians nor will assimilate with them.*

Yes, just think of it! As soon as the ship comes into harbor, a committee of the citizens get on board to present the Chinaman with the freedom of the city (valued at $5). A big crowd gathers at the wharf to receive him with shouts of joy (and showers of stones). The aristocrats of the place flock to his hotel to pay their respects (and to take away things to remember him by). He is so fêted and caressed by Caucasian society that it is a wonder his head is not turned (or twisted off).

In spite of such treatment, the Chinese will keep "themselves to themselves" and snub the American community. Did you know that the Jews accused the Samaritans of refusing to have intercourse with them?

VIII. *The Chinese come and go as pagans.*

Mr. Beecher said in reference to this charge: "We have clubbed them, stoned them, burned their houses, and murdered some of them; yet they refuse to be converted. I do not know any way, except to blow them up with nitro-glycerine, if we are ever to get them to heaven." In spite of these doubtful inducements to become Christians, more than 500 have been admitted to the church.

The Chinese Are Not Criminals

IX. *That the Chinese immigrants are mostly criminals.*

It is not true. I admit that we have a criminal class in China, but the few that got over here came through the neglect of the officers of the Custom-House to enforce the laws.

In 1860 the population of California was 379,994
In 1860 the Chinese population in California was 34,933
The whole number of prisoners was 516
The whole number of Chinese prisoners was 28

While the Chinese population was one in ten, their quota of criminals was only one in eighteen; and that, too, when judges and juries were more or less prejudiced against them. Every fair-minded man can testify that the Chinese are the most law-abiding people in the community, that they are not easily provoked, but are patient (oh, too patient!) under insult and injury. They seldom appear in court-rooms in the character of prisoners. You have never seen one drunk in your life. But, you say, he smokes opium. That, I answer, is his own affair. The law provides no penalties against private vices. You have never heard of Chinamen who organized strikes, stuffed ballot-boxes, and corrupted legislation at the fountain-head. Why, then, are they not as desirable as other immigrants? Is it a crime to be industrious, faithful, law-abiding? wrong to coin one's honest toil into gold, and, instead of wasting one's earnings in drink and debauchery, to support wife and children therewith? This brings me to the next charge.

X. *That the Chinese drain the country annually of large sums.*

Indeed, the California Senate, in its memorial to Congress, November 15, 1877, said that there were 180,000 Chinese in California. The statistics of the Custom-House and the best authorities said there were (in 1877) only 104,000 in the whole country. Of course, while there were only 104,000 in the United States, there were 180,000 in California! The part is greater than the whole. The memorial also said that the 180,000 Chinese drained the country of $180,000,000 annually. Isn't that enough to frighten anybody? Now, 180,000 Chinese sent home on an average $1,000 apiece. Each must have earned $1,250 per year; that is, about $4 per day. You call that cheap labor? Two dollars and fifty cents is fair wages for Caucasians there. You must not think that the august Senate of California meant to lie. Californians are only slightly given to exaggeration. I will now answer the last and most terrible charge.

XI. *That the Chinese bring women of bad character to San Francisco, and that their vices are corrupting the morals of the city.*

How serious a charge this is we cannot realize until we get at all the facts. Just imagine California, the most virtuous of States, and San Francisco, the most immaculate of cities, lying helpless under the upas-tree of Chinese immorality! Have you ever been to San Francisco? Unless you can endure paradise and Eden-like purity, you would better not go there. Why, the Sabbath stillness in that city is simply appalling. The people all go to church, and if you suggest whiskey toddy or a base-ball game on Sunday, they will turn up their eyes, throw up their hands, and pray the Lord to have mercy on you. There are no drunken brawls at any time (except in Chinatown), and it is the policeman's picnic-ground (except in Chinatown). Besides churches, they have numerous temples dedicated to Venus, wherein pious persons work off their surplus devotion. Why is it that these fair vestals wear so little clothing? They are afraid to clog the things of the spirit with the habiliments of sense. Californians are pure, moral, and religious, in all that they do. As for having disreputable houses, or women with loose morals about them, I tell you they are as innocent as lambs. Indeed, Satan could not have made a greater commotion in Eden than the Chinese in California. One would suppose that such a model community would "clean out" those bad Chinese women. But it did not. It deputed a number of special policemen to watch them and arrest them, but it seems that these specials had the marvellous power of transmuting their brass into pure gold, and that, in the exercise of that power, they were as blind as bats. If the virtuous community of San Francisco permitted their morals to be corrupted, it is their own fault.

Such are the charges made against the Chinese. Such were the reasons for legislating against them;—and they still have their influence, as is shown by the utterances of labor organs; by the unreasoning prejudice against the Chinese which finds lodgment in the minds of the people; and by the periodical outbreaks and outrages perpetrated against them without arousing the public conscience.

VIEWPOINT 4

"[Chinese] may in small numbers benefit individual employers, but they breed the germs of a national disease, which spreads as they spread, and grows as they grow."

The Chinese Must Go

James D. Phelan (1861-1930)

James D. Phelan began his career in the family banking business started by his father, who had arrived in California during the Gold Rush. A reform mayor of San Francisco (1897-1901), Phelan attacked the city's corrupt, boss-ridden government; elected to the U.S. Senate (1915-1921) as a Democrat, he supported President Woodrow Wilson's policies. However, perhaps because as a politician he courted labor's vote, he strongly supported a national policy that would exclude Orientals, especially Chinese, from the United States. The following essay is from a series of articles in the *North American Review* in which Chinese consular officers and U.S. politicians debated the issue of Chinese exclusion. Here Phelan attacks many of the points made by Ho Yow, the Chinese consul general.

Excerpted from "Why the Chinese Should Be Excluded," by James D. Phelan, *North American Review* 173 (November 1901): 663-76. Courtesy of the University of Northern Iowa, Cedar Falls.

When Mr. Ho Yow, the Imperial Chinese Consul-General, asked, in the *North American Review*, whether Chinese exclusion is a "benefit or a harm," the interrogation awakened a curious interest. The people most familiar with the subject were disposed to regard the question as not wholly serious. They recalled the patient investigation, full discussion and practically unanimous settlement which it received in 1882, and again in 1892, when Congress granted remedial legislation to cure an acknowledged evil.

The Exclusion Acts then passed were limited to ten years' duration. In May next the latest act will expire by limitation, and Congress will be asked to renew it, because, until now, Chinese exclusion has been regarded in diplomatic circles and elsewhere as the settled policy of the country. Has there been any change in the nature of the evil, or in the sentiments of the people? Certainly not on the Pacific Coast, where the lapse of time has made still more evident the non-assimilative character of the Chinese and their undesirability as citizens.

The Exclusion Act has been reasonably effective, although the Chinese, with more or less success, have employed their well-known cunning in evading its provisions by surreptitiously and fraudulently entering the United States. The law, however, has opposed a barrier to the great volume of immigration which threatened this country for many years prior to 1880. . . .

The influx having been checked, the danger to California has been averted, and, consequently, during the last decade industrial conditions indicate comparative prosperity; whereas it is well known that prior to the Exclusion Laws the State of California suffered acutely from labor troubles and business derangement. Unemployed men, hungry from want of work, marched the streets of the cities, inaugurated political parties, [and] disturbed the peace of communities by riotous outbreaks which threatened at times the foundations of law and order. . . . Accusations were made at that time, which Ho Yow repeats, that the opposition to the Chinese came from demagogues alone. To show the unanimity of the people, I may point out that the Legislature submitted by referendum the question of Chinese immigration to a popular vote. For Chinese immigration 883 votes were polled, and against Chinese immigration 154,638 votes. In the City of San Francisco, representing the wealth and intelligence and containing the skilled-labor organizations of the State, only 224 votes were cast in favor of the immigration and 41,258 votes against it. This result demonstrated clearly that the resident population of California, taking the broad ground of self-preservation, refused to suffer themselves to be dispossessed of their inheritance by Chinese coolies. That is what the verdict meant.

A select committee of Congress, after investigating the question and taking testimony in California, reported in favor of Chinese exclusion, and that policy has been regarded ever since as a peaceful preventive of serious disorders affecting the body politic which would have inevitably ensued had the National Legislature failed to protect the white population of the country. . . .

Mr. Ho Yow, knowing the great demand there is in a new country for common laborers, has ingeniously taken the stand that the Chinese are not skilled and, presumably, are incapable of becoming skilled. Knowing also that skilled labor is organized and is always in the vanguard for the defence and protection of labor rights, he has endeavored to quiet its alarm by arguments of this kind. He thus appeals to the cupidity of the farmer and the orchardist, while he attempts to allay the fears of the mechanic. It is safe to say that his argument is a careful and studied presentation of the case. He attempts to meet the "accusers of his people" by granting with astonishing candor everything that they say. To quote him:

> I shall concede that the Chinese do in a sense work more cheaply than white; that they live more cheaply; that they send their money out of the country to China; that most of them have no intention of remaining in the United States; . . . that they do not adopt American manners, but live in colonies and not after the American fashion.

He then boldly says that on these accounts a condition is created which "is to the highest advantage of this country, and particularly to the highest advantage of those who oppose Chinese labor and at whose instance the laws were passed." He argues—as we have seen, fallaciously—that opposition to the Chinese was the work of "political demagogues"; and he further says that after exclusion, the business of California on that account "dried up," and that trade with China fell off $7,000,000 in two years. Ho Yow is evidently in error, because, after Chinese exclusion, trade with China steadily increased. The total imports and exports in 1880 amounted to $27,999,482, in 1882 to $31,762,313, and in 1900 to $38,130,000. Consul-General Goodnow says (Consular Reports for August, 1901):

> The United States is second only to Great Britain in goods sold to the Chinese. . . . The United States buys more goods from China than does any other nation; and her total trade with China, exports and imports, equals that of Great Britain (not including colonies) and is far ahead of that of any other country.

The exclusion of Chinese has had no appreciable effect on the trade between the two countries. The resident Chinese import for their own consumption dried fish, pickled vegetables and rice; and these commodities have not, according to the Custom House records, fallen off since 1881. Of course, the more Chinese there are in this country the more breadstuffs will be imported, but the commerce in silks and teas goes on irrespective of the presence or absence of a local Chinese population. The same is true of other imports.

WILL IT COME TO THIS ?

In this cartoon, Chinese cheap labor is holding down American labor. However, Chinese laborers are sitting on a keg of dynamite, public opinion, which may soon blow up. This is an example of the virulent anti-Chinese cartoons published during the last third of the nineteenth century.

The fact is, commerce is not sentimental. The Chinese Government, knowing the necessities of the situation, and being familiar with the fact that almost every country has imposed restrictions upon the immigration of Chinese coolies, does not regard our exclusion as necessarily an unfriendly act. Our other relations with China have been more than friendly and have been duly appreciated. . . .

The Chinese are not like other emigrants whose departure from the land that nurtured them in their helpless infancy and childhood is an irrevocable loss. The Chinese emigrant goes out a pauper and unfailingly returns with a competency, and becomes a well-to-do member of the country in which, according to his religious belief, his bones must rest in order to insure eternal peace. This, indeed, is "territorial sectarianism," difficult to overcome, but some would ask America to assume the task.

But it is in the theory that the Chinese question is a labor question that Mr. Ho Yow seems to find his main reliance in advocating the abrogation of the Exclusion Laws. He argues that the opposition is inspired by the laboring masses; that the laboring masses are governed by labor unions; that labor unions are composed of skilled men in various trades and vocations, and that the Chinese are not skilled, and, therefore, are not formidable competitors. . . .

I contend that this is not a mere labor question, not a race question. It is an American question, affecting the perpetuity of our institutions and the standard of our civilization. . . .

One thing certain is that when they come to this country they know little else than manual labor; but they soon acquire a skill which enables them to compete with the trained American workingman. The Chinese in any considerable numbers are, consequently, a great potential danger to skilled labor.

But is the man who tills the soil to be supplanted by the nonassimilative Asiatic? Is husbandry to be abandoned to a servile class? Is land monopoly to follow industrial monopoly, and are large holdings, managed by overseers, to drive the farmers for employment into the cities, where Chinese labor will meet them and there deprive them of the opportunity to work? Pliny says that "large estates ruined Italy." The free population were driven into Rome by slaves, who were forced to cultivate the soil, and, deprived of honorable and useful employment, became the rabble, which finally compassed the destruction of the Republic.

Let it be granted, for the sake of argument, that the Chinese are only common laborers and agriculturalists. Shall they be allowed to enter freely in unlimited numbers to stimulate development, or shall the development of the country be allowed to proceed with equal pace with the settlement of the country by a desirable citizenship? Ho Yow takes the coldly economic view. He modestly says the Chinese by increasing productiveness would open new fields which they themselves would be unable to enter. That is to say, the products of the mine and field would increase the business, for instance, of the transportation lines, the canning industries and the banks. That is very ingenious, but it is predicated upon segregating a servile class, and violently assuming that that class, or its more intelligent members, are incapable of taking up work which involves skill and management. Ho Yow, in this, proves too much.

Consequences of a Permanent Servile Class

The benefits accruing from the presence of a servile class, doing the rough work of a country, always belong, as in slaveholding days, to the few; and when it is considered that the Chinese are migratory and receive wages which they send out of the country, a parallel between the negro slaves and the Chinese coolies is only remarkable in this, that by any fair comparison slavery must be regarded as economically more advantageous to the State. The slaves worked for a comfortable subsistence, and did not drain the soil of its wealth by the exportation of "the wage fund," which was formerly appropriated by the slaveholder, and which, in any event, remained to enrich and develop the country. It is estimated that the Chinese since 1868 have exported from the United States $400,000,000 in gold on this account alone.

Ho Yow says that the Great Wall of China was built to exclude robbers, who gave no return. Our Exclusion Act was erected, he says, to keep out men who gave adequate return for their wages. I hold that the Chinese cannot, in the nature of things, give an adequate return for their wages, not only for the above reason, but because by their presence they exclude a more desirable population.

In an American sense, we cannot regard a laborer, as does Ho Yow, as a human machine. He speaks of the enormous productiveness due to machinery, and he points out the fact that labor-saving devices are encouraged and have increased the sum of human comfort. From this he argues that if the Chinese, on account of their number and the little fuel which they require to keep them going, are in a sense perfect machines, they should be admitted. But there is a limit even to the capacity of a machine. It must have a man behind it. That man is a unit in the government of a free country; and we must insist, in a patriotic sense, as well as in the best economic sense, that his status as an intelligent human being, endowed by his Creator with inalienable rights, shall be preserved. The machine is the creation of intelligence and is only supplementary to the skill of man, whereas the Chinese, knowing nothing but ceaseless and unremitting toil, coming without wives and without appetites, would remain a part of the mechanism and be content. If they were allowed to enter as innocent agriculturists, there is no reason, so imitative are they, why they should not become operatives in our factories and conductors and breakmen, as they are now builders and linemen, on our railroads; as they are now canners and packers of our products, and as they are now sailors upon the sea. They would enter the fields made attractive by the greater production of wealth. . . .

It is no dream in this day of industrial combinations, when we behold the unrestricted power of capital, to foresee that with the abandonment of the policy of exclusion land barons, money captains, commercial kings would reduce American labor to the condition of Oriental servility, and to a standard of living no better than that of the Chinese. This certainly would be the inevitable tendency, and I believe, on account of their tractability, the Chinese would be given preference in employment, which would mean the destruction of the American workingman, and, with the destruction of the American workingman, the destruction of the Republic. . . .

Are the Chinese Desirable as Citizens?

Ho Yow answers the objection that the Chinese "do not assimilate with the American people and do not adopt American methods and ways" by intimating that their provincialism is the result of the refusal of this country to naturalize them. He says: "This whole trouble has been caused by the fact that we are not citizens and voters." He quotes approvingly the words of the Chief Justice of the Dominion of Canada:

> It was a menace to Canada to have a large number of Japanese living in Canada and to exclude them from taking part in the legislation affecting their property and civil rights.

It is, indeed, generally true to say that the United States must admit its Chinese population to the right of suffrage and to all the privileges of American citizenship, if it grants them the privilege of permanent residence. If they are to be admitted into this country freely they cannot be held as a separate class in a state of quasi-bondage or helotry. They are either desirable as citizens or not desirable at all. They must be admitted as ultimate voters, or excluded as being incapable of wisely using the elective franchise and assuming all the rights, duties and obligations of citizenship. It is a false position to discuss them simply as laborers, skilled or unskilled. Therefore, unless America is prepared to receive them as citizens, the Exclusion Act should be renewed, and we should look to the Caucasian race, as we have in the past, for the upbuilding of our industrial, social and political fabric. . . .

Chinese Have No Capacity for the Blessings of Liberty

It is well understood that the invitation of the new Republic was addressed to the people of Europe, and that the Mongolians were not included in it. In interpreting our naturalization laws the Federal courts have held that the Caucasian race was alone contemplated by them, and by special exception, the negro race; that exception was the result of political necessity. The same necessity will arise, in the course of time, to naturalize the Chinese if they are admitted. But the Chinese do not come in the name of liberty as oppressed, nor are they willing to renounce their old allegiance. They are not even *bona fide* settlers. They do not seek the land of the free for the love of it. On the contrary, they are attached to their own country by a superstitious bond, and never think of leaving it permanently. It is also plain that, by their mental organization, they have no capacity for or appreciation of the blessings of liberty.

In fact, few Chinese migrate voluntarily at all, but are brought here under contracts made by their masters. It has been said that if the Six Chinese Companies of California were destroyed immigration would cease. Formerly debtors and criminals were exiled from China under contracts to work out their salvation on American soil. Of such stuff citizens fit for a republic cannot be made.

Their physical assimilation is as repugnant to them as it is undesirable for us. I am informed by the Police Department and by the managers of the Chinese missions in San Francisco that after nearly thirty-five years of intercourse the number of marriages between whites and Chinese do not exceed twenty, and that the offspring are invariably degenerate. The California Legislature, at its last session, amended the Civil Code of the State so as to prohibit, for the first time, the intermarriage of white persons with Mongolians. Heretofore the Code referred only to negroes and mulattoes. They cannot and will not assimilate with the white population; they live in colonies separate and apart, and are in all respects a permanently foreign element.

It follows, from these premises, that there is no obligation on the part of the United States to receive the Chinese as other peoples are received, but that there is an obligation on the United States to exclude them on the ground of duty to others as well as of self-preservation.

Self-Protection Is the Highest Right of the State

The right of a State to exclude an undesirable immigration is fundamental international law. Self-protection yields to no higher law. Therefore it is supreme. The Chinese, by putting a vastly inferior civilization in competition with our own, tend to destroy the population on whom the perpetuity of free government depends. Without homes and families; patronizing neither school, library, church nor theatre; lawbreakers, addicted to vicious habits; indifferent to sanitary regulations and breeding disease; taking no holidays, respecting no traditional anniversaries, but laboring incessantly, and subsisting on practically nothing for food and clothes, a condition to which they have been inured for centuries, they enter the lists against men who have been brought up by our civilization to family life and civic duty. Our civilization having been itself rescued from barbarism by the patriots, martyrs and benefactors of mankind, the question now is: Shall it be imperilled? Is not Chinese immigration a harm?

If it were possible for unmarried white men to compete with

Chinese, they must remain single, by which the State would suffer. If families were reared under the conditions of such a competition, they would gravitate irresistibly and without blame to the poorhouse and the penitentiary. Society must recognize this; to the white man it is only a question of self-support or State support.

If the Chinese are admitted, whence are the ranks of the free population to be recruited? Who shall preserve our civilization and who shall fight our battles? The Chinese may be good laborers, but they are not good citizens. They may in small numbers benefit individual employers, but they breed the germs of a national disease, which spreads as they spread, and grows as they grow.

In this view it matters very little whether with Chinese labor there is increased productiveness or not, nor whether a greater or smaller number of enterprises are inaugurated. The material interests of a State must be subordinated to the social and political interests of the people. Before cheapness and abundance must we consider the status of the men who are called upon to maintain the country's institutions and contribute by their presence to its true wealth. White men are both producers and large consumers, which the Chinese are not. Coolie labor appears to the short-sighted farmer and manufacturer as desirable so long as other people find employment for the white man on whose consumption they depend. But substitute Chinese labor for white labor, and the home market would disappear. What political economy can reconcile this fact with the good of the State? But even political economy must condemn the Chinese. The Chinese leave the results of their labor, it is true, but, let us repeat, they take out of the country the equivalent, and, contrary to those economic laws on whose due observance depends the material wealth of nations, their earnings do not circulate, nor are they reinvested. So what work they perform is paid for doubly by the employer and by the community. . . .

Mistaking America's Mission and Destiny

There are many good people who, mistaking the mission and destiny of their country, in a spirit of brotherhood would welcome the Chinese and every foreign race. Have we not proved by a progressive development that we are sufficient unto ourselves? Is not our duty to the heathen subserved by missionary labors and by establishing American ideas, enterprises and trade in other lands? Must we take them into our own house?

St. Paul said to the Athenians, "God hath made of one blood all nations of men," but he promptly added, "He hath determined the bounds of their habitation." In spite, however, of the warnings of history and the dangers which we of the Pacific Coast have endeavored to point out in the discussion of this question, which is more than one of labor or locality, there are a few men in the East to whom we would politely address ourselves, whose mistaken sense of duty has arrayed them against the American policy of Chinese exclusion. Let them not merit the opprobrium of the poet's reproach:

The steady patriots of the world alone,
The friends of every country but their own.

CHAPTER 5

The Creation of Frontier Mythic Heroes

Chapter Preface

This painting by the Western artist George Calem Bingham depicts Daniel Boone escorting settlers through the Cumberland Gap. The painting romanticizes the pioneer undertaking, the backlighting nearly providing a halo for Boone and his compatriots.

In the concluding paragraph of "The Significance of the Frontier in American History," Frederick Jackson Turner identifies "traits of profound importance" in the American character, "traits of the frontier or . . . [those] called out elsewhere because of the existence of the frontier." Among these traits, which Turner admits do not always have positive consequences, are strength, inventiveness, individualism, and exuberance. These national characteristics developed in part from Americans' attempts to survive in nature; modes of adaptation not necessary in Europe developed rapidly here. Because of the expansiveness of the American continent, physical environments varied greatly. Even on the thin strip of the Atlantic seaboard, a variety of physical environments demanded a variety of survival mechanisms. Each frontier demanded specific skills and inculcated specific ways of thought. A whole panoply of frontier inhabitants evolved, at first a hybrid of European and American, but gradually more and more American. Because of the "unequal rate of advance," the changes did not happen all at once. Thus Turner notes that it is important "to distinguish the frontier into the trader's frontier, the rancher's frontier, . . . the miner's frontier, and the farmer's frontier." With the incremental westering of the frontier, American traits became ever stronger and more pronounced.

Turner's purpose was not to ascribe any heroic dimensions to that procession of frontiersmen moving gradually toward the Rockies and the Pacific. Rather, he wanted to analyze the components and consequences of the frontier process. Why was there an uneven rate of advance of specific types of settlers? How did the relation between people and the land differ from one time and place to another? And, most important, how did the frontier experience shape the American character?

Turner here was concerned with *real* people, people like Mike Fink and Daniel Boone, Christopher Carson, Robert Rogers, and William Frederick Cody, who simply went about their jobs, only later, if at all, considering it extraordinary. However, each of these men and others like them metamorphosed into beings somehow larger than life. As their reality grew more remote in time and space, and as they became subjects of oral tradition and written accounts, they took on the label of Hero. In so doing, they tramped into the mythical as well as the historical past.

It is important to explore how actual historical figures were transformed into mythic heroes. That process is not only complex, but it continues into the present. The frontier—and the heroes it spawns—took on new dimensions in the 1960s and following years. The Space Frontier saw humans challenging environments never dreamed of by Turner. John Glenn, who made the first orbital flight in 1962, captured the public's imagination for his personal courage in mastering a new Unknown, even though rocket technology rather than the Kentucky rifle was his tool. And, just as surely as Andrew Jackson's exploits against the Creeks and the Seminoles catapulted him into the White House, Glenn's exploits in the frontier of space provided a springboard for political success. The politician's requisite birth in a log cabin, a nineteenth-century cliché, was in Glenn's case replaced by travel in a Mercury capsule. Once a new kind of hero existed—a space explorer rather than a Lewis or Clark—the process of mythologizing such heroes could begin. Yet the mythology echoed that of earlier frontiers. The movie *Star Wars* played out many of the same conflicts that had been the stock in trade of the Western film; Luke Skywalker became a late twentieth-century Virginian, hero of Owen Wister's 1902 archetype-establishing cowboy novel.

What is the nature of this transformation of historical figures to mythic heroes? In *The Western Hero in History and Legend*, Kent Steckmesser suggests that elements of this process are evident as early as John Smith, leader of the first permanent English settlement in America. A man "of humble origin [who] loved to travel the unknown wilderness, and made his reputation as a fighter and a man of action," Smith was an "ideal type-figure" for later Western heroes. In *A True Relation* (1608), he left a "brief but valuable narrative of the Jamestown colony." But the historical John Smith was quickly "buried beneath . . . grandiose legends," self-promulgated in *A General Historie of Virginia* (1624). This work, full of literary embellishments and exaggerations, portrays Smith not only as a leader but as a lover and an epic Indian fighter. For example, what was in the 1608 version a fight with one Indian grew by 1624 to a hand-to-hand combat with six or eight of them. Even the romantically dramatic intervention of Pocahontas takes on more prominence in the 1624 narrative. Steckmesser discusses a number of factors contributing to the mythologizing of a man: (1) a basis in fact; (2) literary embellishments by self or others; (3) a distancing that softens harsh realities and lets the character take on epic, often flawless, proportions; and (4) a growth of character, often literally, as his physique enlarges, but certainly a growth in his social significance.

This chapter focuses on two mythic heroes of the frontier—the cowboy and the bandit. Earlier, as we examined Custer and Chivington, we met yet another heroic type—the cavalryman who came to the rescue. For each of these types, the myth developed to serve several simultaneous, perhaps contradictory, functions: to provide safe, vicarious wish fulfillment for the audience, to inculcate or reinforce society's values, and to reveal to a later audience important contemporary issues. Thus, Billy the Kid's four, or seven, or twenty-one, or twenty-three killings gratify society's desire for simple, final justice; his protectiveness toward his mother demonstrates the nineteenth-century value of defending female virtues; and his friendship with the Mexicans who made up part of his gang may be read as a kind of populist support for the underdog in class conflicts.

Moreover, such mythologized characters (and character types) share many traits. They are, first of all, literally larger-than-life; both Custer and Billy the Kid were, in fact, only about 5'8" tall. In life they were often referred to by diminutives; Billy, "the Kid"; Custer, "the Boy General"; and even of the Virginian Owen Wister writes, "In inches he was not a giant." But what these mythic heroes lacked in inches they gained in aura.

This aura was created in part by the hero's role as a clan leader, every bit as much as were those epic heroes of the mythic past, Aeneas or Odysseus. For Custer, the role was literally true; when the Seventh Regiment was assigned to Fort Abraham Lincoln in 1873, Custer had with him his wife, Elizabeth; his brother, Captain Tom Custer; his sister, Margaret; his brother-in-law, Lt. James Calhoun—and his beloved hunting dogs. Billy the Kid, though hounded by the law, had a faithful coterie of Mexican companions. And the Virginian, though a bachelor through most of Wister's novel, provided an effective role model for the greenhorn narrator.

Often the hero could be seen as a misunderstood rebel. The Virginian's early bachelor pranks reflected the chagrin of those resisting change in Wyoming in the late nineteenth century—from a society of rugged male individualism to one of civilized family values. Billy, caught in the political and economic intricacies of the Lincoln County War between rival factions of investors in the cattle business, was, according to one interpretation, a lawman-gone-wrong; others viewed him less charitably, as a hired gun for the Tunstall-McSween faction. And Custer not only graduated at the bottom of his class at West Point with so many demerits he was nearly expelled, but during the Civil War his reckless behavior on the battlefield brought numerous reprimands.

For many heroes, death is an important transfiguring event. Although Walter Woods's play, excerpted in this chapter, has a happy ending, Billy the Kid can really only grow in stature once he is dead. The real Billy, whatever his flaws, fades as ever more exaggerated exploits are recounted. Even better is to die for a cause at a symbolically significant time. Custer, viewed by many under his command as an impetuous despot and even something of a coward for leaving some of his men in the field to face Indians unsupported, took on heroic stature after his death; that the news of the debacle at Little Bighorn reached the East during the centennial celebration of the nation's independence gave him an inflated role as a martyr. A poem by Emma Wheeler Wilcox published in 1895 clearly reveals this: "Greece her Achilles claimed, immortal Custer, we," and "Deeds like that the Christ in man reveal / Let Fame descend her throne at Custer's shrine to kneel."

Wilcox's evocation of Achilles and even Christ suggests the importance of names in the development of a mythic character. After his death, few continued to call Custer the Boy General; the nickname seemed inappropriate for a newly minted martyr. Nat Love, whose autobiography is excerpted in this chapter, *earned* his name "Deadwood Dick" through honest demonstration of his skill; such renaming was in the tradition of the Cooper hero Natty Bumppo/Deerslayer/Hawkeye/Leatherstocking who, like his Indian comrades, valued a name given for his accomplishments more than one bestowed at birth. And the Virginian, never given any other name, becomes Everyman—or at least Everycowboy.

He is allowed this designation because, like other heroes, he represents society's values. Daniel Boone, for example, in the idealized painting at the beginning of this chapter, is the trailblazer bringing Civilization to the wilderness. Joseph McCoy, whose autobiography is excerpted in this chapter, writing when the days of long cattle drives seemed threatened by plows and fences, provides a biblical support of the ranchers' case against encroaching farmers: "Sacred writ plainly tells us that Abel's offering being the product of his stock ranch was more acceptable to [the] Deity than that of his agricultural brother, but it is painful to learn that the Granger Cain should get so . . . jealous of his brother as to let murderous thoughts take possession of him." Custer believed, like many people during the nineteenth century, that it was impossible to civilize the Indian; for those who agreed with him, he died a hero defending civilization against the murderous savages. And John Chivington, the cavalry commander responsible for the massacre at Sand Creek, certainly reflects the paranoia of Denver society in the 1860s and the disdain for formal processes of law. For him, killing Indian women and children was an acceptable act of war; "nits make lice," he is quoted as saying. *The Rocky Mountain News,* reporting in 1883 on one of Chivington's campaign speeches for the legislature, illustrates popular support for him. Of the Sand Creek Massacre the editor wrote:

> Col. Chivington's speech [in which he said, after almost twenty years' reflection, "I stand by Sand Creek"] was received by applause from every pioneer which indicated that they, to a man, heartily approved the course of the colonel twenty years ago in the famous affair in which many of them took part, and the man who applied the scalpel to the ulcer which bid fair to destroy the life of the new colony, in those critical times, was beyond a doubt the hero of the hour.

One final element in the mythologizing process is the omission of evidence. Sometimes love for the subject demands a skewing of data. Elizabeth Custer, for example, dedicated most of her life after her husband's death to gilding his reputation when others seemed determined to tarnish it. In her writings, General Custer is never seen as unreceptive to advice, impetuous, stubborn, or cowardly. For her he always remains the golden-haired hero, the Defender of Civilization. In contrast to Elizabeth Custer's omissions because of love, Owen Wister's portrayal of the mythic cowboy may be based in part on bigotry. Wister, while a student at Harvard and later in Germany, acquired "a passionate attachment to the full-blown mythic romance of Wagner's operas." That musical influence, much later shared by Adolf Hitler, explains Wister's insistence on the "cowboy as a racial . . . type whose potency depended on a pure blood line and a 'clean' environment free from the 'hordes of encroaching alien vermin, that turn our cities into Babels and our citizenship into a hybrid farce.'" This extraordinary comment, from an 1895 article Wister published in *Harper's Monthly*, "The Evolution of the Cow-Puncher," suggests that late-nineteenth-century anti-immigrant feeling flourished not only on the West Coast and was not focused only on the Chinese. It is not surprising that Wister, with such a virulent bias against non-whites and non-Saxons, ignored the actual historical role of the black cowboy as he created his archetypal cowboy, the Virginian.

Whatever their genesis, most mythic beings change, almost organically, as their stories are told and retold. This is, however, less true for the cowboy than for other mythic heroes. Unlike Custer, who had demonstrable major flaws, Wister's cowboy had no actual feet of clay to discover. The legendary cowboy, born as a fictional composite, offers no muck to rake. He remains a defender of a lady's reputation; a believer in man-to-man resolution of conflict, able to kill when necessary, though not indiscriminately; a faithful adherent to a strong moral code if not a particular religious denomination; a respecter of horses and of justice; usually a Southerner, with a Southerner's gentility and sense of decorum; a man confident of his skill but not boastful. And, when such a cowboy occasionally behaves badly, perhaps shooting up a town after drinking too much, it may be excused as release from a daily life that is almost puritanically monastic. Because the mythic cowboy, whatever his race, supports the traditional values of society, he comes down to us as an unqualifiedly *good* hero.

We are more ambivalent about the bandit-as-hero. How, after all, does a nation of believers in law and order accept such an anti-hero? The reality, however, is that, from the very beginning, at least some frontiersmen chose to live beyond settled areas, seeking to avoid social and legal restrictions. The renegade, as much as the pathfinder, represents our frontier heritage. Moreover, there is a long tradition of the Robin Hood bandit, robbing the rich—if not to give to the poor, at least not preying on them. Such an interpretation may well have become more popular at the end of the nineteenth century with the rise of the robber barons and the Trusts. As monopolies, armed with political power and seemingly inexhaustible wealth, began to dominate the economy, "little people," remembering the promise of the frontier and frustrated by its curtailment, may have fantasized about bank robbers and bandits as agents of justice.

An even more bitter ambivalence has washed over the frontier cliché of the cavalry to the rescue. Recent history, especially the war in Vietnam, has produced a re-examination of the military, once viewed unquestioningly as an illustration of the best of American values. The movie *Soldier Blue*, produced in 1974, was a bitter castigation of the Chivington-engineered massacre at Sand Creek and, by extrapolation, the My Lais of more recent history. Philip Caputo's *A Rumor of War* (1977), describing his experiences as a young Marine infantry officer sent to Vietnam in 1965, forcefully argues that society's moral veneer, peeled away at Sand Creek, may be no stronger today. He writes of interrogating an apparently uncooperative Vietnamese woman: "I had my first violence fantasy then, a hint that I was breaking down under the strains and frustrations peculiar to that war." He imagines slapping her bloody, beating the truth from her about the location of the Viet Cong. "There was no one out there to stop me from actually doing it, no one and nothing except that inner system of moral checks called conscience. That was still operating, so I did not touch the old woman." That "system of moral checks" did not hold for all in Vietnam—or at Sand Creek. In both operations there were those who plunged through a ragged moral safety net while others maintained honor and decency.

It is, perhaps, this archetypal struggle between good and evil, however defined, that becomes the universal component of the myth-making process.

VIEWPOINT 1

"Few occupations are more cheerful, lively and pleasant than that of the cow-boy on a fine day or night; but when the storm comes, then is his manhood and often his skill and bravery put to test."

The White Cowboy Helped Win the West

Joseph G. McCoy (1837-1915)

In 1874 when Joseph G. McCoy published *Historic Sketches of the Cattle Trade*, the largest livestock owners were Texans, and McCoy was among their leaders. Cattle ranching had become a business, with few of the owners actually living on the ranch, but usually in a nearby "post-office village." Ranching now involved acquiring financing necessary to buy good grazing land and an adequate foundation herd, logistical skill to get the cattle from range to market in condition to garner the best possible price, and some diplomatic skills as southern cattle were driven to northern markets in post-Civil War years. In his book, McCoy, often credited with being "the father of the Chisholm trail," describes every aspect of the cattle business, from branding new calves to driving the beef to Abilene. He even describes the workings of the Plankington and Armour Packing Company. He also provides sketches of many leaders of the cattle industry, analyzes the impact of the railroads, and comments on the Panic of 1873 which wiped out many Western cattlemen. In the following selection, McCoy provides detailed descriptions of the cowboy at work and at play.

Excerpted from *Historic Sketches of the Cattle Trade of the West and Southwest* by Joseph G. McCoy. Kansas City, MO: Ramsey, Millett & Hudson, 1874.

[Texas cowboys] are, as a class, not liberally educated, and but few of them are extensive readers, but they are possessed of strong natural sense, well skilled in judging human nature, close observers of all events passing before them, thoroughly drilled in the customs of frontier life, more clannish than the Scotch, more suspicious than need be yet often easily gulled by promises of large prices for their stock; very prone to put an erroneous construction upon the acts and words of a Northern man, inclined to sympathize with one from their own State as against another from the North, no matter what the Southern man may have been guilty of. To beat a Northern man in a business transaction was perfectly legitimate, and regarded all such as their natural enemies of whom nothing good was to be expected. Nothing could arouse their suspicions to a greater extent than a disinterested act of kindness. Fond of a practical joke, always pleased with a good story, and not offended if it was of an immoral character; universal tiplers, but seldom drunkards; cosmopolitan in their loves; . . . always chivalrously courteous to a modest lady; possessing a strong, innate sense of right and wrong, a quick, impulsive temper, great lovers of a horse and always good riders and good horsemen; always free to spend their money lavishly for such objects or purposes as best please them; very quick to detect an injury or insult, and not slow to avenge it nor quick to forget it; always ready to help a comrade out of a scrape, full of life and fun; would illy brook rules of restraint, free and easy.

Cowboy Character Shaped by Environment

Such were some of the traits of character often met with in the early days of Abilene's glory, but there were good reasons for all these phases and eccentricities of character. Their home and early life was in a wild frontier country, where schools were few and far between, their facilities for attaining news by the daily press exceedingly limited. They had just passed through a bitter civil war, which graduated their former education of hatred and suspicion of Northern men, and above all, the long and bitter experiences they had endured in Southern Kansas and Missouri, swindling, outrage, robbery, rapine, and murder were full sufficient to embitter beings more than human. But we are not disposed to do the character of Texan drovers injustice, for the most of them are honorable men, and regard their pledged word of honor or their verbal contract as inviolable, sacred, and not to be broken under any circumstances whatever. Often transactions involving many thousands of dollars are made verbally only, and complied with to the letter. Indeed, if this were not so they would often experience great hardships in transacting their business as well as getting through the country with their stock. We remember but few instances where a Texan, after selling his herd, went off home without paying all his business obligations. . . .

Riding Herd

One remarkable feature is observable as being worthy of note, and that is how completely the herd becomes broken to follow the trail. Certain cattle will take the lead, and others will select certain places in the line, and certain ones bring up the rear, and the same cattle can be seen at their post, marching along like a column of soldiers, every day during the entire journey, unless they become lame, when they will fall back to the rear. A herd of one thousand cattle will stretch out from one to two miles whilst traveling on the trail, and is a very beautiful sight, inspiring the drover with enthusiasm akin to that enkindled in the breast of the military hero by the sight of marching columns of men. Certain cow-boys are appointed to ride beside the leaders and so control the herd, whilst others ride beside and behind, keeping everything in its place and moving on, the camp wagon and "cavvie-yard" bringing up the rear. When an ordinary creek or small river is reached the leaders are usually easily induced to go in, and although it may be swimming, yet they scarce hesitate, but plunge through to the northern shore and continue the journey, the balance of the herd following as fast as they arrive. Often, however, at large rivers, when swollen by floods, difficulty is experienced in getting over, especially is this the case when the herd gets massed together. Then they become unwieldy and are hard to induce to take the water. Sometimes days are spent, and much damage to the condition of the herd done, in getting across a single stream. But if the herd is well broken and properly managed, this difficulty is not often experienced.

As soon as the leaders can be induced to take to the water, and strike out for the opposite shore, the balance will follow with but little trouble. Often the drover can induce the leaders to follow him into and across the river, by riding ahead of them into the water and, if need be, swimming his horse in the lead to the opposite shore, whilst the entire herd follow much in the same order that it travels on the trail. . . . When the herd gets to milling in the water—to break this mill and induce the leaders to launch out for the shore—the drover swims his cow pony into the center of the mill and, if possible, frightens the mass of struggling whirling cattle, into separation. Not unfrequently the drover is unhorsed and compelled to swim for his life; often taking a swimming steer by the tail, and thus be safely and speedily towed to the shore.

Swimming herds of cattle across swollen rivers is not listed as one of the pleasurable events in the drover's trip to the northern market. . . . When the herd is over the stream the next job is to get the camp wagon over. This is done by drawing it near the water's edge and, after detaching the oxen and swimming them over, a number of picket ropes are tied together, sufficient to reach across the river, and attached to the wagon which is then pushed into the water and drawn to the opposite shore, whereupon the team is attached and the wagon drawn on to solid ground.

Storm and Stampede

Few occupations are more cheerful, lively and pleasant than that of the cow-boy on a fine day or night; but when the storm comes, then is his manhood and often his skill and bravery put to test. When the night is inky dark and the lurid lightning flashes its zigzag course athwart the heavens, and the coarse thunder jars the earth, the winds moan fresh and lively over the prairie, the electric balls dance from tip to tip of the cattle's horns—then the position of the cow-boy on duty is trying far more than romantic.

North Wind Picture Archives

Cowboys often found respite from their lonely, dangerous life on the trail by kicking up their heels in a dance hall like this.

When the storm breaks over his head, the least occurrence unusual, such as the breaking of a dry weed or stick, or a sudden and near flash of lightning, will start the herd, as if by magic, all at an instant, upon a wild rush, and woe to the horse, or man, or camp that may be in their path. The only possible show for safety is to mount and ride with them until you can get outside the stampeding column. It is customary to train cattle to listen to the noise of the herder, who sings in a voice more sonorous than musical a lullaby consisting of a few short monosyllables. A stranger to the business of stock-driving will scarce credit the statement that the wildest herd will not run so long as they can hear distinctly the voice of the herder above the din of the storm. But if by any mishap the herd gets off on a real stampede, it is by bold, dashing, reckless riding in the darkest of nights, and by adroit, skillful management that it is checked and brought under control. The moment the herd is off, the cow-boy turns his horse at full speed down the retreating column, and seeks to get up beside the leaders, which he does not attempt to stop suddenly, for such an effort would be futile, but turns them to the left or right hand, and gradually curves them into a circle, the circumference of which is narrowed down as fast as possible, until the whole herd is rushing wildly round and round on as small a piece of ground as possible for them to occupy. Then the cow-boy begins his lullaby note in a loud voice, which has a great effect in quieting the herd. When all is still, and the herd well over its scare, they are returned to their bed-ground, or held where stopped until daylight. . . .

The Cowboy's Life in the City

After a drive of twenty-five to one hundred days, the herd arrives in Western Kansas, whither, in advance, its owner has come. . . .

No sooner had it become a conceded fact that Abilene, as a cattle depot, was a success, than trades' people from all points came to the village and, after putting up temporary houses, went into business. Of course the saloon, the billiard table, the ten-pin alley, the gambling table—in short, every possible device for obtaining money in both an honest and dishonest manner, were abundant.

Fully seventy-five thousand cattle arrived at Abilene during the summer of 1868, and at the opening of the market in the spring fine prices were realized and snug fortunes were made by such drovers as were able to effect a sale of their herds. It was the custom to locate herds as near the village as good water and plenty of grass could be found. . . .

The herd is brought upon its herd ground and carefully watched during the day, but allowed to scatter out over sufficient territory to feed. At nightfall it is gathered to a spot selected near the tent, and there rounded up and held during the night. One or more cow-boys are on duty all the while, being relieved at regular hours by relays fresh aroused from slumber, and mounted on rested ponies, and for a given number of hours they ride slowly and quietly around the herd, which, soon as it is dusk, lies down to rest and ruminate. About midnight every animal will arise, turn about for a few moments, and then lie down again near where it arose, only changing sides so as to rest. But if no one should be watching to prevent straggling, it would be but a short time before the entire herd would be up and following off the leader, or some uneasy one that would rather travel than sleep or rest. All this is easily checked by the cow-boy on duty. But when storm is imminent, every man is required to have his horse saddled ready for an emergency. . . . Day after day the cattle are held under herd and cared for by the cow-boys, whilst the drover is looking out for a purchaser for his herd. . . .

The Cowboy at Play in Abilene

Whilst the herd is being held upon the same grazing grounds, often one or more of the cow-boys, not on duty, will mount their ponies and go to the village nearest camp and spend a few hours; learn all the items of news or gossip concerning other herds and the cow-boys belonging thereto. Besides seeing the sights, he gets such little articles as may be wanted by himself and comrades at camp; of these a supply of tobacco, both chewing and smoking forms one of the principal, and often recurring wants. The cowboy almost invariably smokes or chews tobacco—generally both; for the time drags dull at camp or herd ground. There is nothing new or exciting occurring to break the monotony of daily routine events. Sometimes the cow-boys off duty will go to town late in the evening and there join with some party of cow-boys—whose herd is sold and they preparing to start home—in having a jolly time. Often one or more of them will imbibe too much poison whisky and straightway go on the "war path." Then mounting his pony he is ready to shoot anybody or anything; or rather than not shoot at all, would fire up into the air, all the while yelling as only a semi-civilized being can. At such times it is not safe to be on the streets, or for that matter within a house, for the drunk cow-boy would as soon shoot into a house as at anything else. . . .

The life of the cow-boy in camp is routine and dull. His food is largely of the "regulation" order, but a feast of vegetables he wants and must have, or scurvy would ensue. Onions and potatoes are his favorites, but any kind of vegetables will disappear in haste when put within his reach. In camp, on the trail, on the ranch in Texas, with their countless thousands of cattle, milk and butter are almost unknown, not even milk or cream for the coffee is had. Pure shiftlessness and the lack of energy are the only reasons for this privation and to the same reasons can be assigned much of the privations and hardships incident to ranching.

It would cost but little effort or expense to add a hundred comforts, not to say luxuries, to the life of a drover and his cow-boys. They sleep on the ground, with a pair of blankets for bed and cover. No tent is used, scarcely any cooking utensils, and such a thing as a camp cook-stove is unknown. The warm water of the branch or the standing pool is drank, often it is yellow with alkali and other poisons. No wonder the cow-boy gets sallow and unhealthy, and deteriorates in manhood until often he becomes capable of any contemptible thing; no wonder he should become half-civilized only, and take to whisky with a love excelled scarcely by the barbarous Indian.

Barbarians at Heart

Emerson Hough, one of the premier writers on the American cowboy, wrote The Story of the Cowboy *in 1897. In this excerpt he analyzes why the cowboy appeals to the American public.*

If we care truly to see the cowboy as he was, and seek to give our wish the dignity of a real purpose, the first intention should be to study the cowboy in connection with his surroundings. Then perhaps we may not fail in our purpose, but come near to seeing him as he actually was, the product of primitive, chaotic, elemental forces, rough, barbarous, and strong. Then we shall love him because at heart each of us is a barbarian, too, and longing for that past the ictus of whose heredity we can never eliminate from out our blood.

When the herd is sold and delivered to the purchaser, a day of rejoicing to the cow-boy has come, for then he can go free and have a jolly time; and it is a jolly time they have. Straightway after settling with their employers the barber shop is visited; and three to six months' growth of hair is shorn off, their long-grown, sunburnt beard "set" in due shape, and properly blacked; next a clothing store of the Israelitish style is "gone through," and the cow-boy emerges a new man, in outward appearance, everything being new, not excepting the hat and boots, with star decorations about the tops, also a new ——, well in short everything new. Then for fun and frolic. The bar-room, the theatre, the gambling-room, the bawdy house, the dance house, each and all come in for their full share of attention. In any of these places an affront, or a slight, real or imaginary, is cause sufficient for him to unlimber one or more "mountain howitzers," invariably found strapped to his person, and proceed to deal out death in unbroken doses to such as may be in range of his pistols, whether real friends or enemies, no matter, his anger and bad whisky urge him on to deeds of blood and death.

At frontier towns where are centered many cattle and, as a natural result, considerable business is transacted, and many strangers congregate, there are always to be found a number of bad characters, both male and female; of the very worst class in the universe, such as have fallen below the level of the lowest type of the brute creation. Men who live a soulless, aimless life, dependent upon the turn of a card for the means of living. They wear out a purposeless life, ever looking blear-eyed and dissipated; to whom life, from various causes, has long since become worse than a total blank; beings in the form of man whose outward appearance would betoken gentlemen, but whose heartstrings are but a wisp of base sounding chords, upon which the touch of the higher and purer life have long since ceased to be felt. Beings without whom the world would be better, richer and more desirable. And with them are always found their counterparts in the opposite sex; those who have fallen low, alas! how low! They, too, are found in the frontier cattle town; and that institution known in the west as a dance house, is there found also. When the darkness of the night is come to shroud their orgies from public gaze, these miserable beings gather into the halls of the dance house, and "trip the fantastic toe" to wretched music, ground out of dilapidated instruments, by beings fully as degraded as the most vile. In this vortex of dissipation the average cow-boy plunges with great delight. Few more wild, reckless scenes of abandoned debauchery can be seen on the civilized earth, than a dance house in full blast in one of the many frontier towns. To say they dance wildly or in an abandoned manner is putting it mild. Their manner of practising the terpsichorean as would put the French "Can-Can" to shame.

Enthusiastic Dancing

The cow-boy enters the dance with a peculiar zest, not stopping to divest himself of his sombrero, spurs, or pistols, but just as he dismounts off of his cow pony, so he goes into the dance. A more odd, not to say comical sight, is not often seen than the dancing cow-boy; with the front of his sombrero lifted at an angle of fully forty-five degrees; his huge spurs jingling at every step or motion; his revolvers flapping up and down like a retreating sheep's tail; his eyes lit up with excitement, liquor and lust; he plunges in and "hoes it down," at a terrible rate, in the most approved yet awkward country style; often swinging "his partner" clear off the floor for an entire circle, then "balance all" with an occasional demoniacal yell, near akin to the war whoop of the savage Indian. All this he does, entirely oblivious to the whole world "and the balance of mankind." After dancing furiously, the entire "set" is called to "waltz to the bar," where the boy is required to treat his partner, and, of course, himself also, which he does not hesitate to do time and again, although it costs him fifty cents each time. Yet if it cost ten times that amount he would not hesitate, but the more he dances and drinks, the less common sense he will have, and the more completely his animal passions will control him. Such is the manner in which the cow-boy spends his hard earned dollars. And such is the entertainment that many young men—from the North and the South, of superior parentage and youthful advantages in life—give themselves up to, and often more, their lives are made to pay the forfeit of their sinful foolishness.

After a few days of frolic and debauchery, the cow-boy is ready, in company with his comrades, to start back to Texas, often not having one dollar left of his summer's wages.

VIEWPOINT 2

"The assembled crowd named me Deadwood Dick and proclaimed me champion roper of the western cattle country."

The Black Cowboy Was the Equal of His White Brother

Nat Love (1854-1921)

Nat Love was born in a Tennessee slave cabin in 1854. At fifteen, disgruntled by the lack of opportunity for a black man in the Reconstruction South, he headed west to Dodge City, Kansas, at that time "a typical frontier city with a great many saloons, dance halls, and gambling houses" that apparently cared not at all whether patrons had white or black skin as long as their money was green. Soon after his arrival, Love landed a job as a cowpuncher and, for the better part of a generation, he took part in the long cattle drives from Texas to Kansas. In his accounts of his life as a cowboy, he mentions no incidents of racial discrimination; however, when the railroads made long cattle drives an anachronism, Nat Love became a Pullman porter, one of the few jobs open at the time to Negroes. It may be of coincidental interest that Love left the range in 1890, the very year the frontier was declared closed. This passage is typical of his autobiography, for

From *The Life and Adventures of Nat Love, Better Known in the Cattle Country as "Deadwood Dick"* by Nat Love. Los Angeles: n.p., 1907.

he not only describes life as a cowboy but constantly comments on contemporary events and famous people he met. It may be noted that the rodeo, seen in Nat Love's and Bill Pickett's careers, was yet another means of transforming the working cowboy into a popular hero.

Our plantation was situated in the heart of the black belt of the south, and on the plantations all around us were thousands of slaves, all engaged in garnering the dollars that kept up the so-called aristocracy of the south, and many of the proud old families owe their standing and wealth to the toil and sweat of the black man's brow, where if they had to pay the regular rate of wages to hire laborers to cultivate their large estates, their wealth would not have amounted to a third of what it was. Wealth was created, commerce carried on, cities built, and the new world well started on the career that has led to its present greatness and standing in the world of nations. All this was accomplished by the sweat of the black man's brow. By black man I do not mean to say only the black men, but the black woman and black child all helped to make the proud south what it was, the boast of every white man and woman, with a drop of southern blood in their veins, and what did the black man get in return? His keep and care you say? Ye gods and little fishes! Is there a man living today who would be willing to do the work performed by the slaves of that time for the same returns, his care and keep? No, my friends, we did it because we were forced to do it by the dominant race. . . .

It was on the tenth day of February, 1869, that I left the old home, near Nashville, Tennessee. I was at that time about fifteen years old, and though while young in years the hard work and farm life had made me strong and hearty, much beyond my years, and I had full confidence in myself as being able to take care of myself and making my way.

I at once struck out for Kansas of which I had heard something. And believing it was a good place in which to seek employment. It was in the West, and it was the great West I wanted to see, and so by walking and occasional lifts from farmers going my way and taking advantage of every thing that promised to assist me on my way, I eventually brought up at Dodge City, Kansas, which at that time was a typical frontier city, with a great many saloons, dance halls, and gambling houses, and very little of anything else. When I arrived the town was full of cow boys from the sur-rounding ranches, and from Texas and other parts of the west. As

Kansas was a great cattle center and market, the wild cow boy, prancing horses of which I was very fond, and the wild life generally, all had their attractions for me, and I decided to try for a place with them. . . .

Rumors of Little Bighorn

We had not been on the trail long before we met other outfits, who told us that General Custer was out after the Indians and that a big fight was expected when the Seventh U.S. Cavalry, General Custer's command, met the Crow tribe and other Indians under the leadership of Sitting Bull, Rain-in-the-Face, Old Chief Joseph, and other chiefs of lesser prominence, who had for a long time been terrorizing the settlers of that section and defying the Government.

It is significant that this is clearly a posed studio shot, an illustration of how some Western heroes mythologized themselves. Love's photo is similar in intent to Custer's writing.

As we proceeded on our journey it became evident to us that we were only a short distance behind the soldiers. When finally the Indians and soldiers met in the memorable battle or rather massacre in the Little Big Horn Basin on the Little Big Horn River in northern Wyoming, we were only two days behind them, or within 60 miles, but we did not know that at the time or we would have gone to Custer's assistance. We did not know of the fight or the outcome until several days after it was over. It was freely claimed at the time by cattle men who were in a position to know and with whom I talked that if Reno had gone to Custer's aid as he promised to do, Custer would not have lost his entire command and his life.

It was claimed Reno did not obey his orders, however that may be, it was one of the most bloody massacres in the history of this country. We went on our way to Deadwood with our herd, where we arrived on the 3rd of July, 1876, eight days after the Custer massacre took place.

The Custer Battle was June 25, '76, the battle commenced on Sunday afternoon and lasted about two hours. That was the last of General Custer and his Seventh Cavalry. How I know this so well is because we had orders from one of the Government scouts to go in camp, that if we went any farther north we were liable to be captured by the Indians.

We arrived in Deadwood in good condition without having had any trouble with the Indians on the way up. We turned our cattle over to their new owners at once, then proceeded to take in the town. The next morning, July 4th, the gamblers and mining men made up a purse of $200 for a roping contest between the cow boys that were then in town, and as it was a holiday nearly all the cow boys for miles around were assembled there that day. It did not take long to arrange the details for the contest and contestants, six of them being colored cow boys, including myself. Our trail boss was chosen to pick out the mustangs from a herd of wild horses just off the range, and he picked out twelve of the most wild and vicious horses that he could find.

The conditions of the contest were that each of us who were mounted was to rope, throw, tie, bridle and saddle and mount the particular horse picked for us in the shortest time possible. The man accomplishing the feat in the quickest time to be declared the winner.

It seems to me that the horse chosen for me was the most vicious of the lot. Everything being in readiness, the "45" cracked and we all sprang forward together, each of us making for our particular mustang.

"Deadwood Dick"

I roped, threw, tied, bridled, saddled and mounted my mustang in exactly nine minutes from the crack of the gun. The time of the next nearest competitor was twelve minutes and thirty seconds. This gave me the record and championship of the West, which I held up to the time I quit the business in 1890, and my record has

Bill Pickett, Bulldogger

Bill Pickett, another black cowboy, is credited with inventing one of the seven standard rodeo events, bulldogging, or wrestling a steer to the ground. Pickett's unique technique, however, was to grab the bull with his teeth rather than his hands. The following is a newspaper account of his feat.

The great event of the celebration this year was the remarkable feat of Will Pickett, a Negro hailing from Taylor, Texas, who gave his exhibition while 20,000 people watched with wonder and admiration a mere man, unarmed and without a device or appliance of any kind, attack a fiery, wild-eyed, and powerful steer and throw it by his teeth. With the aid of a helper, Pickett chased the steer until he was in front of the grand stand. Then he jumped from the saddle and landed on the back of the animal, grasped its horns, and brought it to a stop within a dozen feet. By a remarkable display of strength he twisted the steer's head until its nose pointed straight into the air, the animal bellowing with pain and its tongue protruding in its effort to secure air. Again and again the Negro was jerked from his feet and tossed into the air, but his grip on the horns never once loosened, and the steer failed in its efforts to gore him. Cowboys with their lariats rushed to Pickett's assistance but the action of the combat was too rapid for them. Before help could be given, Pickett, who had forced the steer's nose into the mud and shut off its wind, slipped, and was tossed aside like a piece of paper. There was a scattering of cowboys as he jumped to his feet and ran for his horse. Taking the saddle without touching the stirrup, he ran the steer to a point opposite the judges stand, again jumped on its back, and threw it. Twice was the Negro lifted from his feet, but he held on with the tenacity of a bulldog. Suddenly Pickett dropped the steer's head and grasped the upper lip of the animal with his teeth, threw his arms wide apart to show that he was not using his hands, and sank slowly upon his back. The steer lost its footing and rolled upon its back, completely covering the Negro's body with its own. The crowd was speechless with horror, many believing that the Negro had been crushed: but a second later the steer rolled to its other side, and Pickett arose uninjured, bowing and smiling. So great was the applause that the [Negro] again attacked the steer, which had staggered to its feet, and again threw it after a desperate struggle.

never been beaten. It is worthy of passing remark that I never had a horse pitch with me so much as that mustang, but I never stopped sticking my spurs in him and using my quirt on his flanks until I proved his master. Right there the assembled crowd named me Deadwood Dick and proclaimed me champion roper of the western cattle country.

The roping contest over, a dispute arose over the shooting question with the result that a contest was arranged for the afternoon, as there happened to be some of the best shots with rifle and revolver in the West present that day. Among them were Stormy Jim, who claimed the championship; Powder Horn Bill, who had the reputation of never missing what he shot at; also White Head, a half breed, who generally hit what he shot at, and many other men who knew how to hand a rifle or 45-Colt.

The range was measured off 100 and 250 yards for the rifle and 150 for the Colt 45. At this distance a bulls eye about the size of an apple was put up. Each man was to have 14 shots at each range with the rifle and 12 shots with the Colts 45. I placed every one of my 14 shots with the rifle in the bulls eye with ease, all shots being made from the hip; but with the 45 Colts I missed it twice, only placing 10 shots in the small circle, Stormy Jim being my nearest competitor, only placing 8 bullets in the bulls eye clear, the rest being quite close, while with the 45 he placed 5 bullets in the charmed circle. This gave me the championship of rifle and revolver shooting as well as the roping contest, and for that day I was the hero of Deadwood, and the purse of $200 which I had won on the roping contest went toward keeping things moving, and they did move as only a large crowd of cattle men can move things. This lasted for several days when most of the cattle men had to return to their respective ranches, as it was the busy season, accordingly our outfit began to make preparations to return to Arizona.

In the meantime news had reached us of the Custer massacre, and the indignation and sorrow was universal, as General Custer was personally known to a large number of the cattle men of the West. But we could do nothing now, as the Indians were out in such strong force. There was nothing to do but let Uncle Sam revenge the loss of the General and his brave command, but it is safe to say not one of us would have hesitated a moment in taking the trail in pursuit of the blood thirsty red skins had the opportunity offered.

Everything now being in readiness with us we took the trail homeward bound, and left Deadwood in a blaze of glory. On our way home we visited the Custer battle field in the Little Big Horn Basin.

There was ample evidence of the desperate and bloody fight that had taken place a few days before. We arrived home in Arizona in a short time without further incident, except that on the way back we met and talked with many of the famous Government scouts of that region, among them Buffalo Bill (William F. Cody), Yellowstone Kelley, and many others of that day, some of whom are now living, while others lost their lives in the line of duty, and a finer or braver body of men never lived than these scouts of the West. It was my pleasure to meet Buffalo Bill often in the early 70s, and he was as fine a man as one could wish to meet, kind, generous, true and brave.

Buffalo Bill got his name from the fact that in the early days he was engaged in hunting buffalo for their hides and furnishing U.P. Railroad graders with meat, hence the name Buffalo Bill. Buffalo Bill, Yellowstone Kelley, with many others were at this time serving under Gen. C.C. Miles.

The name of Deadwood Dick was given to me by the people of Deadwood, South Dakota, July 4, 1876, after I had proven myself worthy to carry it, and after I had defeated all comers in riding, roping, and shooting, and I have always carried the name with honor since that time.

We arrived at the home ranch again on our return from the trip to Deadwood about the middle of September, it taking us a little over two months to make the return journey, as we stopped in Cheyenne for several days and at other places, where we always found a hearty welcome, especially so on this trip, as the news had preceded us, and I received enough attention to have given me the big head, but my head had constantly refused to get enlarged again ever since the time I sampled the demijohn in the sweet corn patch at home.

Arriving at home, we received a send off from our boss and our comrades of the home ranch, every man of whom on hearing the news turned loose his voice and his artillery in a grand demonstration in my honor.

But they said it was no surprise to them, as they had long known of my ability with the rope, rifle and 45 Colt, but just the same it was gratifying to know I had defeated the best men of the West, and brought the record home to the home ranch in Arizona. After a good rest we proceeded to ride the range again, getting our herds in good condition for the winter now at hand.

VIEWPOINT 3

"Ther gal ain't no fool ef she do wear breeches."

"Calamity Jane" Was Any Man's Equal

Edward L. Wheeler (1854-1885)

In a 1937 *Yale Review* article, historian Merle Curti wrote of dime novels: "[They] must be taken into account particularly by those interested in the democratization of culture . . . in the rise and reinforcement of our tradition of adventure and rugged individualism, in the development of class consciousness, and in the growth of American patriotism and nationalism." Because they were more widely read than was serious literature, these usually melodramatic paperbacks reflected and reinforced the people's values.

Dime novels, first published by the house of Beadle & Adams in 1860, were so popular that it is reported they were shipped by the freight-car load to Union soldiers. The first dime novel, *Malaeska, The Indian Wife of the White Hunter* by Mrs. Ann S. Stephens, earlier printed serially in *The Ladies Companion*, was set in the Catskills in early colonial days. The frontier became an immensely popular subject for Beadle & Adams's readers. Literary historian Philip Durham categorized 1,531 novels (there were 3,158 original novels in the Beadle & Adams series) according to subject matter. He found 30 percent dealing with the West in general; 10 percent with miners, mining, and mining camps; 6 percent with Texas life; 6 percent with city life; 6 percent with the sea; 5 percent with city detectives; 5 percent with Western detec-

From *Deadwood Dick on Deck; or, Calamity Jane, the Heroine of Whoop-Up* by Edward L. Wheeler. New York: Beadle and Adams, 1885.

tives; 4 percent with Indian life; 4 percent with border life before the Civil War; 3 percent with Indian scouts; 3 percent with the American Revolution; 2 percent with fur trappers; 2 percent with overland journeys; 2 percent with the southern Mississippi River; 1 percent with Mexico; and the rest with miscellaneous topics. Clearly the American public of the last four decades of the nineteenth century had an insatiable appetite for popular fiction about the frontier, both to read about days gone by and to vicariously experience events others were still living.

Edward L. Wheeler, author of the Deadwood Dick series, was one of Beadle & Adams's most prolific authors. The following selection comes from his eighth Deadwood Dick novel, first published on December 17, 1878. Admittedly cliché-ridden, the novel reflects the sympathies of its mass audience: A Danite is cast as a villain, exploiting anti-Mormon feelings of the day, and the heroes' insistence on keeping out of the capitalistic corporation by selling parts of their mining holdings to individuals was an appeal to the average person during a period of strife between labor and capital. In Calamity Jane, Wheeler portrays the real-life Martha Connarray and legitimizes a nontraditional role for women in the process.

Martha Connarray, like Phoebe Anne Mozee, captured the late-nineteenth-century imagination. To achieve their public personae, both women were rechristened. Little Phoebe, who at age nine had demonstrated her prowess with a rifle by shooting the heads off squirrels to feed her impoverished family in Ohio, became Annie Oakley in Col. William F. Cody's Wild West Show. While Buffalo Bill promoted Annie for her trick shooting (she sometimes used a mirror to aim at a target behind her), Martha Connarray shamelessly promoted herself. As Calamity Jane she claimed to be the army's only female scout and a fearless Indian fighter. In reality, she was known as a drunk and a sometime prostitute. She claimed to be married to Wild Bill Hickock, a legend in his own right, but no evidence exists that such a marriage occurred. When she died in 1903, however, she was buried beside him. At her death, the legend was authenticated; reality was buried with her.

In the following excerpt, from the first chapter of the novel, it is less important whether Wheeler is biographically accurate than that he creates a heroine who can attract a mass audience. Unconventional women fascinated his readers despite—or more likely because of—their flaunting of society's conventions. While the Elizabeth Custers and Bessie Rehwinkels might be more acceptable in polite society, the boardinghouse operators and madams and criminals reflected part of the reality of the frontier and captured readers' interest.

[As the novel opens, two miners, camped near Deadwood, hear a clear soprano voice exulting in an independent life in the woods, panning for gold, breaking horses, and sending back "cold lead" at any who would threaten her.]

The two men alluded to were sitting upon the bank of the stream, and they did not move until the songstress had ceased her melody; then they looked up and exchanged glances.

"Beautiful, wasn't it, Sandy?"

"Yes," replied the younger of the twain, as he resumed his pipe, his eyes roving out over the noisy river, dreamily. "I was not aware you had such musical stars out here in your mining districts. A woman, wa'n't it?"

"Yas, a woman," replied Colonel Joe Tubbs, knocking the ashes out of his pipe, and refilling it with chipped plug. "At least they say she's o' the feminine sex, fer w'ich I can't sw'ar, purtic'lar. An' ef she's a weemon, thar ain't many better lukers 'twixt hayr, Deadwood, an' ther risin' sun."

"What reason have you to doubt that she is not a woman, colonel?"

"Wal, Sandy, I ken't say as I really doubt et, fer I s'pect et's a solid fac' that she ar' one o'ther lineal descendents of thet leetls fruitful scrape in a certain garden, yeers ago, afore ther Antediluve. But ye see how it is: in the gelorius State o' Ohio, from which I war imported ter this side o' ther hemisphere, ther female sex ginnerally war begarbed in petticoats, an' left ther male representatives to wear ther breeches!"

"Humph!" and a little smile came to Sandy's lips, "then this nightingale who has just favored us, wears the breeches herself, does she?"

"You pile up yer chips an' bet thet she do, Sandy, and ef you warn't an Eastern chap, an' but leetle used ter sech weemon as we hev in this delectable Black Hills kentry, I'd say, 'Sandy, galoot, pile yer frunt foot for'a'd, and go in for Janie.'"

"Janie—that is her name, eh?"

"Wal, I reckon—Calamity Jane for short. I don't allow thar's many who do know who she is, aside from her title, Sandy, tho' she don't cum no furder off than up in Nevada. She's a brick, Sandy, and jest let et pop right inter yer noddle right hayr, that she ain't no fool ef she do wear breeches. An' ef ye ever have occasion ter meet ther gal, Sandy, jest remember ther words uv Colorado Joe Tubbs on thes 'ere eventful night—'Ther gal ain't no fool ef she do wear breeches.'"

"I will, pardner. I don't suppose because a woman wears male

213

A photograph of the real Calamity Jane reveals that Edward Wheeler's romantic description of her took a bit of poetic license. Unlike Wheeler's more alluring depiction, the real Jane sports boots, a buckskin jacket, and a shirt buttoned to her chin. Both depictions have her armed with a rifle and a six-gun.

attire that she is necessarily a fool; though why a female must lower her sex by appearing in man's garb, I see not. She must be an eccentric creature—rather a hard case, is she not?" with a little curl of his lip.

A Dare-Devil

"'Hard case,' Sandy?" and here the veteran paused to close one eye, and blow out a cloud of fragrant smoke; "wal, no, when ye ask my jedgment in ther matter. She's a woman, Sandy, an' tho' thar's many who lay claim ter that name who ar' below par, I don't reckon Janie ar' quite that fur gone. She's a dare-devil, Sandy, an' no mistake. She ar' the most reckless buchario in ther Hills, kin drink whisky, shute, play keerds, or sw'ar, ef et comes ter et; but, 'twixt you and me, I reckon ther gal's got honor left wi' her grit, out o' ther wreck o' a young life. Oncet an' awhile thar is a story whispered about that she war deserted up at Virginny City, an' tuk ter thes rovin' life ter hunt down her false lover; another thet she

214

hed bin married ter a Nevada brute, an' kim over inter these deestrict ter escape him; then thar's bin sum hard stories o' her up at Deadwood an' Hayward, but I never b'lieved 'em 'case they were ginneraly invented by a gang o' toughs who hed a grudge ag'in' her. I never b'lieved 'em, Sandy, because she war a woman; an' once I hed a wife an' little golden-haired daughter—she luked like you, Sandy—an' I know'd 'em ter be good; thet's why I nevyr kim ter believe all about Calamity Jane!" and the old man bowed his head on his arm, at some sad recollection.

"No! no!" he went on, after a few moments of silence. "Janie's not as bad as ther world would have her; because she's got grit an' ain't afeared to shute ther galot as crosses her, people condemn her. I reckon ye kno' how et is, out hayr in ther Hills, Sandy—ef a female ken't stand up and fight fer her rights, et's durned little aid she'll git."

"So I should conclude from what observations I have been able to make, since I came West," was the reply of the young miner. "Is this Calamity Jane pretty, colonel?"

"Wal, some might say so, Sandy; I am not partial ter givin' opinions o' ther external merits of ther female line, o' late years. Hed sum experience in thet line a couple o' years ago, afore I left Angelina, my second, ter come out hayr—war just tellin' her how purty a certain widder war, when—well, I never quite knew what struck me, but I finally waked up ter find myself carved up inter steaks an' ther ha'r on to o' my head gone. Likewise, my Angelina. She had eloped wi' another galoot. Since then I allus withhold my opinion on ther beauty or humblyness o' ther opposite sex."

"Well, I suppose you wa'n't sorry, eh?" observed Sandy, as he arose, with a yawn, and picked up his handsome Sharpe's rifle.

"Wal, no; I ken't say's I am, sence et turns out thet ther Black Hills affords me more comfort an' enjoyment than hum uster wi' Angelina everlastingly browsin' me down wi' a mop-stick.". . .

After the conclusion of the beautiful yet weird mountaineer's song, which Joe Tubbs had declared came from the lips of Calamity Jane, a person on horseback descended a dizzy zig-zag path that led from one of the mountain peaks, into a narrow dark defile, but the matter of a mile or so above Canyon Gulch, and the infant city of Satan's Bend.

"Whoa! Steady, Trick—none o' yer funny business, now. Don't ye perceive thet ef yer were to tumble down this declivity with me, there'd be no guardian angel in the Black Hills?" and here a merry peal of laughter escaped the red lips of the speaker.

"Steady—a little further—there! Good for you, old fellow! We're on safe footing, at last. I wonder if any one's around in these parts?" and the dark eyes peered sharply into every shadow in her immediate vicinity. "No; I reckon the coast is all clear, and we must get a-going for Deadwood, Trick, for there is no telling how soon that delightful population may need us to quell some row or do a suffering pilgrim good."

Calamity Jane Described

We have described the eccentric dare-devil of the Black Hills in other works of this series, but as some may not have read them, it will require but little time to describe her again.

A female of no given age, although she might have ranged safely anywhere between seventeen and twenty-three, she was the possessor of a form both graceful and womanly, and a face that was peculiarly handsome and attractive, though upon it were lines drawn by the unmistakable hand of dissipation and hard usage, lines never to be erased from a face that in innocent childhood had been a pretty one. The lips and eyes still retained in themselves their girlish beauty; the lips their full, rosy plumpness, and the eyes their dark, magnetic sparkle, and the face proper had the power to become stern, grave or jolly in expression, wreathed partially as it was in a semi-framework of long, raven hair that reached below a faultless waist.

Her dress was buckskin trowsers, met at the knee by fancifully beaded leggings, with slippers of dainty pattern upon the feet; a velvet vest and one of those luxuries of the mines, a boiled shirt, open at the throat, partially revealing a breast of alabaster purity; a short, velvet jacket, and Spanish broad-brimmed hat, slouched upon one side of a regally beautiful head. There were diamond rings upon her hands, a diamond pin in her shirt-bosom, a massive gold chain strung across her vest front.

For she had riches, this girl, and none knew better than she how to find them in the auriferous earth or at the gaming-table of Deadwood, the third Baden Baden of two continents.

A belt around her waist contained a solitary revolver of large caliber; and this, along with a rifle strapped to her back, comprised her outfit, except we mention the fiery little Mexican black she rode, and the accompanying trappings, which were richly decorated and bespangled, after lavish Mexican taste.

"I guess the coast is clear, Trick; so go ahead," and a jerk at the cruel Spanish bit and an application of spurs sent the spiteful cayuse clattering wildly down the canyon, while Calamity Jane rocked not ungracefully from side to side with the reckless freedom peculiar to the California buchario. Indeed, I think that any person who has witnessed the dare-devil riding of this eccentric girl, in her mad career through the Black Hills country, will agree with me that she has of her sex no peer in the saddle or on horseback.

The first time it was ever my fortune to see her, was when Deadwood was but an infant city of a few shanties, but many tents.

She dashed madly down through the gulch one day, standing erect upon the back of her unsaddled cayuse, and the animal running at the top of its speed, leaping sluices and other obstructions—still the dare-devil retained her position as if glued to the animal's back, her hair flowing wildly back from beneath her slouch hat, her eyes dancing occasionally with excitement, as she recognized some wondering pilgrim, every now and then her lips giving vent to a ringing whoop, which was creditable in imitation if not in volume and force to that of a full-blown Comanche warrior.

Sporting Women

After her husband, George, was blown up in a mine accident, Anne Ellis was left on her own to raise and provide for her children. She had a little with which to start: The mine gave her six hundred dollars; each man working in the mine contributed a day's wages; and working-class neighbors brought food for the wake and flannel for the baby's petticoat. Needing a steady income, Anne started baking bread, cakes, and pies for women in a nearby brothel; later she was convinced by the mine owners to open a boardinghouse. Despite one incident when she considered suicide, Ellis's Life of an Ordinary Woman *is a testimony to the will to survive. In this excerpt, she describes the "sporting women" living next door.*

In these early days we took the sporting women as we did the saloons, as a matter of course. They, like the saloons, never bothered us, so we had no feeling for or against them, and even now, when I hear talk of raiding or running them out of town, I never pay any attention, considering it none of my business. At one time in my married life their house was just back of mine on the mountain-side, a flight of steps running up to it. Nights when they and their friends would be drunk and fighting, I have heard curses, screams, the break of falling glass, wild laughter—some of them have the shrillest, emptiest, most cutting and unfeeling laugh—then the sound of people falling down this long flight of steps, bumping and cursing each step, till, in the morning, when I opened my door, I expected to see the ground strewn with maimed people. But—much to my disappointment—there is nothing in sight.

Now, she dashed away through the narrow gulch, catching with delight long breaths of the perfume of flowers which met her nostrils at every onward leap of her horse, piercing the gloom of the night with her dark lovely eyes, searchingly, lest she should be surprised; lighting a cigar at full motion—dashing on, on, this strange girl of the Hills went, on her flying steed.

The glowing end of her cigar attracted the notice of four men who were crouching in the dense shadows, further down the gulch, even as the hoofstrokes broke upon their hearing.

"That's her!" growled one, knocking the ashes out of his pipe, with an oath. "Reckoned she wouldn't be all night, ef we only hed patience. Grab yer weepons, an' git ready, boys. She mustn't escape us this time."

Calamity Jane came on; she was not aware of her danger, until she saw four dark shadows cross her path, and her cayuse reared upon its haunches.

"Whoa! Trick; don't git skeered; hold up, you devils. I reckon you're barkin' up ther wrong tree!" she cried.

Then there were three flashes of light in the darkness followed by as many pistol-shots—howls of pain and rage, and curses too vile to repeat here—a yell, wild and clear, a snort from the horse—then the dare-devil rode down the man at the bits, and dashed away down the canyon, with a yell of laughter that echoed and re-echoed up and down the canyon walls.

"I wonder who composed thet worthy quartette?" Calamity mused, as she gazed back over her shoulder. "Reckon at least a couple of 'em bit ther dust, ef not more. Could it have been—but no! I do not believe so. Deadwood Dick's men ain't on the rampage any more, and it couldn't hev been them. Whoever it was wanted my life, that's plain, and I shall have to look out fer breakers ahead, or next time I shall not get off with a simple scratch."

VIEWPOINT 4

"The guilty shall be made to suffer."

Billy the Kid Was a Folk Hero

Walter Woods (1873-1942)

SHOT WELL, HE DID,
AND OUT OF MANY
A TIGHT PLACE HE SLID
$5000 ON HIS HEAD
CATCH HIM
EITHER ALIVE OR DEAD,

SEE:

THE FAMOUS BANDIT HORSE, "SILVER HEELS"
THE BATTLE IN THE DARK
THE HAIRBREADTH ESCAPE OF BILLY THE KID
THE KISS AUCTION
THE SOUL STIRRING BRAVERY OF THE BOY BANDIT
THE FAMOUS BROKEN HEART SALOON

Excerpted from *Billy the Kid* by Walter Woods. In *The Great Diamond Robbery and Other Recent Melodramas*, edited by Garrett H. Leverton. America's Lost Plays, vol. 8. Princeton, NJ: Princeton University Press, 1940. Copyright 1968, Indiana University Press. Reprinted with permission of Indiana University Press.

So read part of the announcement for the play *Billy the Kid*. Written by Walter Woods, it opened at the New Star Theater in New York on August 13, 1906. The *Dramatic News* proclaimed it "better than *The Girl of the Golden West* and the best melodrama I expect to see this season." It was a tremendous box office success, running for twelve consecutive seasons. As is evident from the following segments of Act I, "The Oath of Vengeance," the interpretation of Billy is quite sympathetic: he is the child of a woman done wrong by the play's villain, Denver Boyd, who tricks Billy into stealing from his stepfather and who later in the play tries to kill him. Justice triumphs, however, when Boyd, wearing Billy's coat, is shot by mistake and Billy rides off with his sweetheart. Like many melodramas, this play builds its conflict between Good and Bad, the Hero and the Villain. Audiences loved to be titillated by the deviousness of the bad guy but roared with approval when Good triumphed. Denver Boyd is all the more evil because he destroyed Billy's innocence, forcing him into a life of violence to achieve vengeance.

CHARACTERS

Bill: Billy the Kid; son of Mary Wright
Stephen *Wright*: a ranch owner; Billy's stepfather
Con Hanley: a ranch hand
*Den*ver Boyd: an eastern gentleman; Billy's biological father
Mary Wright: wife of Stephen Wright; Billy's mother
Moses Moore: former military orderly
Col. Wayne Bradley: retired army officer
Nellie: Billy's sweetheart

Act I.

Scene: *Landscape in 5. Picket fence at back. Large Southern home with porch L. Canary in cage hanging from porch. Well curbing, foot and a half high, up L. Table and chair R. Discovered: Con seated on well curb, smoking. Enter Maid from house, with bottles and glasses. Puts them on table. Enter Wright R.U.E. followed by Denver.*

Wri. Con! [*Con jumps up and gets busy*]

Con. Yis, sor.

Wri. Have the niggers bring up a few loads of gravel and fill that old well. [*Goes to table, sits L; Denver sits R.*]

Con. Well, well. All's well that ends well.

Wri. What's that, suh?

Con. I said, very well, sor. That would end the well, sor. [*Exit L.*]

Wri. [*Pouring drinks*] Somebody will fall in there yet. It's a nuisance. It's thirty feet deep and dry as a bone. We get all our water from the artesian well, yonder.

Den. Thirty feet deep? A dangerous hole.

Wri. Yes, suh. Why a person could fall in there and no one would ever know what became of him.

Den. [*Half to himself*] Excellent.

Wri. What's that, suh?

Den. The—ah—whiskey is excellent.

Wri. You're a gentleman, suh. Any man who is a judge of whiskey is a friend of mine. [*They shake hands*]

Den. I'd often heard of your Southern hospitality, and rather doubted its existence myself; but during my short stay here you have converted me for life.

Wri. Tut, tut, tut, suh! You have only received the treatment that any gentleman may expect. Have another drink. And remember, until you are ready to leave this—rather dismal landscape, you are my honored guest.

Den. It's a beautiful spot—beautiful. And you have a charming wife and a wonderful son. No wonder you are contented.

Wri. Contented? Contented is not the word, suh. Happy, suh, downright happy!

Den. [*Slight sneer*] Indeed?

Wri. Yes, suh. Why hang it, I'd like to see the man who could *help* but be happy with Mary for a wife. A lady, suh—one of your sort from up North. How she ever came to care for an old codger like me, is more than I can guess.

Den. You underrate yourself.

Wri. Not a bit of it. My youth is far behind. I'm rough in my ways, and I never took a prize in a beauty show. [*Denver laughs*] Although I am well fixed financially—

Den. [*Still laughing*] Well, there, there! That last remark doubtless—

Wri. Hold on, my friend. I was going to say that although I am well fixed financially, Mary would never wed for money, and if any man was to hint at such a thing, I believe I would kill him. [*Denver suddenly ceases laughing; he looks at Wright*]

Den. [*Intense*] I believe you would.

Wri. [*Light*] You and she must become great friends, suh. Perhaps—perhaps she sometimes feels sort of lonesome, way out here in the West, and you two can talk over New York until this ranch will seem like a suburb of the great city.

Den. I am sure Mrs. Wright and myself will become great friends but I hardly think we will discuss the East. During our

221

short interview this morning, I could see that her whole interest lies with her home, husband and boy.

Wri. [*Huskily*] That's kind of you to say that, suh. Yes, suh—[*Fills glass to hide his emotion, spills liquor*] Yes, suh.

Con. [*Enters L.U.E.*] For the love of Hiven, don't spill it. . . .

Wri. [*Rises, crosses to Con, C., laughing*] Help yourself, but go light on it. [*Goes up L. Con crosses to table, takes bottle and glass, all the time watching Wright. Seeing his back turned, is about to drink from bottle when he turns and sees Denver watching him*]

Con. Turn yer head, can't ye? What do ye want to be watching a man drink for? [*Growling*] Old Tom the peeper! My, my, but it's a beautiful pair of eyes ye have in your head. I love to look at 'em. [*Pours glass full and drinks*] Well, how did ye like the way I did it?

Den. You seem to have taken a dislike to me, Con.

Con. I have not. I wouldn't take the trouble.

Den. [*Low*] One word to Wright of your insolence to me today and he would kick you off the place.

Con. One word to him about the little talk I overheard ye having wid his wife this morning and ye would never leave the place alive.

Den. [*Rises, uneasy*] What did you hear?

Con. That's none of your dom business. Turn yer head, will ye? I want another drink. [*Denver turns, agitated. Con drinks from bottle*]

Den. Have another, Con?

Con. What's the use? The more I drink the less I talk.

Den. [*Hurriedly*] Before you tell Wright anything I wish to see you alone.

Con. No, I'm not going to tell him. That seems to relieve ye, don't it? No, I wouldn't spoil his happiness for the world. But I'll keep me eye on you, my laddy buck, while ye stay here—which had better not be long.

Den. Meet me here, in an hour—alone.

Con. All right. In the meantime, me and the well will proceed to get full together. [*Goes up stage*]

Den. [*Aside*] And you, my friend, will be at the bottom of it.

Wri. [*As Con joins him*] Will the niggers start on the well at once? [*Con shakes his head*] No, suh? Why not, suh?

Con. Billy is using 'em for cattle, sor. He's learning to be a roper, sor.

Wri. I'll rope him. Tell him I want him. Tell him—*tell him.*

Con. T'ell with him.

Wri. What?

Con. I said I'd tell him, sor—[*Exit L.U.E. Wright laughs*]

Den. The servant seems on excellent terms with the master.

Wri. [*Comes down*] Servants? Haven't a one on the place; they are all my friends. Master? There is but one Master—above. [*Crosses to table*]

Den. [*Up L.*] And one servant who never fails us—below. [*Looks in well*] A dangerous hole, dark and deep. . . .

Wri. [*Enters*] Hello, Con. Did you tell Billy? Is he coming?

Con. Yes, sor. No, sor.

Wri. Yes, suh—no, suh! What do you mean?

Con. Yes, sor, I told him. No, sor, he ain't coming.

Wri. Why not?

Con. He's practising wid his revolver. He wants to be a crack shot.

Wri. I'll crack him when I see him, confound him.

Con. Yes, confound him, but Con couldn't bring him wid a yoke of oxen. [*Exit L.U.E.*]

Den. [*Crosses to table*] That boy of yours, Billy, seems full of mischief.

Wri. Full of life, love and kindness, sir. A better boy never lived. A little wild perhaps but that will wear off in time. Brave and reckless as any cowpuncher on the ranch; a hard rider, a good roper and a sure shot. But he ain't mine, more's the pity. You see, Mary was a widow when I married her. Had a little boy baby. But he's grown up just like mine and will never know the difference.

Den. [*Surprised*] She had a child when she married you?

Wri. Yes, poor thing. She had married a cur, a sneak who deserted her. Then he died, which I reckon was the only decent thing he ever did in his whole life.

[*The audience later learns it is Denver Boyd who fathered Billy and abandoned Mary*]

Den. [*Aside*] She had a child.

Wri. Mary is only half my age, suh. But our love is as young as a honeymoon. There's only one mar to my happiness. I'm sorry the scoundrel who caused her such unhappiness is dead. I should like the pleasure of killing him. [*Crosses to house*]

Den. [*Aside*] A dangerous fool. I must be careful. . . .

[*Later*]

Con. Supper's waiting for ye, Billy.

Bill. Well, I'll wait till you go, to keep you out of temptation. Besides, I want to tell you how well I'm getting on with my shooting. I hit the bull's eye ten times hand running.

Con. Ye did?

Bill. And I roped seven niggers out of eight.

Con. Billy boy!

Mose. Better study your schooling. All them things won't do you no good.

Bill. Won't eh? Oh, yes, it will 'cause I'm going to be a pirate.

Mose and Con. A what?

Bill. A pirate on the high seas. I'm going to hold up trains and stages.

Mose. What? On the high seas?

Bill. No-o. I'm mixed. The book I've been reading last was about a knight of the road, not a pirate.

Mose. Leave them books alone, son. They'll fill your head with trash.

Bill. No trash about this. I'm going to be one of 'em and Con is going to be my lieutenant. Ain't you, Con?

Con. [*Winking at Mose*] Sure thing, Billy.

Bill. No fooling now.

Con. Divil a bit.

Bill. Put her there. [*Holds out hand*]

Con. [*Wiping his hand on his pants*] Wait a bit, Billy; I shook wid a blackguard a while ago. [*He shakes his hand*]

Mose. Now, Con, don't go putting that boy up to any foolishness.

Bill. This ain't foolishness, Mose. We're going to hold up only the rich people and carry them off to our cave for ransom.

Con. What is a ransom, Billy?

Bill. I don't know.

Con. Well, how in blazes are ye going to hold 'em for it if you don't know what it is?

Bill. Oh, it means—death; hold 'em until they die, see?

Con. Well I think that will be a heap of trouble. Why not take a gun and ransom 'em as soon as we capture 'em?

Mose. Con, stop teasing the boy.

Bill. Then we'll capture Nellie and I'll marry her.

Con. Oh, ho! Nellie is it? Sure yer stuck on her.

Bill. Never you mind, Con. She's going to be my wife some day.

Mose. Great guns. What notions—Pirates, ransoms and matrimony. . . .

[*All exit. Mary and Denver enter.*]

Mary. You wish to speak to me alone? Speak quickly, I can grant you but a moment.

Den. Indeed? [*C. Looks at her*] What a change. How—happy you must be.

Mary. Why—why did you come here. To torture me?

Den. Bosh! I torture? I am going to take you away from this life of monotony to one of pleasure.

Mary. I am happy with my husband.

Den. Your husband? You flatter me. You were never divorced to my knowledge. I still bear that title.

Mary. [*Putting hand to head*] Oh, I had forgotten. I fear I shall go mad—I thought you dead. This morning when you came like a black cloud from the wretched past, my heart stopped beating. I would gladly have died. After a little, rather than cause my—the man whose name I bear—the sorrow that your real identity would bring him, I decided to remain silent. But do not torture me more with your presence. My patience has a limit, and rather than endure your sneers and insinuations, I will tell Mr. Wright all.

The real-life Billy the Kid. A legendary figure of the Old West, Billy seems to have been both folk hero and sociopath.

Den. [*Frightened*] You would tell him? Have you forgotten the love you once bore me?

Mary. [*Sits on steps*] Yes. As completely as you did when you so cruelly deserted me. Oh, my struggles for an honorable living were bitter but I bore them, until an honest love crept into my barren life and showed me true happiness. [*Wearily*] And now—it is all over.

Den. Nonsense. I don't want you to leave him—that is, not yet.

Mary. And do you suppose I would pass another day under his roof knowing that I am not his wife?

Den. Why not? He has certain deeds [to property] that I must get. You can help me in this. Then we will clear out forever.

Mary. Shame! When will your evil heart grasp the fact that I am not your tool?

Den. Sh-h! [*Wright appears at door*] As you say, your husband is a prince among men. I do not wonder you are proud of him. [*Wright, thinking he has been unobserved, quietly exits house*]

Mary. What treachery!

Den. [*Smiling*] Diplomacy, my dear.

Mary. One word from me to the man you are so basely deceiving, and he would kill you.

Den. Yes. I am aware of his bloodthirsty tendencies, therefore I have no thought of allowing you to tell him. Suppose I took to supplying him with past history. For instance, you spoke of your virtuous struggles from the time I left you until you married Wright, but I learned today that when you came to him you had a child.

Mary. Why that child is—

Den. There, there. I don't care for explanations; they are tiresome. Enough that I know you—and you know me. At present I am in something of a hole—shady transaction back East. I had to leave suddenly. Wright has the very deeds I was supposed to have forged. By hook or crook I must have them. I came here, never dreaming of finding my charming consort of sixteen years ago. Fortune favors me. You will be of great assistance.

Mary. [*Rises*] Enough. I will at once inform my husband. [*Starts*]

Den. He is not your husband. You are a bigamist. One word from me will land you in jail.

Mary. Do you think I care for that? I will tell the truth. Take the consequences—and let you do the same.

Den. But the boy—he has a home, a *name*. What would he think of you if he knew.

Mary. My boy!

Den. Be reasonable—for his sake.

Mary. I will keep your secret today. Tonight I will take my boy and leave this place forever.

Den. You'll help me get the papers and go with me, eh?

Mary. You contemptible cur—*No*, I would rather die.

Den. Curse your tongue. Take care or I'll—[*Raises hand to strike*]

Mary. Oh, no, you won't. You are too cowardly to strike me. You know there are those who would call you to a swift account for assaulting me. You will vent your spite on the woman you have so cruelly wronged, in a more cowardly fashion and at a time when there will be no one to aid her.

Den. You're right, I will. [*Mary exits*] Oh, I'll get even. I'll touch her heart. She's soft on her boy. Mothers always are. [*Laughs*] I'll lead that boy to a life of dissipation—crime, if I can manage it.

226

Oh, I'll touch her to the quick. I'll shrivel her heart up like the blackened embers of a discarded camp fire. How I hate her brat. I could kill him by inches. I'd like to tear his heart out! I'd like to—[*His hand is raised above his head. Enter Bill L.I.E. Denver changes manner*]—to take you by the hand, my dear boy. I've heard so much of you. [*They shake hands*]

Bill. From Con?

Den. Why—ah—yes, from Con.

Bill. Well, don't believe anything he tells you. He's the biggest liar in the state.

Den. [*Laughs*] I don't believe he exaggerated in your case.

Bill. Well, if he didn't, it was an accident but he means it for the best. He's my pal.

Den. Considerable difference in your ages, for pals, don't you think?

Bill. Oh, that don't make any difference. You see I never had any boys to associate with. I have been brought up with men. [*Crosses to table*]

Den. Con said you were as much of a man as any of them. What do you intend to become—a scout?

Bill. A pirate.

Den. [*Laughs*] A pirate?

Bill. That's what Con and I play we are going to be. [*Laughs*] It's only in fun, sir.

Den. But you are too big and brave a lad to play at adventure, why not have a real one? Let's have a drink?

Bill. No, sir, I never—

Den. What! You don't mean to say that a man like you never—? Oh I see, don't want the old folks to know, eh? Well, you can trust me. Here, take a drink.

Bill. [*Flattered, takes bottle*] Guess I can stand a pull. [*Drinks*]

Den. The people around here don't appreciate you, not even your father. I hear you are a fine shot.

Bill. Oh, I can shoot some, sir.

Den. I'll wager you can. What sort of a gun do you use?

Bill. This one. [*Shows Colt*]

Den. [*Takes it*] Oh, a Colt. An old out-of-date pattern, too. [*Tosses it on table*] Let me show you something modern. [*Takes pistol from pocket*] See; a double-acting, self-cocking, shell-extracting revolver. [*Hands it to Bill*]

Bill. Gee! What a beauty!

Den. It shall be yours if you are the lad of spirit I take you to be. [*Takes pistol, puts it in pocket*] Now let's play a little joke on your father, just to show him the stuff you are made of.

Bill. [*Drinks. Shows a recklessness from the effects*] I'm your man—what is it?

Den. You know he keeps his private papers in the—ah—

Bill. Little safe in his bedroom.

Den. That's it. Of course you don't know the combination—

Bill. Oh, but I do though.

Den. All the better. Now here's the plan. Your father has boasted there is not a man in the state who would dare hold him up for anything. And as for cracksmen, he defies the cream of them to get anything from his safe. Now, if you will get all his papers—don't touch the money, that would be stealing—but just the papers, and bring them to me, I will tell your father there is one man in the state that was a match for him and show him the papers to support my statement. He, of course, will be thunderstruck, and when he asks who this wonderful fellow is, I will introduce, Billy, the Prince of the Road. [*Laughs*] What do you think of it?

Bill. [*Laughs*] That would be a fine joke, wouldn't it? I believe I'll try it.

Den. Of course you'll try it. You couldn't let such an opportunity slip.

Bill. When shall we do it?

Den. Tonight. They will all leave the house in a few moments to see the Colonel start for home. That is our opportunity. Get a piece of black cloth and make yourself a mask. Saddle your horse and tie him yonder. After the folks leave the house, you slip in the back way. Now go.

Bill. [*Starts*] Won't Con be surprised? My, but that stuff makes you dizzy, don't it?—and Mose laughed at me. I'll make them all proud of me yet. [*Exits L.U.E.*]

Den. Fool! When I get the papers, I'll set the officers on his track. Two birds with one stone—the papers, and the mother's heart broken over a worthless boy. . . .

[*Enter Mary from the house, followed by Wright*]

Wri. Mary! For God's sake listen to me. You do not—you cannot mean that you are going to leave me forever.

Mary. Don't question me, I must.

Wri. Oh, I do not need an explanation. [*Bitterly*] Youth weds with old age. It could not last. I might have known it.

Mary. Stephen, it is not that. God knows I love you better than all the world. But I must leave you.

Wri. But why—why if you love me?

Mary. I cannot explain. It would kill me—it would kill us both.

Wri. You do not mean—disgrace?

Mary. Yes. [*Wright sinks on porch, overcome*] My heart is breaking. I must go. [*Staggers to C.*]

Den. [*Enter R.U.E. not seeing Wright*] Yes, and you go alone.

Mary. I am going with my boy.

Den. You can't. He's going to jail.

Mary. What do you mean?

Den. That I acted on your suggestion, refrained from blows and struck at your heart. By this time your son is a criminal and answerable to the law.

Mary. [*Half screams*] What have you done?

Den. Revenged myself—on your son.

Mary. And yours as well. Fool, could not your cold heart have prompted the truth? He was your own child. You have sent your own flesh and blood to destruction.

Den. You lie.

Mary. I speak the truth.

Wri. [*Who has overheard. Rising*] What does this mean? [*Denver frightened*]

Mary. It means that there stands the man who blighted my past as well as my present happiness. It means that he is Boyd Bradley, my husband, and the father of my boy.

Wri. Wait a bit, wait a bit. I can't seem to get these things straight somehow.

Den. [*Drawing revolver*] Then get it through your head quickly. She is my wife and she is going with me.

Wri. [*Low and intense*] So—this is the man who caused my Mary's unhappiness—the man we thought dead. And now he returns to wreck afresh the life of the woman who trusted him. [*Slowly approaches Denver*]

Den. Be careful. Keep your distance. I am armed.

Wri. And do you think I care for that? All the weapons this side of Hell couldn't keep my fingers from your throat. [*Wright grapples with Denver. They struggle. Mary screams, goes down R. Revolver explodes, killing Mary. They struggle toward the well. Denver gets his pistol hand free and shoots Wright. He falls half in well, head first. Denver stands frightened, looking around*]

Den. It was self-defense—he tried to murder me—he threatened to kill me—Mary heard him. [*Sees Mary*] Mary! Fainted! [*Goes to her*] Dead! God! I did not mean it. I did not mean it. [*Overcome, sinks on knees. Suddenly starts up*] They'll lynch me. [*Crying*] I am innocent. It was an accident and self-defense. They'll not believe it—they'll not believe it. [*In frenzy*] I must get rid of the bodies somehow. The old well—thirty feet deep and dark as a pocket. [*Throws Wright in*] My revolver, this must not be found. [*Drops it in well*] They will fill the well and all traces will be lost. His property will go to my wife—she is dead. But the boy—he stands between me and a fortune. Pshaw! He is an outlaw! I will put him where he will never trouble me again.

Bill. [*Enters from house, black mask on*] Here are the papers—why, what is the matter? [*Drops papers*] Mother! [*Runs to her*] Mother,

Mother, speak to me! [*Looks up in agony, husky voice*] Mr. Denver—look at me—look me in the face. What has done this?

Den. I—I—don't—know.

Bill. You are not speaking the truth. Where is my father?

Den. You mother was going to leave him—they had a quarrel—and—

Bill. [*Half screams*] Answer me. Did my father do this?

Den. Your father! Your father? [*Realizing that he is the boy's father*] Your—father—yes!

Bill. [*Strong, but not loud*] I do not believe it.

Den. As God is my judge, I speak the truth.

Bill. My father shall be found. From his lips I will learn the truth.

Den. But you have no time for this. Do you realize that you are an outlaw? You have robbed your father's safe. Who will believe you did not kill your mother in an attempt to escape?

Bill. You scoundrel!

Den. I know you are innocent, but will the law believe it, too? Make good your escape and leave me to find your father. I will take good charge of these. [*Stoops for papers Bill has dropped*]

Bill. [*Takes pistol from table*] Drop those papers. [*Denver does so*] My mind is dazed by this calamity. But one thing I know, the guilty shall be made to suffer. It shall be the one object of my life. [*Kneels before Mary*] Mother, if you can hear me from above, record my oath of vengeance. And you—[*To Denver*] You who have plotted my destruction shall live to hear the outlaw you have created. Go, and leave me with my dead. [*Falls over body of Mary*] Mother! Mother! [*Denver slinks off L.U.E.*]

230

"He would sacrifice the lives of a hundred men who stood between him and liberty, when the gallows stared him in the face."

Billy the Kid Was a Sociopath

Pat Garrett (1850-1908)

Sheriff Pat Garrett put an end to the career of Billy the Kid (William Bonney), shooting him on July 14, 1881. The Kid's death, however, only began another life, in legend. One of the first to capitalize on Bonney's notoriety, Garrett published *The Authentic Life . . .* in 1882. One would think Garrett, having firsthand knowledge of the Kid, would write either an objective account or one strongly biased against him. Instead, the book expresses both admiration and revulsion for the man Garrett later killed. Garrett portrays Billy as starting his outlaw life as the result of a misguided sense of chivalry toward his mother. However, even in depicting this act of chivalry, Garrett shows Billy's lack of regret at shedding blood.

Garrett's book was largely ghostwritten by an eastern newspaperman, Ash Upsom, who in all likelihood dramatized people and events to keep the interest of his largely eastern readers. Nevertheless, his portrayal, through Garrett's eyes, shows Billy the Kid to be an unremitting sociopath.

From *The Authentic Life of Billy, the Kid* by Pat Garrett. New edition © 1954 by the University of Oklahoma Press.

When young Bonney was about twelve years of age, he first imbrued his hand in human blood. This affair, it may be said, was the turning point in his life, outlawed him, and gave him over a victim of his worser impulses and passions.

As Billy's mother was passing a knot of idlers on the street, a filthy loafer in the crowd made an insulting remark about her. Billy heard it and quick as thought, with blazing eyes, he planted a stinging blow on the blackguard's mouth, then springing to the street, stooped for a rock. The brute made a rush for him, but as he passed Ed. Moulton, a well-known citizen of Silver City, he received a stunning blow on the ear which felled him, whilst Billy was caught and restrained. However, the punishment inflicted on the offender by no means satisfied Billy. Burning for revenge, he visited a miner's cabin, procured a Sharp's rifle, and started in search of his intended victim. By good fortune, Moulton saw him with the gun, and, with some difficulty, persuaded him to return it.

Some three weeks subsequent to this adventure, Moulton, who was a wonderfully powerful and active man, skilled in the art of self-defense, and with something of the prize-fighter in his composition, became involved in a rough-and-tumble bar-room fight, at Joe Dyer's saloon. He had two shoulder-strikers to contend with and was getting the best of both of them, when Billy's "antipathy" [the man who had insulted his mother]—the man who had been the recipient of one of Moulton's "lifters," standing by, thought he saw an opportunity to take cowardly revenge on Moulton, and rushed upon him with a heavy bar-room chair upraised. Billy was usually a spectator, when not a principal, to any fight which might occur in the town, and this one was no exception. He saw the motion, and like lightning darted beneath the chair—once, twice, thrice, his arm rose and fell—then, rushing through the crowd, his right hand above his head, grasping a pocket-knife, its blade dripping with gore, he went out into the night, an outcast and a wanderer, a murderer, self-baptized in human blood. He went out like banished Cain, yet less fortunate than the first murderer, there was no curse pronounced against his slayer. His hand was now against every man, and every man's hand against him. He went out forever from the care, the love, and influence of a fond mother, for he was never to see her face again—she who had so lovingly reared him, and whom he had so tenderly and reverently loved. Never more shall her soft hand smooth his ruffled brow, whilst soothing words charm from his swelling heart the wrath he nurses. No mentor, no love to restrain his evil passion or check his desperate hand—what must be his fate? . . .

The Kid Escapes from Jail

[Several years later] on the evening of April 28, 1881, Olinger took all the other prisoners across the street to supper, leaving Bell in charge of the Kid in the guard-room. We have but the Kid's tale, and the sparse information elicited from Mr. Geiss, a German employed about the building, to determine the facts in regard to events immediately following Olinger's departure. From circumstances, indications, information from Geiss, and the Kid's admissions, the popular conclusion is that:

At the Kid's request, Bell accompanied him down stairs and into the back corral. As they returned, Bell allowed the Kid to get considerably in advance. As the Kid turned on the landing of the stairs, he was hidden from Bell. He was light and active, and, with a few noiseless bounds, reached the head of the stairs, turned to the right, put his shoulder to the door of the room used as an armory (though locked, this door was well known to open by a firm push), entered, seized a six-shooter, returned to the head of the stairs just as Bell faced him on the landing of the staircase, some twelve steps beneath, and fired. Bell turned, ran out into the corral and towards the little gate. He fell dead before reaching it. The Kid ran to the window at the south end of the hall, saw Bell fall, then slipped his handcuffs over his hands, threw them at the body, and said:—"Here, d—n you, take these, too." He then ran to my office and got a double-barreled shotgun. This gun was a very fine one, a breech-loader, and belonged to Olinger. He had loaded it that morning, in presence of the Kid, putting eighteen buckshot in each barrel, and remarked:—"The man that gets one of those loads will feel it." The Kid then entered the guard-room and stationed himself at the east window, opening on the yard.

Olinger heard the shot and started back across the street, accompanied by L.M. Clements. Olinger entered the gate leading into the yard, as Geiss appeared at the little corral gate and said, "Bob, the Kid has killed Bell." At the same instant the Kid's voice was heard above: "Hello, old boy," said he. "Yes, and he's killed me, too," exclaimed Olinger, and fell dead, with eighteen buckshot in his right shoulder and breast and side. The Kid went back through the guard-room, through my office, into the hall, and out on the balcony. From here he could see the body of Olinger, as it lay on the projecting corner of the yard, near the gate. He took deliberate aim and fired the other barrel, the charge taking effect in nearly the same place as the first; then breaking the gun across the railing of the balcony, he threw the pieces at Olinger, saying:—"Take it, d—n you, you won't follow me any more with that gun." He then returned to the back room, armed himself

Obituaries

Billy the Kid's death was widely reported. In these two obituaries, he is shown as a bloodthirsty young outlaw.

DESPERADO DIES IN WESTERN GUN PLAY

W.H. Bonney, known as Billy the Kid, the scourge of the south-west, met his death from a bullet fired by Patrick F. Garrett, sheriff of Lincoln County, New Mexico, when the latter met him face to face in the dining room of the home of Pedro B. Maxwell, wealthy Pecos Valley cattle man. Garrett's quick action saved Maxwell's life, for the blood thirsty young outlaw had ridden into Fort Sumner with murder in his heart. Maxwell refused to admit that the Kid had made any attempt upon his life, but it is a well-known fact that the former murderer had boasted that he had several men yet to kill, among them such notable figures as John Chisum and Governor Lew Wallace.

Bonney, who was born in Brooklyn, had slain twenty-one men and was twenty-one years old when Garrett's shot ended his fiendish career.

—The New York *Sun*

DESPERADO TRAPPED IN LAIR OF LUXURY

With fangs snarling and firing a revolver like a maniac, W.H. Bonney (alias Billy the Kid) fought his way out of his ambushed robber castle at Stinking Spring where he lived in luxury of his ill gotten gains with his Mexican beauties, only to meet his end at a bullet from Sheriff Pat F. Garrett. The outlaw's gang fled over the prairie and Garrett's posse gave chase, but with their youthful leader in his death throes the lesser desperadoes surrendered. Billy the Kid had built up a criminal organization worthy of the underworld of any of the European capitals. He defied the law to stop him and he stole, robbed, raped, and pillaged the countryside until his name became synonymous with that of the grim reaper himself. A Robin Hood with no mercy, a Richard the Lion Hearted who feasted on blood, he became, in the short span of his twenty-one years, the master criminal of the American Southwest. His passing marks the end of wild west lawlessness and Sheriff Garrett well earns the stunning fortune awaiting the man who had the courage to capture this desperado, dead or alive.

—The *Daily Graphic*

with a Winchester and two revolvers. He was still encumbered with his shackles, but hailing old man Geiss, he commanded him to bring a file. Geiss did so, and threw it up to him in the window. The Kid then ordered the old man to go and saddle a horse that was in the stable, the property of Billy Burt, deputy clerk of probate, then went to a front window, commanding a view of the street, seated himself, and filed the shackles from one leg. Bob. Brookshire came out on the street from the hotel opposite, and started down towards the plaza. The Kid brought his Winchester down on him and said:—"Go back, young fellow, go back. I don't want to hurt you, but I am fighting for my life. I don't want to see anybody leave that house."

In the meantime, Geiss was having trouble with the horse, which broke loose and ran around the corral and yard awhile, but was at last brought to the front of the house. The Kid was all over the building, on the porch, and watching from the windows. He danced about the balcony, laughed, and shouted as though he had not a care on earth. He remained at the house for nearly an hour after the killing before he made a motion to leave. As he approached to mount, the horse again broke loose and ran towards the Rio Bonito. The Kid called to Andrew Nimley, a prisoner, who was standing by, to go and catch him. Nimley hesitated, but a quick, imperative motion by the Kid started him. He brought the horse back and the Kid remarked:—"Old fellow, if you hadn't gone for this horse, I would have killed you." And now he mounted and said to those in hearing:—"Tell Billy Burt I will send his horse back to him," then galloped away, the shackles still hanging to one leg. He was armed with a Winchester and two revolvers. He took the road west, leading to Fort Stanton, but turned north about four miles from town and rode in the direction of Las Tablas.

It is in order to again visit the scene of this tragedy. It was found that Bell was hit under the right arm, the ball passing through the body and coming out under the left arm. On examination it was evident that the Kid had made a very poor shot, for him, and his hitting Bell at all was a scratch. The ball had hit the wall on Bell's right, caromed, passed through his body, and buried itself in an adobe on his left. There was other proof besides the marks on the wall. The ball had surely been indented and creased before it entered the body, as these scars were filled with flesh. The Kid afterwards told Peter Maxwell that Bell shot at him twice and just missed him. There is no doubt but this statement was false. One other shot was heard before Olinger appeared on the scene, but it is believed to have been an accidental one by the Kid whilst prospecting with the arms. Olinger was shot in the right shoulder, breast, and side. He was literally riddled by thirty-six buckshot.

The inhabitants of the whole town of Lincoln appeared to be terror-stricken. The Kid, it is my firm belief, could have ridden up and down the plaza until dark without a shot having been fired at him, nor an attempt made to arrest him. A little sympathy might have actuated some of them, but most of the people were, doubtless, paralyzed with fear when it was whispered that the dreaded desperado, the Kid, was at liberty and had slain his guards.

This, to me, was a most distressing calamity, for which I do not hold myself guiltless. The Kid's escape, and the murder of his two guards, was the result of mismanagement and carelessness, to a great extent. I knew the desperate character of the man whom the authorities would look for at my hands on the 13th day of May—that he was daring and unscrupulous, and that he would sacrifice the lives of a hundred men who stood between him and liberty, when the gallows stared him in the face, with as little compunction as he would kill a coyote.

CHAPTER 6

The Frontier and Today's Popular Culture

Chapter Preface

Those who gathered at the annual meeting of the American Historical Association in 1893 in Chicago listened to a number of papers, among them Frederick Jackson Turner's "The Significance of the Frontier in American History." But after the meetings were over, the delegates found all kinds of entertainment at the World's Columbian Exposition on the shores of Lake Michigan. They could ride the Ferris wheel, ogle belly dancers, or dance to the ragtime music of Scott Joplin. They could enjoy reenactments of stagecoach robberies and Indian war dances at Buffalo Bill Cody's Wild West Show. Or they could gaze in awe at a segment of the 2500-year-old General Noble Tree, a giant sequoia felled for the exhibition to create national pride—and to encourage tourism. In short, the historians, like throngs of other fairgoers, could have immersed themselves in the popular culture of the day. Thus it is appropriate that this chapter, examining the impact of the frontier on today's popular culture, concludes a volume that began with Turner.

One hundred years after Turner presented his paper, the frontier and its influence permeate American society. Elements of the frontier sustain us—literally and figuratively. We barbecue; we pour Log Cabin syrup on our pancakes; we snack on Tombstone pizza and "run for the border" to Taco Bell. Though most of us may be ignorant of which end of a cow to lasso, we wear blue jeans, blanket coats, and cowboy boots; splash on Chaps or Stetson cologne; and take lessons in country line dancing. Broncos and Cherokees and Trailblazers line our driveways. Our sports teams—the Cowboys and Forty-Niners and Redskins—echo our frontier heritage and, sometimes, its hurts, as was seen in some native American responses to the Atlanta Braves' baseball fans' "tomahawk chop." The Warner Brothers catalog offers Looney Tunes characters, replete with cowboy hats, on a set of six barbecue skewers; Disney has a Mickey Mouse lariat watch. Dozens of local historical societies sponsor reenactments like the "Market and Musket Days at the David Crabill Homestead . . . a hands-on chance to learn about life on the Ohio frontier." All this, of course, is in addition to scores of books, a resurgence of Western films (*Dances with Wolves, The Last of the Mohicans, Unforgiven, Posse*), and the enormously popular TV series *Dr. Quinn, Medicine Woman*. The frontier seems to be everywhere.

Pop culture is predicated on knowledge and familiarity. Its vitality comes from the shock of recognition that occurs when a society looks at itself in the mirror. It echoes the hopes, dreams, and aspirations, values, strengths, and pride of a people. Looking at pop culture closely gives insights into who we are. William H. Savage Jr. wrote of cowboy songs: "Songs are demonstrably social documents. . . . Lyric analysis is one way to identify attitudes in social history." And so it is with movies, fashion, and advertising as explored in this chapter.

The frontier is part of our national history, yes, helping to define us as a people, but it is also a touchstone for a redefinition and reaffirmation of ourselves. In this sense, it is no less a catalyst for intellectual discussion and popular entertainment than it was a century ago.

VIEWPOINT 1

"If the Western hero had been conceived as an Arthurian knight of the plains, he ended up more closely resembling a cocaine dealer in cowboy drag."

The Western Film Is Merely Entertainment

Geoffrey O'Brien

The current proliferation of Western films and TV series, as well as scholarly and popular books on the frontier, suggests that Americans are once again finding the frontier a source of entertainment and a valid subject for research. Geoffrey O'Brien, writing in the *New York Review*, uses his discussion of five new books (*West of Everything: The Inner Life of Westerns* by Jane Tompkins, *Western Films: A Complete Guide* by Brian Garfield, *Box-Office Buckaroos: The Cowboy Hero from the Wild West Show to the Silver Screen* by Robert Heide and John Gilman, *The BFI Companion to the Western* edited by Edward Buscombe, and *The Western* edited by Phil Hardy) as the springboard for a general discussion of the Western film. He argues that Western movies were simplistic clichés, providing a "delusory aura of realness," giving a wide variety of people simple diversion, and suggesting underlying boredom, claustrophobia, emotional deprivation, and male domination.

If, as Brian Garfield's reviewed book suggests, one may distinguish between "New Yorkers and Europeans" on the one hand and "real Westerners" on the other, this review clearly belongs to the former. We might remember that, from the very beginning of the frontier experience, some people preferred to remain comfortably in an urban setting while others lived the frontier experience. John Jacob Astor and Francis Chardon are only one illustration of this dichotomy between "real Westerners" and others. O'Brien, like Astor, profits vicariously.

What did Josef Stalin and Douglas MacArthur, Ludwig Wittgenstein and Sherwood Anderson, Jorge Luis Borges, Akira Kurosawa, and the janitor of a rooming house I once lived in have in common? They all loved Westerns. Such a taste was a leveling factor of modern culture, cutting across classes and nationalities. Whether as pulp stories, novels, movies, or television shows, Westerns were basic cultural wallpaper for most of the century, offering the simplest of simple pleasures: a fist fight on the roof of a stagecoach, a body falling out of a window, a man drinking from a river, a horse crossing a plain at full gallop.

Westerns were reliable, minimal, direct, mindless, a series of clear actions occurring in an empty world where there was ultimately nothing to worry about. Indians, outlaws, rustlers, and crooked railroad men emerged out of nowhere and were duly erased. A Western was not expected to depart from precedent any more than a baseball game would experiment with new rules or novel plays. The genre was an antidote to complexity, enjoyed precisely because of its apparent lack of any subtext to parse or interpret. Ironically, the simplest of genres ultimately succumbed to a host of problems it had never anticipated: problems with history, with gender roles, with racial stereotypes, with faded notions of heroism and honor.

When Jean-Luc Godard, in an enthusiastic review of Anthony Mann's *Man of the West* (1958), called the Western "the most cinematic of cinematic genres" he did not add that it is also the most generic, or consider whether repetition and formula might be crucial to his notion of the "cinematic." All that movies really have in the way of tradition has come from reenacting the same situations, the same fights and chases and fires, decade after decade. In 1958 a movie like *Man of the West* exerted emotional power simply by being there, by displaying its monolithic title on the marquee, by starring an aging Gary Cooper, whose face belonged, according to Godard, to "the mineral kingdom." Having maintained its simple repertoire of images and devices with less visible change than any other genre, the Western was symbolic home, a last living link with the primordial pre-cinematic world.

The movies were of course only the most prominent feature of a huge stretch of territory encompassing battle sites, ghost towns, and federally protected rock formations; tourist attractions ranging from Walt Disney's Frontierland to woebegone theme parks like New Jersey's Wild West City, where you can still see the marshall confront the outlaws on Main Street at high noon; plastic figurines of cowboys and Indians, toy six-guns, tom-toms, war bonnets; Vaughan Monroe singing "Ghost Riders in the Sky" and Sonny Rollins playing "I'm an Old Cow Hand." The clichés have been so thoroughly absorbed that they are almost ready to become exotic again, as exotic as childhood pictures of one's grandparents.

Whatever aura of authenticity Westerns possessed arose from the piling up of fantasies in a cultural compost: Buffalo Bill dime novels, the lyrics of "Get Along Old Paint" and "Streets of Laredo," the paintings of Remington and Russell, Owen Wister's Virginian, Zane Grey's Lassiter, Clarence Mulford's Hopalong Cassidy, movie heroes from William S. Hart and Tom Mix to Gene Autry and Roy Rogers, the radio exploits of The Lone Ranger. After a while it seemed as if there must be something real at the bottom of all that. How else could it have stayed around so long?

The Beginning of the End of the Western

In the period after World War II Westerns enjoyed renewed popularity, indicating perhaps a nostalgia for the certitudes they had once offered; but they also evolved and mutated at a pace suggesting a desire to try out all the genre's possibilities, to get to the root of it once and for all. The years between 1945 and 1960 encompassed the golden age of a form which turned out to be ideally suited to the entertainment needs of cold war America, offering history as escape, violence as morality, and "adult" and "psychological" elements as proof that everyone had gotten a little bit more mature.

They also, in an era of ostensible political consensus, provided a field where ambiguity and dissension could flourish. Since from the outside they all looked the same, Westerns made excellent cover for a wide range of peculiarities and hidden messages. There were McCarthyist Westerns (*Springfield Rifle*), anti-McCarthyist Westerns (*Silver Lode*), antiracist Westerns (*Walk the Proud Land*), racist Westerns (*Arrowhead*), homoerotic Westerns (*Johnny Guitar*), sadomasochist Westerns (*Valerie*). From a commercial point of view they were all salable. Location shooting, flexible color cinematography, and wide-screen formats gave even the oldest plots a new look, making it possible to remake old B pictures as major-motion-picture events. Along the way an astonishing number of excellent movies, large and small, managed to get made.

Just at that moment, when the Western's durability was becoming an axiom of film criticism, it was in reality nearly exhausted. A decade of cinematic oversaturation was followed by an onslaught of television shows: *Have Gun Will Travel, Maverick, Gunsmoke, The Rifleman, Rawhide.* In 1958 there were thirty-one Westerns running in prime time. This sustained plundering of the genre's resources had by 1960 pretty much run it dry. The generation that grew up in the 1950s knew the mechanics and conventions so well that new forms of excess and rule breaking were required to maintain excitement.

The fifteen-year decline and fall of the Western (roughly between 1960 and 1975) was for many more interesting than what came before, punctuated as it was by the spectacular contributions of Sam Peckinpah and Sergio Leone. It certainly featured more unrestrained violence, went to new lengths to create an aura of historical accuracy, and agonized in unprecedented fashion over the ultimate purpose and significance of the form. Far more conscious creative effort went into the Western's decadence than was expended on its heyday. Even the worst of the "revisionist" and "dirty" anti-Westerns were at least remarkable for the pretentiousness of their ambitions. Unfortunately, when the rules went, audience interest went not long afterward. A genre that was essentially based on seeing how many changes could be rung on a small set of unvarying elements lost its point when granted absolute freedom.

One of the things that helped kill off the Western was the quest for realism and historical accuracy. Westerns had always had a connection, however oblique, to a notion of reality. As Jane Tompkins remarks in her study *West of Everything: The Inner Life of Westerns,* "Westerns satisfy a hunger to be in touch with something absolutely real," a statement as applicable to *The Great Train Robbery* as to *Dances with Wolves.* Even the gushingly sentimental novels of Zane Grey satisfy, in between times, a craving for grittiness: skillets, stirrups, cattle tracks, dry boulders, the smell of sagebrush and leather. Western writers and film makers often practiced a stringent but selective accuracy with regard to the minutiae of horses or firearms or wagon wheels, no matter how fantastic and ahistorical the context in which those details were set.

"Delusory Realness"

That delusory aura of realness was the product that was being sold. Westerns were created for the benefit of audiences remote—at first geographically, and then temporally—from the settling of the West. From history the genre borrowed settings and props for a game of make-believe; it has had little further connection with anything that actually happened in the nineteenth-century West. Not that Westerns are indifferent to history; on the contrary, they are excited by it, and by the pretense that they are connected to it. Its artifacts, from watch fobs to Winchesters, provide fetishistic embellishment for narratives that otherwise exist completely outside of history.

Actor Gary Cooper (foreground) shoots it out in the 1950s Western Man of the West. *Movies have tended to romanticize life in the Old West.*

From time to time, fresh infusions of the real helped spice the fantasy. For one generation, authenticity might be represented by the folksy humor of Gabby Hayes or Smiley Burnett, for another by the luxurious pseudohistoricism of romantic pageants like *Jesse James* (1939) and *They Died with Their Boots On* (1942). The innovative although vague psychosexual furies of *Duel in the Sun* (1946) and *Pursued* (1947) gave way to the self-congratulatory tolerance of *Broken Arrow* (1951) and the "mature" social questioning of *High Noon* (1952). By the late 1950s, the Western tended to demonstrate its maturity by introducing themes of sexual violence (*Jubal, The Bravados, Man of the West, Last Train from Gun Hill*) and racial conflict (*Trooper Hook, Flaming Star, Sergeant Rutledge, The Unforgiven*). It was only when film makers began to suffer from the delusion that they were reconstructing the way things really were that the genre started to lose its reason for existing.

One might possibly be able to make a movie that hewed closely to the known facts of life in the Old West, but such a movie would have nothing in common with Westerns, and it is unlikely that many people would go to see it. "The West was not dull," writes Evan S. Connell in *Son of the Morning Star*. "It was stupendously dull, and when it was not dull it was murderous." Speaking of the southwestern cavalry life that provides the setting for so many movies, an actual participant (Second Lieutenant John G. Bourke) lingers on "sickness, heat, bad water, flies, sand-storms, and utter isolation," and concludes: "The humdrum life of any post in Arizona in those days was enough to drive one crazy." The question then is not so much whether it would be possible to recreate such a past as what would be the point of doing so. The Western had a point, ignoble as it might appear: to provide a rather simple diversion for the widest number of people, in which deserts and mountains, functioned more or less as the seacoast of Bohemia or the forest of Arden. Any deeper concern with history, myth, or moral struggle evolved late in the game.

America Does Not Own the Western

Yet no one can let it rest quite like that. The Western is a largely childish entertainment that trespasses on something that almost everyone wants a piece of. It's history whether it wants to be or not, if only the history of its own diffusion: it speaks for a huge stretch of still contested territory. So the critical corpus that has grown up around it reflects a more or less openly acknowledged state of war. What's up for grabs is the story that will be told about America and by extension about the modern world: the Western is, by default, the heritage of the global communications tribe which this century has created, a tribe flung together haphazardly by the forces of technology and mass culture.

In that culture, the Western is common property that anyone can appropriate, an international artifact making itself at home in anyone's culture. *Shane* is as much a Japanese movie as it is American, and *Django* as much a Jamaican movie as it is Italian. For that matter, Billy the Kid belongs as much to modernist artists like Aaron Copland and Jack Spicer as to King Vidor and Sam Peckinpah. The process has been international and self-consciously aesthetic from the start. Balzac absorbed Cooper, Karl May created Teutonic transpositions of the frontier myth which continue to fuel a subculture of German Wild West aficionados. Puccini turned the Golden West into aria. A comprehensive history of the Western would not pass over the childlike pulp novelist in Renoir's *Le Crime de Monsieur Lange* (1935), exulting in his fantasies of Arizona Jim, or Anna Magnani in Visconti's *Bellissima* (1951), watching *Red River* in a Roman slum and becoming jubilant over a scene of cattle wading through a river: "Look! The cows are all getting wet! It's marvelous!"

America does not own the Western any more than the "real" Westerners do. This is not to deny the special qualities associated with that all-male subculture of genre specialists chiefly responsible for the Western's greatest glories, described by the screenwriter Burt Kennedy as "a kind of dynasty, to which those New York types who make all the movies nowadays will never belong." The dynasty was real—as immersed in the conventions of the cowboy picture as a Noh actor in the contemplation of his mask—but it was a dynasty of tricksters and fabricators. They knew all there was to know about how a hero should seem.

Brian Garfield, a writer of Western novels (including the excellent *Sliphammer*) and author of the knowledgeable but singularly ill-tempered *Western Films: A Complete Guide*, distinguishes between "New Yorkers and Europeans" on the one hand and real Westerners on the other, among whom he is careful to include "others, not born to the saddle, [who] westernized themselves so thoroughly that—like religious converts—they became more native than the natives themselves"—this latter obviously a crucial category, since it includes John Wayne, John Ford, and Randolph Scott. The reference to religious conversion establishes the zealous undertone of Garfield's remarks, with their desire to exclude the inauthentic and unworthy from the claim he has staked.

What's at issue is not so much the right to assert what really happened in history as the right to fool around with history, a right jealously guarded. What actually exists within the protected zone of those who felt themselves privileged to interpret the West turns out, if we look at the biographies of Ford or Peckinpah, to be little more than a boy's world of drunken brawls and rough practical jokes. John Wayne pouring vodka on Ward Bond's chest and setting it on fire, or an increasingly sodden and coked-up Sam Peckinpah practicing between takes the manly art of knife throwing. As Louis L'Amour put it, "When you open a rough, hard country, you don't open it with a lot of pantywaists." What can the land tamers do then, after the country has been opened, except go to seed or make Westerns?

Psychological Dysfunction in the Western

Random violence and drunkenness suggest the underlying boredom which is the emotional basis of Westerns. They are basically about killing time; they are what there was to do in town, in America, year after year. Jane Tompkins's *West of Everything*, a disarmingly direct, utterly unironic look at what makes the genre tick, raises the right kind of questions. Rather than getting caught up in the mare's nest of historical accuracy, she considers first of all not where the Western gets its images from, but what use readers and viewers make of those images: "One must begin with their impact on the body and the emotions."

She begins by talking about pleasure and so naturally within a few paragraphs she is talking about pain: the pain of horses, of cattle, of women condemned to powerlessness and men self-condemned to silence and punishment. With reference to Louis L'Amour's heroes she writes:

> It is the ability to endure pain for a long time that saves him. . . . Protagonists crawl across deserts on their hands and knees, climb rock faces in the blinding sun, starve in snowbound cabins in the mountains, walk or ride for miles on end with all but mortal wounds, survive for long periods of time without water, without shelter, without sleep.

If the Western is in some fundamental sense a meditation on deprivation and suffering, the chief deprivation is emotional. The dryness and rigidity of the Western hero has to do with a refusal to express feeling in words: "The Western itself is the language of men, what they do vicariously, instead of speaking." Aissa Wayne's memoir, *John Wayne, My Father*, chimes in, as if in confirmation: "What made living with my father hard, and unnerving, was that he mostly suppressed what was churning inside him. To his family, he rarely expressed his inner feelings, or even admitted he had them. With all that bottled emotion, its release often came in the form of misdirected rage."

Tompkins sees the genre as part of a war on women's words, on the women's culture of temperance and etiquette and civic responsibility, on nineteenth-century Christian culture as a female stronghold. "The Western doesn't have anything to do with the West as such. . . . It is about men's fear of losing their mastery, and hence their identity, both of which the Western tirelessly reinvents." But of course it isn't all invention: Westerns invent very little, tending rather to reenact the tensions and anxieties that define the universal male culture of playgrounds, locker rooms, army barracks, and prison yards. If the Western hero is on the run, it isn't only from women but also from the aggression of other men.

The openness of the wide open spaces serves as a means of protection. The Western landscape is a place where the hero can get lost, hide out forever from everything, starting with language. (Tompkins speaks of the desert as "the place where language fails and rocks assert themselves.") It may be hard for generations who have grown up in a world without Westerns to realize how much the childish perception of landscape was formerly colored by the Western's use of forest, canyon, and mesa. Cowboy pictures provided an education in what space is for.

Or rather they repackaged an education initiated by generations of explorers, like John Wesley Powell writing in the Grand

Canyon: "After dinner we pass through a region of the wildest desolation." The marketing of wilderness, with Indians removed and guard rails in place, opened up a new space for fantasy in the minds of consumers. The extraordinarily popular fiction of Zane Grey used real locations as the basis for a world as fantastic as Tolkien's, a misty kingdom given over to "the flutter of aspen-leaves and the soft, continuous splash of falling water."

Grey's titles alone convey the dreamlike quality of his books: *The Wanderer of the Wasteland, The Light of Western Stars, Stairs of Sand, Valley of Wild Horses.* In *Riders of the Purple Sage* (1912) he conjures up a Surprise Valley in which hero and heroine can become Adam and Eve again, and seal the transformation by literally sealing themselves in the valley, rolling a giant rock down the mountain to cut off the only egress. The escape from history could not be more complete, nor would it ever be so complete again. Zane Grey represents a romantic height from which the genre has been devolving ever since. As Jane Tompkins points out, "the land is never represented in Westerns in this way again. . . . In the Western novels and movies that succeed Grey's, the landscape hardens."

Landscape makes Westerns look different from other movies, and location shooting gives an epic spaciousness to otherwise small-scale pictures like *The Naked Spur* (1953) and *Ride Lonesome* (1959). The obligatory vistas, whether of keelboats going up the Missouri (*The Big Sky*) or of canoes skirting the Everglades (*Distant Drums*), are often reason enough to watch a film, and Kevin Costner's *Dances with Wolves* acknowledges this by allowing landscape to assume virtual creative control. Yet for the most part Western movies have had little real use for wilderness or exploration. They never linger long enough, not even John Ford's movies; they are always in too much of a hurry to get back to the closed human worlds of the fort, the town, the mining camp, the stagecoach station.

The classic Western is customarily less epic than it is a study in claustrophobia and repetition, offering not wide open spaces but dead ends, the canyons and defiles of ambush, the mesa beyond which there's nowhere else to hide, the alleys and stables where men on the run are cornered. "They've got this whole town boxed up." Open space being lyrical rather than dramatic, the Western's formal problem becomes one of making space ever tighter and narrower.

Just as the figures are hemmed in by their landscape, they are caught within their rather limited behavioral rules. There are no corners to hide in, no room to back up: the aesthetic of the prison yard again. It is a system of traps where there is really only one plot: the man whose hand is forced, who *must* shoot to kill. If he were simply free and strong and able to go wherever he liked there would be no story.

The title of a 1970s horror movie makes explicit the underlying menace of Westerns: *The Hills Have Eyes*, whether they belong to cattle rustlers or thirst-crazed army deserters dragging a load of gold bullion through Death Valley or a Comanche raiding party. "When you can't see 'em, they're lookin' at you" (*Run of the Arrow*, 1956). The Western hero has little real freedom, since he must forever watch his back and keep an eye on the rimline. The landscape is a book full of ominous coded messages: embers, broken twigs, suspicious bird calls.

The country where masked men ride is itself a mask. Or it is a painted face: the face of the Indian suddenly looming up out of the underbrush, a favorite shot in the 1950s, particularly suited for 3-D. It is hardly necessary to add that not even the most liberal and well-intentioned of Westerns bothered to attempt even minimal accuracy in the presentation of Native American cultures and artifacts. Indians served as supremely efficacious decorative elements, a blend of war paint as fright mask and continual drumming: *Distant Drums, Apache Drums, Yaqui Drums, A Thunder of Drums, Drum Beat*.

The heroes themselves were equally decorative. Cowboy regalia provided an opportunity for a display of male plumage which became perfect material for fetishist obsession, as amply displayed in *Box-Office Buckaroos*, a densely packed catalog of cowboy collectibles, from a Tom Mix white plastic cowboy belt to Gene Autry rubber galoshes. What with scarf, boots, lariat, stirrups, holsters, belt, string tie, and hat—not to mention the horse, the gun, the walk, and the talk—the Western hero was burdened with as foppish and hieratic a dress code as anything this side of a Renaissance courtier.

A Final Decline

People who write about Westerns tend to talk about heroes and history, whereas hard-core fans generally paid more attention to the bad guys and the action. History was never more than a pretext, and the hero was often a blunt object for a range of interesting evil to bump up against. The ostensible moral seriousness of 1950s Westerns like *High Noon, The Gunfighter, 3:10 to Yuma*, and *The Bravados* was consistently undercut by their delight in a fauna of male evil and dysfunction: Robert Ryan, Ernest Borgnine, Jack Palance, Jack Elam, Neville Brand, Charles McGraw, Lee Van Cleef, Leo Gordon, Ray Teal, Earl Holliman, Lee Marvin, Charles Bronson. (Marvin and Bronson were constant presences throughout the 1950s and 1960s before finally becoming stars, as if to belatedly acknowledge the scarred and downbeat level of reality they represented.)

The title *Garden of Evil* appropriately tags the Western's catalog of the many ways in which males can fail to measure up: spineless gamblers, equivocating lawyers, businessmen huffing and puffing in the face of Indian trouble, young hotshots too quick on the trigger, reservation agents conducting a black-market trade in rifles and whiskey, dying cavalry commanders blinded by pride, alcoholic mutineers, sadistic desperadoes liberated by the absence of law. Cowardice, cruelty, fanaticism, petty thievery, just plain goofing off: these were the raw materials out of which a commander (Gregory Peck in *Only the Valiant* or Randolph Scott in *Seventh Cavalry*) had to make a functioning unit.

The losers finally broke out and took over in the era of the "dirty Western": *Rio Conchos* (1964), *The Professionals* (1966), *The Wild Bunch* (1969), and the more than three hundred Spaghetti Westerns produced between 1963 and 1969. When Americans looked in the distorting mirrors of *Django* and *Sabata*, they found a more congenially nasty image than what had been filtered through the pieties of *Gunsmoke* and *Bonanza:* an unhypocritical defense of eye gouging and below-the-belt punches, served up by frankly self-serving, lecherous heroes who (unlike James Stewart in *The Naked Spur* or Gregory Peck in *The Bravados*) positively relished the opportunity for revenge.

If the Western hero had once been conceived as an Arthurian knight of the plains, he ended up more closely resembling a cocaine dealer in cowboy drag. The Western had always sought to blur the line between hero and outlaw, and now it had been erased altogether. Since an examination of a photograph of the real-life Jesse James reveals someone who more resembles a serial killer than he does Tyrone Power or Robert Wagner, that might be the most fitting way to close the circle. In any event that is where the Western reaches the end of its trajectory, unless its recent escapist (*Silverado*) or utopian (*Dances with Wolves*) manifestations are indeed harbingers of a reviving genre rather than wishful footnotes to a closed history.

VIEWPOINT 2

"What appears to make Westerns meaningful to Indians is the fantasy of being free and independent like the cowboy."

The Western Film Provides Cultural Insights

JoEllen Shively

In many of the classic Western films, "righteous violence" was an important motif: right—virtue—*had* to triumph. While in many films the conflict was between the law and bandits, in others the conflict was between Indians and whites. One might think that Caucasian viewers of Western movies would identify with and approve of the cowboy hero and that native Americans would be offended by the mostly negative portrayals of their ancestors. However, JoEllen Shively, a Chippewa Indian and assistant professor of sociology and faculty associate at the Center for Research on Social Organization at the University of Michigan, conducted a study of viewers' reactions to Westerns and made some surprising discoveries: that plot rather than ethnicity determines whom reservation Indians and Anglos will root for in a Western while among Indian college students, ethnicity is a far more important factor.

The dominant approach to understanding cultural products typically selects a particular popular genre for analysis in the hope of generating conclusions about the societal values expressed in the cultural product. For example, [John] Cawelti [*The Six-Gun Mystique*], on the basis of his reading of Western novels, concluded that these novels are a vehicle for exploring value conflicts, such as communal ideas versus individualistic impulses, and traditional ways of life versus progress. Cawelti argued that Westerns are formulaic works that provide readers with a vehicle for escape and moral fantasy.

In the major sociological study of Western films, [Will] Wright [*Sixguns and Society*] used his own viewing of the most popular Western movies from 1931 to 1972 to argue that Westerns resemble primitive myths. Drawing on Levi-Strauss, Wright developed a cognitive theory of mythic structures in which "the receivers of the Western myth learn how to act by recognizing their own situation in it." Wright's main thesis is that the narrative themes of the Western resolve crucial contradictions in modern capitalism and provide viewers with strategies to deal with their economic worlds. The popularity of Westerns, Wright argued, lies in the genre's reflection of the changing economic system, which allows the viewers to use the Western as a guide for living.

These explanations of the Western's popularity attend to cultural texts but ignore the viewers, whose motives and experiences are crucial. The lack of solid data about audience interpretations of various formulas renders existing models of the cultural significance of Westerns and other genres speculative.

While growing up on an Indian reservation in the midwestern United States, I observed that fellow Indians loved Western movies and paperbacks. Subsequently, I observed this phenomenon on Indian reservations in Oregon and North Dakota, as well as among Indians who lived off the reservations. As scholars have noted . . . American Indians have always lived in a culturally, economically, and politically marginal subculture and are ambivalent about American values of achievement and acquisition of material wealth. Thus, it seemed unlikely that Indians who like Westerns would need them as conceptual guides for economic action as Wright alleged. The popularity of Westerns among Indians must be explained in other ways.

In an argument similar to Wright's, [Ann] Swidler suggested that cultural works are tools used by people to contend with immediate problems. Swidler discussed "culture" in a broad sense as comprising "symbolic vehicles of meaning including beliefs, ritual practices, art forms, ceremonies as well as language, gossip, stories and rituals of daily life." Swidler was concerned with how culture shapes action and with how people "use" culture. Assuming that Western movies are a story or an art form, how do American Indians use this cultural product?

I address several issues that previous studies have made assumptions about, but have not addressed clearly. One issue is the general question of how different groups appropriate and find meaning in cultural products. In particular, does Wright's theory about the cultural use of Westerns hold true for American Indians watching a "cowboys vs. Indians" film? Is the mythic structure of a drama—the "good guy/bad guy" opposition in the Western—more salient than the ethnic aspect of the cultural product, or do Indians in the audience identify with Indians on the screen, regardless of who the good guys and bad guys are? Do Indians prefer Westerns that portray sympathetic and positive images of Indians, e.g., *Broken Arrow*? . . . Do Indians like only Westerns that show a tribal group other than their own as the villains? Fundamentally, how do Indians link their own ethnic identity to the Western, or limit this identity so they can enter the narrative frame of the Western?

Research Design

Matched samples of 20 Indian males and 20 Anglo [non-Indian white Americans not of Spanish or Mexican descent] males living in a town on an Indian reservation on the Western Plains of the United States watched a Western film, *The Searchers*. Ethnically pure groups were assembled by one Anglo informant and one Indian informant who invited five ethnically similar friends to their homes to watch the film. Written questionnaires were administered immediately after the film, followed by focus-group interviews. An Anglo female conducted the focus-group interviews with Anglos; I conducted the focus-group interviews with Indians. (I am Chippewa.) (Transcripts of the focus interviews are available from the author on request.)

Respondents were asked why they liked or did not like *The Searchers* in particular and Western movies in general. . . .

Because I wanted to avoid the possible ambiguity of asking how mixed-bloods understand Westerns, all Indians in my sample claim to be "full-blood" Sioux, and all Anglos claim to be white. Because the Western genre is primarily about males, only males were included in the sample.

The respondents did not constitute a representative sample, but were assembled in an effort to create roughly matched groups. I attempted to match Indians and Anglos on age, income, years of education, occupation, and employment status, but succeeded in matching mainly on age, education, and occupation, and was less successful on income and employment status. In the analysis, neither employment status nor income appear to affect the dependent variables. Matching Indians and Anglos on education required me to exclude college-educated respondents. All subjects were between the ages of 36 and 64—the average age of Indian respondents was 51, and the average age of Anglo respondents was 52. Most of the respondents were married.

I chose *The Searchers* (1956) as the Western film to show because its major conflict is between cowboys and Indians. According to Wright (1977), *The Searchers* was one of the period's top-grossing films, a sign of mythical resonance. The film stars John Wayne—a critical advantage for a Western according to Indian and Anglo informants. Briefly, *The Searchers* is about Indian-hating Ethan Edwards's (John Wayne) and Martin Polly's (Jeff Hunter) five-year search to find Debbie Edwards, Ethan's niece (Natalie Wood), who has been kidnapped by Comanche Chief Scar (Henry Brandon). In the end, Scar is killed, and Debbie, who was married to Scar, is taken back to the white civilized world.

Findings

I began my research with the assumption that people understand movies based on their own cultural backgrounds. Therefore, the experience of watching Western movies should be different for Indians and Anglos, especially when watching scenes in which Indians are portrayed in distorted, negative ways. My most striking finding, however, is an overall similarity in the ways Indians and Anglos experienced *The Searchers*.

All respondents—Indians and Anglos—indicated that they liked Western movies in general. Furthermore, in the focus interviews, they said they wished more Westerns were being produced in Hollywood. I asked the respondents to rank the three types of films they most liked to watch from a list of 10 (musical, gangster, horror, and so on). All 40 subjects—both Anglo and Indian—ranked Westerns first or second; the Western was far and away the most popular genre. Seventy-five percent ranked Westerns first. Combat movies were a distant second, and science fiction movies were third.

On both the written questionnaires and in the focus interviews, all respondents indicated that they liked *The Searchers* and considered it a typical Western. One Indian and two Anglos reported that they had seen the film before.

In response to the question, "With whom did you identify most in the film?," 60 percent of the Indians and 50 percent of the Anglos identified with John Wayne, while 40 percent of the Indians and 45 percent of the Anglos identified with Jeff Hunter. None of the Indians (or Anglos) identified with the Indian chief, Scar. Indians did not link their own ethnic identity to Scar and his band of Indians, but instead distanced themselves from the Indians in the film. The Indians, like the Anglos, identified with the characters that the narrative structure tells them to identify with—the good guys. In the focus-group interviews, both Indians and Anglos reiterated their fondness for John Wayne. For both audiences, the Indians in the film were either neutral or negative. What stood out was not that there were Indians on the screen, but that the Indians were the "bad guys." For example, in the focus groups respondents were asked, "Do you ever root for the Indians?" Both Indians and Anglos consistently responded, "Sometimes, when they're the good guys." Their responses suggest that there is no strong ethnic bias governing whom the respondents root for and identify with. Instead, antagonism is directed against the bad guys. The structure of oppositions that defines the heroes in the film seems to guide viewers' identification with the characters in the film and overrides any ethnic empathy. . . .

Although Indians and Anglos relied on cues in *The Searchers* about whom to identify with, in other ways the fictional frame of the film did not completely capture these viewers. When discussing *The Searchers*, Indians and Anglos rarely used the main characters' story names. Instead they used the actors' names—John Wayne and Jeff Hunter—which suggests a strong "star effect." . . .

Both Indians and Anglos reported that they liked all of John Wayne's movies, whether he played a boxing champion, a pilot, or a cowboy. In all of his films, they see the strong personality characteristics of "the Duke," or "Dude," as some of the respondents referred to him. For both Indians and Anglos on this reservation, being called "cowboy" or one of John Wayne's nicknames, often "Dude" or "Duke," is a token of respect. Indians often see themselves as "cowboys," greeting each other with, "How ya doing, cowboy?," or "Long time no see, cowboy," and refer to their girlfriends or wives as "cowgirls." . . .

The respondents talked about John Wayne as if he were one of them and they knew him personally—like a good friend. Believing in John Wayne the man is part of the charisma attached to the cowboy role. It is a self-reinforcing cycle: Because John Wayne always plays good guys—characters with whom viewers empathize—it is easy to identify with John Wayne and all he represents. [Emanuel] Levy [*And the Winner Is . . . The History and Politics of the Oscar Awards*] noted that, "because acting involves actual role playing and because of the 'realistic' nature of motion pictures, audiences sometimes fail to separate between players' roles onscreen and their real lives offscreen. The difference between life on and offscreen seems to blur." For respondents, John Wayne *is* the Cowboy, both in his movies and in real life. . . .

The Real and the Fictional: Patterns of Differences

Although Anglos and Indians responded in similar ways to the structure of oppositions in the narrative, the two groups interpreted and valued characteristics of the cultural product differently once they "entered" the narrative. The narrative was (re)interpreted to fit their own interests. Although both Indians and Anglos saw some aspects of *The Searchers* as real and others as fictional, the two groups differed on what they saw as authentic and what they saw as fictional.

Cowboys and Indians

Table 1. Ranks of Reasons for Liking The Searchers, *by Ethnicity*

	American Indians				Anglos			
Reason	Ranked 1st	Ranked 2nd	Ranked 3rd	Weighted Sum of Ranks[a]	Ranked 1st	Ranked 2nd	Ranked 3rd	Weighted Sum of Ranks[a]
Action/fights	2	4	5	19	2	6	4	22
John Wayne	5	3	2	23	2	3	0	12
It had cowboys and Indians	6	5	3	31	3	2	5	18
Scenery/landscape	6	3	2	26	3	5	6	25
Humor	1	5	6	19	0	1	1	3
Romance	0	0	1	1	0	0	1	1
Authentic portrayal of Old West	0	0	0	0	10	3	3	39
Other	0	0	1	1	0	0	0	0

[a] Ranks are weighted: 1st × 3; 2nd × 2; 3rd × 1.

Table 1 shows how the two groups responded when asked to rank their three most important reasons for liking the film. The Kendall rank-order correlation coefficient of $\tau = .29$ indicates that Indians' and Anglos' reasons often differed. The two groups agreed on the importance of "action and fights," "it had cowboys and Indians," and "the scenery and landscape" as reasons for liking the film. They also agreed that "romance" was not an important reason for liking the film. But the differences between Indians and Anglos in Table 1 are striking: None of the Indians ranked "authentic portrayal of the Old West" as an important reason for liking the movie, while 50 percent of the Anglos ranked it as the most important reason.

The results in Table 1 suggest that the distinctive appeal of the Western for Indians has two elements: (1) the cowboy's way of life—the idealized Western lifestyle seems to make this cultural product resonate for Indians; and (2) the setting of the film, the beauty of the landscape (Monument Valley) moves Indian viewers. When asked in the focus groups, "Why did you like this film, and what makes Westerns better (or worse) than other kinds of movies?" Indians reported: "Westerns relate to the way I wish I could live"; "The cowboy is free"; "He's not tied down to an eight-to-five job, day after day"; "He's his own man"; and "He has friends who are like him." What makes Westerns meaningful to Indians is the fantasy of being free and independent like the cowboy and the familiarity of the landscape or setting.

The setting also resonated for Anglos, but Anglos perceived these films as authentic portrayals of their past. In the focus groups, Anglos, but not Indians, talked about Westerns as accurate chronicles of their history. When asked, "Why did you like this film, and what makes Westerns better (or worse) than other kinds of movies?" Anglos said, "My grandparents were immigrants and Westerns show us the hard life they had"; "Westerns are about my heritage and how we settled the frontier and is about all the problems they had"; "Westerns give us an idea about how things were in the old days"; and "Westerns are true to life." What is meaningful to Anglos is not the fantasy of an idealized lifestyle, but that Western films link Anglos to their own history. For them, Western films are like primitive myths: They affirm and justify that their ancestors' actions when "settling this country" were right and good and necessary.

Indians seemed ambivalent about how the Old West was portrayed in *The Searchers*. In the focus groups, I asked Indians if the film was an authentic portrayal of the Old West and they responded:

> As far as the cowboy's life goes, it's real, but you don't get to know the Indians, so it's hard to say it's totally authentic. (Bartender, age 42)

> I think it's real in some ways, like when you see the cowboy and how he was. (Mechanic, age 51)

> The cowboys are real to me. That's the way they were. But I don't know about the Indians 'cause you never see much of them. (Farm worker, age 50)

> Yeah, the movie is more about the good guys than the bad guys. I mean, the bad guys are there, but you don't get to know them very well. Mostly the movie is about the cowboys, the good guys, anyway. (Carpenter, age 48)

For Indians, the film was more about cowboys than about Indians. This does not hinder their enjoyment of the film or make it less meaningful, because they did not view the Indians on the screen as real Indians.

Both Indians and Anglos were asked, "Are Indians and cowboys in this film like Indians and cowboys in the past?" and, "Are they like Indians and cowboys today?" Anglos replied:

> I think the cowboys and the settlers are pretty much like those in the old days. It's hard to say if the Indians are like Indians in the past. (Mechanic, age 39)

> They're not like Indians today. (Foreman, age 56)

> Indians don't go around kidnapping white women and children these days. (Bartender, age 48)

> Probably they're similar to how some of the Indians were in the past, I mean Indians really did scalp white men. (Postal worker, age 49)

> Yeah, and they kidnapped white children and white women. My grandparents used to tell stories about how their parents told them to be careful when they played outside. They had to stay close to their homes, 'cause the Indians used to kidnap children. (Bus driver, age 49)

Anglos thought the cowboys in the Western were similar to cowboys of the past, and they suggested that Indians in the film were similar to Indians in the past. However, they did not think Indians today are like Indians in the film.

When asked the same questions about whether Indians and cowboys in the film are like Indians and cowboys today and in the past, Indians replied somewhat differently:

> The cowboys are like cowboys in the past. Maybe some Indians in the past were like the Indians in the films. (Bartender, age 58)

> They're not like Indians today. I mean, the only time Indians dress up is for powwows. (Cook, age 60)

> In this movie and other movies with Indians, you don't get to know them. I mean, they're not really people, like the cowboys are. It's hard to say they're like Indians in the past. For sure they're not like Indians today. (Bartender, age 42)

> The Indians aren't at all like any of the Indians I know. (Unemployed factory worker, age 44)

> Indians today are the cowboys. (Bartender, age 42)

The phrase "Indians today are the cowboys," means that contemporary Indians are more like cowboys than Anglos are, in the sense that it is Indians who preserve some commitment to an autonomous way of life that is not fully tied to modern industrial society. Indians want to be, and value being, independent and free—separate from society—more than Anglos do.

Because *The Searchers* portrays Indians not as human beings, but as "wild, blood-thirsty animals," Indians might be expected to report that the Indians on the screen are not like Indians they know today or like Indians in the past. How could they identify with the Indians on the screen when Indians are portrayed in such a caricatured fashion? The only connections that Indians made between the Indians on the screen and Indians of the past and present were with the costumes worn by the Indians on the screen.

On some deeper level, however, Indian respondents may have identified with the Indians on the screen. For example, when asked in the focus groups, "What's a bad Western like?" Indians reported that they like all Westerns except for films like *Soldier Blue*. All of the Indian respondents were familiar with this film. *Soldier Blue* is a 1970 film based on the Sand Creek massacre of 1864, when Colonel Chivington of the U.S. Cavalry ambushed and slaughtered a village of peaceful Arapaho and Cheyenne children, women, and men in Colorado. In all of the Indian focus groups, this title was mentioned as one Western they did not like. This suggests that when films are too realistic and evoke unpleasant emotions, they are no longer enjoyable. . . .

Another striking difference revealed in Table 1 is that Indians cited "humor" as an important reason for liking the film, while Anglos did not. In the focus groups, Indians talked about several comic scenes in the film. When asked if humor was important in Western films, they all said, "Yeah." They reported that they liked humor and wit in Western movies and valued this trait in their friends. Humor is a source of joy for them—a gift.

Anglos, in contrast, never mentioned John Wayne's humor. Why did Indians and not Anglos respond to the humor? If Anglos perceived the film as an authentic story of their past, they may have concentrated on the serious problems in the film, i.e., getting the white girl back. Perhaps Anglos were so preoccupied with the film as an affirmation of their past that they were unable to focus on the intended humor, or at least other characteristics of the film were more important. On the other hand, Indians, who did not see the film as an authentic story of their own past, may have focused more on the intended humor in the film.

Ideal Heroes

Indians and Anglos also valued individual traits of the cowboy differently. Table 2 shows how the two groups responded when asked to rank the three most important qualities that make a good hero in a good Western. A Kendall rank-order correlation coefficient of $\tau = .167$ shows little agreement between Indian and Anglo rankings. Indians ranked "toughness" and "bravery" as the two most important qualities of a good hero in a good Western, whereas Anglos ranked "integrity/honesty" and "intelligence" as most important. Perhaps audiences look for exceptional character-istics in a good hero—qualities they would like to see in them-selves. To live free and close to the land like Indians wish to live, exceptional bravery and toughness are necessary. Because Anglos do not want to live like cowboys, bravery and toughness are not as important. Responses of Indians in Table 2 are similar to re-sponses in Table 1 and to the oral responses. For example, when the Indians described John Wayne as a reason why they liked *The Searchers*, they concentrated on John Wayne's toughness.

Cowboys and Indians

Table 2. Ranks of Qualities That Make a Good Hero in a Good West-ern, by Ethnicity

	American Indians				Anglos			
Quality	Ranked 1st	Ranked 2nd	Ranked 3rd	Weighted Sum of Ranks[a]	Ranked 1st	Ranked 2nd	Ranked 3rd	Weighted Sum of Ranks[a]
Bravery	8	6	4	40	3	4	1	18
Integrity/honesty	2	2	0	10	8	9	5	47
Independence	0	0	2	2	0	0	1	1
Toughness	8	8	4	44	0	0	0	0
Sense of humor	0	2	8	12	0	1	1	3
Strength	2	0	0	6	0	0	0	0
Loyalty	0	0	0	0	1	0	7	10
Intelligence	0	2	2	6	8	6	5	41
Other	0	0	0	0	0	0	0	0

[a] Ranks are weighted: 1st × 3; 2nd × 2; 3rd × 1.

While the two groups differed on the qualities that make a good hero, Indians and Anglos tended to agree on the characteristics of a good Western. When asked what characteristics they liked in a good Western, a Kendall rank-order correlation coefficient be-tween Indian and Anglo responses was high, $\tau = .78$, i.e., there were no pronounced differences between Indians and Anglos. For both groups, the three most important characteristics of a good Western were: "a happy ending"; "action/fights"; and "authentic portrayal of Old West.". . . Indian and Anglo viewers ranked "a happy ending" as the most desirable characteristic of a good West-ern. The essential happy ending for my respondents may be re-lated to Cawelti's "epic moment" when the villain is conquered, the wilderness is subdued, and civilization is established. . . .

For Indians, the importance of a "happy ending" in a good West-ern film also reflects on their evaluation of *Soldier Blue* as a bad

Western—*Soldier Blue* does not fulfill the "happy ending" criterion of a good Western. Although Indians like action or fights, they are discerning about what kinds of action or fights they enjoy.

For both Anglos and Indians, the three least liked characteristics of a good Western were: "hero rides off into the sunset alone"; "Indians as bad guys"; and "romance between hero and woman." Both groups preferred that "the hero settles down.". . .

Some Indians *do* identify with the Indians in the Western and are not affected by the film's signals about whom to identify with. Before taking my research procedures into the field, I pretested them with 15 American Indian college students at a West Coast university (10 males, 5 females). Because Indians in the reservation sample differed in important characteristics from the Indians in the pretests (9 of the Indian students were "mixed-bloods"), systematic comparisons were not possible.

However, Indian students responded differently from Indians in the reservation sample. Ethnicity was a salient issue for the majority of the students. The narrative of *The Searchers* did not "work" for the students and they were unable to fully enter the drama. For example, unlike the reservation Indians, a majority of the Indian students identified with and rooted for Scar and his Indians or Debbie, the kidnapped girl. They thought Debbie should have been allowed to stay with Scar and that the search should not have taken place at all.

Like the reservation Indians, the college-educated Indians did not view *The Searchers* as an authentic portrayal of the "Old West" and were quick to point out stereotypical portrayals of Indians in the film. They reacted against the negative message in the film that "the only good Indian is a dead one." They also pointed out many inaccuracies in the film, such as the use of Navajos and the Navajo language for Comanche, "Comanche" Indians wearing Sioux war bonnets, and Indians sometimes wearing war bonnets while fishing. Neither the Indians nor the Anglos in the reservation sample mentioned any of these inaccuracies.

All students but one reported that they liked Westerns in general, but preferred Westerns whose plots are about "cowboys vs. cowboys" or "Indians vs. Indians," or a "cowboys vs. Indians" plot in which the Indian point of view is shown. Several male students indicated that they and their friends often rent Western videos and named the video stores nearest the university that had the best selection of Westerns.

None of the students particularly liked John Wayne. Like the reservation sample, the students talked about John Wayne in "real life" and referred to what they considered racist statements he made off-screen in various interviews.

I asked each student, "Do Indians back home on the reservation like Westerns?" and "Do they root for the cowboys?" All of them said, "Oh yeah, sure." One Sioux student said his father had most of John Wayne's films on video, and a Chippewa said that his uncle was named after John Wayne. One Navajo said of his reservation town, "Ever since they closed down the movie theater several years ago, every Friday night they show a movie in the cafeteria room at the high school, and most of the time it's a Western. Everybody goes."

The heightened ethnic awareness of the college students interferes with, or overrides, their responses to the Western so that they do not get caught up in the structure of oppositions in the narrative. Because they identify with their ethnic group, they see *The Searchers* through a different lens. Education increases their awareness of anti-Indian bias in the film, producing a "revised eye" that frames these films in ethnic terms. In this context, ethnicity is a construct of a particular culture or subculture.

Although it would seem problematic for Indians to know which characters to identify with in *The Searchers*, it was not a problem for them at all—they identified with the cowboy and his lifestyle. Indians did not focus on the Indians, who are often portrayed onscreen as a faceless, screaming horde. Instead, they saw the cowboys as they want to see themselves—as the good guys.

What appears to make Westerns meaningful to Indians is the fantasy of being free and independent like the cowboy. In addition, the familiarity of the setting is important. Anglos, on the other hand, respond to the Western as a story about their past and their ancestors. The Western narrative becomes an affirmation of their own social experience—the way they are and what their ancestors strove for and imposed on the West are "good." Thus, for Anglos, the Western resembles a primitive myth. But it is not a myth in this sense for Indians—Indians do not view the Western as authentic.

Both Indians and Anglos find a fantasy in the cowboy story in which the important parts of their ways of life triumph and are morally good, validating their own cultural group in the context of a dramatically satisfying story. Perhaps this motive for ethnic group validation is more general and not peculiar to cowboy movies.

Oppositions in the Western narrative are important to viewers. Indians and Anglos both root for and identify with the good guys. . . .

The Indian college students, who by attending college have opted for some of the values of white society, find other meanings in *The Searchers*. Because they are immersed in the intellectual world of the university, the symbolic importance of the film for them lies in its false representation of their ancestry and history.

VIEWPOINT 3

"Ride 'em, cow bro."

Some Western Films Clarify the Historical Record

Susan Wloszczyna

In the following viewpoint, Susan Wloszczyna, film reviewer for *USA Today*, presents little-known information on the role of blacks in the West as she discusses Mario Van Peebles's *Posse*. She perceives the film as a corrective to the "lily-white John Wayne adventure story." In her discussion, Ms. Wloszczyna emphasizes that the frontier provided challenges and opportunities to men and women of a wide variety of ethnic backgrounds.

Old Jack City. Unfo'given. Boyz N the Saddle.

Yeah, yeah. Mario Van Peebles has heard all those cowpoke jokes already, cracked by uptight-in-the-saddle studio types who scoffed at the idea of a black-themed Western.

The actor/director, who quickly was dubbed "Mario, bay-bee!" by Hollywood bigwigs after his 1991 urban drama *New Jack City* scored $40-million-plus at the box office, just hitched his wagon to a smaller and more appreciative British company instead.

But the other day, he got a taste of how the actual public might brand his latest movie.

Co-screenwriter Dario Scardapane called to report, "I was standing outside a movie theater, and these two ladies were looking at the *Posse* poster. And one said, 'Oh, they're cute.' But the other one said, 'Yeah, but black cowboys. Who are they kidding?'"

No one. *Posse*, galloping into theaters, isn't just a horse opera of a different color. This is a hefty slice of American pie that somehow got left behind in the cinematic sagebrush.

The story of Jessie Lee (a highly Clintonian figure—as in Eastwood, not Bill—played with steely-eyed grit by Van Peebles) and his wild bunch may be the stuff of pulp fiction. We're talking gold bullets cast from purloined coins, bawdy-house brouhahas and shootouts with six-guns a-blazing.

Photofest

The 1993 movie Posse *depicted the lives of black cowboys.*

But details like the front-line status of segregated black cavalrymen during the Spanish-American War and the rise of all-black utopian communities represented by the fictional Freemanville in *Posse* are rooted in fact.

"It's so important that the West be pictured as it was, not some lily-white John Wayne adventure story," says William Loren Katz, author of *The Black West* (Open Hand Press) and *Black People Who Made the Old West* (Africa World Press). "A whole heritage has been lost to generation after generation of schoolchildren, black and white."

Well, Pilgrim, did you know that almost 1 out of 3 cowboys who roamed the range was black? And that of the first 44 settlers of Los Angeles, 26 were black? And 30 all-black towns were built in Oklahoma between 1890 and 1910?

Even Tone-Loc, the rapper/actor who's Angel in *Posse*, swallowed the white-bread version of the West while growing up in Texas. And he has relatives who migrated to California and were cowboys.

"I never wondered how come there were no brothers in Westerns," he says. "The way they had you believe, (the white cowboys) were the only ones around. Basically, you just accepted it—until now."

Just how did this part of the West go un-won in textbooks and in Tinseltown? Katz believes it comes from a long-ingrained inclination to portray blacks and other minorities as second-class citizens for economic and social reasons. "The tale of frontier blood, sacrifice and conquest has bonded white citizens and established exactly who built the country—and who didn't."

Even in classrooms today, Katz says, "Books make it seem like, after the Civil War, blacks went home and went to sleep and didn't wake up until Martin Luther King."

Of course, Hollywood's further whitewashing of the West clouded the picture even more. One of the more blatant examples: *Tomahawk* (1951), which featured white actor Jack Oakie as legendary black frontiersman Jim Beckwourth. As Katz says, "Audiences learned Beckwourth was important, but not that he was black."

Throughout the years, the movies occasionally served up blacks in Westerns, even if ignoring the historical events. These offerings vary from the singing cowboys in "race" films of the '30s and '40s (*Bronze Buckaroo, Harlem Rides the Range*) to the racially relevant Westerns of the '60s (*The Professionals, Major Dundee*) to '70s-style blaxploitation (Fred Williamson in *The Legend of Nigger Charley*) and liberalism (Sidney Poitier's *Buck and the Preacher*).

In the '80s, it was common to cast black stars in Westerns without reference to race (*Silverado*, TV's *Lonesome Dove*), a tradition carried on by Eastwood's Oscar-winning *Unforgiven*. But it's a portrayal that author Donald Bogle (*Blacks in American Films and Television*, Simon & Schuster) finds unsatisfying. After all, with the passage of post-Reconstruction laws that denied land ownership and voting rights to blacks, racism thrived in the West as well.

"It's good to know that any actor could play the roles they play and that the black actor has a chance. But, for me, it was disappointing when Gene Hackman brutalized Morgan Freeman with no reference to his race. They had no trouble referring to the women as bitches and whores."

Posse, on the other hand, is fairly steeped in race, although Van Peebles shuns the label "black Western"—as he points out, no one called *Unforgiven* a "white Western." He took care to cast one white actor (Stephen Baldwin of TV's *The Young Riders*) as part of Jessie Lee's gang and give Jessie a half-Indian love interest. "Unless we see the world a little like a Benetton ad, no one is moving forward."

But how do you make today's audiences feel at home on the range? With plenty of sex and skin (including a butt-naked swim scene), gunfire that explodes like a Fourth-of-July sky and contemporary references (echoing Rodney King, comic veteran Nipsey Russell implores, "Can't we all just get along?").

Who's Who Among Rogues and Heroes

Meet real-life black heroes and villains of the West:

• *Nate Love*, aka Deadwood Dick, was an ex-slave turned cowboy who hung out with Bat Masterson and braved dangerous cattle drives.

• *Cherokee Bill* was an Indian scout and outlaw counterpart to Billy the Kid. His wicked ways landed him in a noose a month before he turned 20.

• *Mary Fields*, aka Stagecoach Mary, was a strapping 6-footer who never shied from a shootout. A fearless mail carrier while in her 60s, she spent much of her final years in a Cascade, Mont., saloon playing cards with the boys.

• *Ben Hodges* was a notorious card sharp who was the equal of another Dodge City citizen, Wyatt Earp. He was buried in the Maple Grove Cemetery alongside many other old-time cowboys and cattlemen. Said one pallbearer: "We wanted him where they could keep a good eye on him."

• *Bill Pickett* claimed to have invented bulldogging, which involved wrestling a steer by the horns, and he starred in silent films. A big rodeo draw in the early 1900s, his assistants included Will Rogers and Tom Mix. Until he was famous, he disguised himself as a Mexican toreador to enter rodeos that refused blacks. In 1971, he became the first black voted into Oklahoma City's Cowboy Hall of Fame.

But Van Peebles also makes a nod to the old, with vintage cameos (Pam Grier, Robert Hooks, Isaac Hayes, Mario's dad, Melvin) plus homage to probably the greatest black Western star ever—Woody Strode, who lends his trademark dignity to the beginning and end of *Posse*. While never an actor of the caliber of a

Sidney Poitier, "He does represent a major shift of images," Bogle says. "Visually, he made a great statement. There was nothing servile about him."

Says Van Peebles of Strode, who appeared in John Ford's *The Man Who Shot Liberty Valance* and Sergio Leone's *Once Upon a Time in the West* as well as non-oaters like *Spartacus:* "He's the granddaddy. He was the first black cowboy I remember who didn't shuffle."

Strode, a 6-foot-plus former football star and wrestler who turn[ed] 79 in July 1993, remains an imposing figure in his *Posse* role, which he calls a "bookend."

But *Posse* can't compare to the high point of his career: 1960's *Sergeant Rutledge*, the Ford Western that finally arriv[ed] on video in June 1993.

"If it hadn't been for John Ford, I would never have been on a horse," Strode says. With *Rutledge*, the tale of a black cavalry soldier wrongly accused of rape and murder who turns out to be a heroic figure, Ford appeared to be making amends for earlier films that exploited the likes of Stepin Fetchit. As Strode once observed: "You never seen a Negro come off a mountain like John Wayne before."

Strode, who calls Ford "Papa," says, "He was like a father to me. I told him, 'You're going to turn into Abraham Lincoln.'" Strode also appeared in Ford's *Two Rode West* and *Seven Women*.

With some 60 Westerns posed to mine the same gold as *Unforgiven*, at least *Posse* is the first to stake a claim with movie audiences. But historian Katz believes it's an important step. "*Posse* opens a small door on a vast history."

And just like in *Posse*, perhaps it's best to let Strode speak last. "It's amazing that I got to live to see a black kid star in his own picture and get studio money and be a director. Then I know there've been some changes."

Ride 'em, cow bro.

VIEWPOINT 4

"The most successful Marlboro men were pilots. . . . Because pilots seem to have a little wrinkle around the eyes."

The Cowboy in Advertising

This book has already explored the transformation of historical reality to myth. When the myth was deeply enough embedded in the popular consciousness, and associated with positive qualities, it could become an effective element of advertising. Such was the case with the cowboy and the Philip Morris Marlboro man campaign. In popular iconography, the cowboy was strong and skilled, a man in touch with nature, capable of conquering it as well as human challenges, a man willing to do right and occasionally to "bust loose." In short, in the popular conception, the cowboy was a man's man. It was this essence of masculinity that the Marlboro ad campaign played upon. The campaign was so successful that the Marlboro man himself became part of twentieth-century American iconography and thus could be a target of parody. The process illustrated in this segment on advertising illustrates that once an image becomes familiar, it can be used to manipulate an audience. As one examines contemporary society, it becomes clear how many images of the frontier have been so used.

The First Cowboy in Tobacco Ads

The first use of the cowboy in advertising utilized an objective photograph. In the above photograph, an anonymous cowboy relaxes from his work and rolls a cigarette. Prior to 1881, when James Buchanan Duke, benefactor of Duke University, began to mass-produce prefabricated cigarettes, they were made in relatively small numbers in New York City by Russian immigrants. Bull Durham tobacco dominated the market from the Civil War to the outbreak of World War I. Sold loose in a drawstring pouch with its trademark Durham bull, the tobacco was shaken into a cigarette paper, rolled, and sealed with a lick before smoking. Those very adept at the process could do it one-handed. This photograph captures a moment in an ordinary cowboy's life.

The Marlboro Man Was a Positive Image to Attract Male Smokers

Charles Goodrum and Helen Dalrymple discuss the Marlboro campaign in their fascinating *Advertising in America: The First Two Hundred Years*. In a chapter on tobacco they include a wealth of Americana: for example, the fact that the original Lucky Strike was meant to suggest the discovery of a vein of gold, or that the Camel trademark was modeled after an actual dromedary named "Old Joe" in the Barnum and Bailey menagerie. "Marlboro Country," of course, still presents images of an archetypal American West.

The Marlboro campaign, believed by many advertising professionals to be Number One among the All-Time Greats, started in 1954 when Philip Morris moved an uninspired account to Leo Burnett in Chicago. By 1954, there were already six filter-tip cigarettes on the market. Marlboro then had a red paper "beauty tip" to camouflage lipstick, came in a white pack bearing the slogan, "Mild as May," and, not surprisingly, sold mostly to women. It held less than one quarter of one percent share of the cigarette market.

Burnett decided to go for the macho. The agency redesigned the pack to a flip-top box, changed the color to strong red and white, and chose the cowboy as the most effective shorthand symbol for the masculine image. (For the first ten years the cowboy always had a tattoo on the back of one hand.)

The original photographer of the series, Constantin Joffe, recalls that "the most successful Marlboro men were pilots, and do you know why? Because pilots seem to have a little wrinkle around the eyes."

At the time of this writing, the Marlboro series [was] the longest running modern campaign and [had] higher brand identification and recall than any other advertising theme in the marketplace.

Mocking the Ads

Although tobacco use in America has historic roots (Columbus described Indians smoking), it began to come into disfavor in the mid 1960s. Prior to that time, according to Goodrum and Dalrymple, much tobacco advertising implied benefits, or at least an absence of harm: "Not a cough in a carload!" (Old Golds), and "More doctors smoke Camels." But in 1964 the Surgeon General of the United States issued the first report suggesting a link between smoking and increased mortality rates. Since then, increasingly strong warning labels have been required on tobacco packaging. This cartoon reflects this trend.

VIEWPOINT 5

"The denim pants—known as 'waist overalls'—became as popular as the original canvas variety."

Levi Strauss Invented Western Work Clothes for Miners, Cowboys, and Engineers

Lynn Downey

Around the world, Levi's® jeans are a uniquely American icon. For decades, American tourists have been happily accosted all over the world by young people wanting to beg, borrow, or barter for their denim pants. Somehow wearing Levi's® jeans has allowed people in Greece and Spain and Russia to capture a little bit of the American dream, to share in the image of the American West as a place of adventure and fresh starts. A product created out of practical necessity has been transformed into an almost mythic symbol. The following biography of the founder of the company, Levi Strauss, reflects many of the frontier motifs: the impact of the gold rush as an economic and demographic catalyst; the immigrant's succeeding through hard work and determination; the progressive westering—from New York to Kentucky

From *Levi Strauss* by Lynn Downey, Levi Strauss & Co. historian. Reprinted with permission from the Levi Strauss & Co. archives, San Francisco, California.

to California; the changes wrought by technology; the battles humans must fight against the forces of nature; the existence of a strong San Francisco Jewish community, suggesting the diversity of the nation; and a strong sense of philanthropy. This biography unites many of the themes already explored in this book; Strauss, like his Levi's® jeans, becomes a symbol of the American frontier tradition.

Levi Strauss, the inventor of what many consider to be the quintessential American garment—the blue jean—was born in Buttenheim, Bavaria, on February 26, 1829, to Hirsch Strauss and his second wife, Rebecca Haas Strauss. Hirsch, a dry goods peddler, already had four children with his first wife, who had died a few years earlier: Jacob, Jonas, Louis, and Mathilde. Levi—named "Loeb" at birth—and his older sister Fanny were the last of the Strauss children; Hirsch succumbed to tuberculosis in 1845.

Two years after his death Rebecca, Loeb, Fanny, and Mathilde emigrated to New York. There, they were met by Jonas and Louis, who had already made the journey and had started a dry goods business. Loeb Strauss soon became known as Levi and by 1848 he was living in Kentucky, learning the dry goods trade. For nearly five years he tramped through the hills carrying packs loaded with thread, scissors, yards, combs, buttons, and bolts of fabric. The year 1850—considered the founding date of Levi Strauss & Co.—saw Levi well-established in his trade, working closely with his prosperous brothers.

Levi's sister Fanny married David Stern, also a dry goods merchant, and the two of them moved to San Francisco soon after news of the California gold rush had spread to the East. The city also beckoned to young Levi and in March of 1853 he arrived in the bustling, noisy town to establish a dry goods business with his brother-in-law. Their first store was a small building on California Street between Sansome and Battery; in 1853 this location was close to the waterfront, very handy for receiving and selling the goods that arrived by ship from the Strauss Brothers store in New York. Around 1856 the business moved to 117 Sacramento Street and then to 63 & 65 Sacramento as its trade and reputation expanded. In 1866 the company moved again, to even larger quarters at 14-16 Battery Street.

Levi spent $25,000 to add gaslight chandeliers, a freight elevator and other amenities to the new location. It was the headquarters of the now-prosperous firm; the Eastern sales office remained with the Strauss brothers in New York. In his mid-thirties, Levi was already a well-known figure around the city. He was active in the business and cultural life of San Francisco, and actively supported the Jewish community. He belonged to Temple Emanu-El, the city's first synagogue, and was a contributor to the gold medal given annually to the best Sabbath School student. He now had four nephews, the children of his sister Fanny: Jacob, Sigmund, Louis, and Abraham Stern. Despite his stature as an important business man, he insisted that his employees call him Levi, and not Mr. Strauss.

This illustration is from a turn-of-the-century Levi Strauss & Co. catalog.

Sometime after his arrival in San Francisco in 1853, Levi had hit upon the idea of making sturdy work pants out of some of the canvas material he had on hand. Whether he was asked to make the pants by the miners who frequented the city or whether he observed that their trousers didn't hold up well in the diggings is not known. However they came about, his innovative work pants quickly became popular, especially after he took to the road again as a peddler, traveling the small towns in the gold country. By the 1860s Levi was buying denim from a mill in New Hampshire and the denim pants—known as "waist overalls"—became as popular as the original canvas variety. They were made under the supervision of the Strauss brothers in New York and shipped to San

Francisco for sale.

In 1872, Levi received a letter that changed the course of the company's history, as well as the history of his famous pants. Jacob Davis, a tailor living in Nevada, had started placing metal rivets at the points of strain on the pants he was making for his customers. He regularly purchased bolts of cloth from Levi Strauss & Co., and in 1872 he wrote to the company, telling them about his invention and suggesting that they patent the process together. Levi was enthusiastic about the idea and the patent was granted on May 20, 1873.

They knew that demand would be great for the now-sturdier waist overalls, so Levi brought Jacob Davis to San Francisco to oversee the first West Coast manufacturing facility. Initially, Davis supervised the cutting of material and its delivery to individual seamstresses who worked out of their homes. But the demand for overalls made it impossible to maintain this system, and a factory on Fremont Street was opened.

As the end of the 19th century approached, Levi stepped back from the day-to-day workings of the business, leaving it to his nephews. David Stern had died in 1874 and around 1876 Jacob and Louis Stern entered the company; Sigmund joined the firm around 1881. In 1890—the year that the lot number "501" first appeared on the denim overalls—Levi and his nephews officially incorporated the company, though by this time the 61-year-old businessman had begun to concentrate on other business and philanthropic pursuits.

Levi Strauss, Philanthropist

Levi had been a charter member and treasurer of the San Francisco Board of Trade since 1877. He was a director of the Nevada Bank; the Liverpool, London and Globe Insurance Company; and the San Francisco Gas and Electric Company. In 1874 Levi and two associates purchased the Mission and Pacific Woolen Mills from the estate of former silver millionaire William Ralston; much of the mill's fabric was used to make the Levi Strauss & Co. "blanket-lined" pants and coats. Levi was a contributor to the Pacific Hebrew Orphan Asylum and Home, the Eureka Benevolent Society, and the Hebrew Board of Relief. In 1897 he provided the funds for twenty-eight scholarships at the University of California, Berkeley.

During the week of September 22, 1902, Levi began to complain of ill health but by Friday evening the 26th, he felt well enough to attend the family dinner at the home on Leavenworth Street which he shared with his nephews and their families. He awakened briefly in the night; he told the nurse in attendance that he felt "as comfortable as I can under the circumstances" and then, peacefully, died.

His death was headline news in the Sunday, September 28, edition of the San Francisco *Call*. On Monday, the day of his funeral, local businesses were temporarily closed so that their proprietors could attend the services. The eulogy was read by Rabbi Jacob Voorsanger of Temple Emanu-El at Levi's home; afterward, company employees escorted the casket to the Southern Pacific railway station, where it was transported to the Hills of Eternity Cemetery in Colma, south of San Francisco.

Levi's estate amounted to nearly $6 million, the bulk of which was left to his four nephews and other family members. Other bequests were made to the Pacific Hebrew Orphan Asylum, the Home for Aged Israelites, the Roman Catholic and Protestant Orphan asylums, Eureka Benevolent Society, and the Emanu-El Sisterhood.

In summing up Levi's life and the establishment of his business, the San Francisco *Call* stated: "Fairness and integrity in his dealings with his Eastern factors and his customers and liberality toward his employees soon gave the house a standing second to none on the coast." An even more fitting testimonial was pronounced by the San Francisco Board of Trade in a special resolution:

> The great causes of education and charity have likewise suffered a signal loss in the death of Mr. Strauss, whose splendid endowments to the University of California will be an enduring testimonial of his worth as a liberal, public-minded citizen and whose numberless unostentatious acts of charity in which neither race nor creed were recognized, exemplified his broad and generous love for and sympathy with humanity.

On April 18, 1906, San Francisco was devastated by a massive earthquake and fire. Counted among the buildings which did not survive the catastrophe was the headquarters of Levi Strauss & Co. on Battery Street. The gas chandeliers, installed with such pride by Levi himself, were shaken from the walls and the escaping gas added to the already dangerous fire hazard. The building was rocked to its foundations, burned, and all the goods inside lost. The factory on Fremont Street suffered the same fate.

It was a great loss; but it did not signal the end to the company. As the ashes cooled, the Stern brothers made plans for a new facility and a new factory, as their uncle Levi would no doubt have done. They also continued to pay employee salaries and extended credit to other, less fortunate merchants until they could get back on their feet. For though the building itself fell, the company built by Levi Strauss was bedrock solid, due to his foresight, his business sense, and his unswerving devotion to quality.

VIEWPOINT 6

"[Ralph] Lauren is the latest in a long line of entrepreneurs who have been able to turn a profit with metaphoric evocations of a frontier past."

Ralph Lauren Appropriated Western Work Clothes for Modern Consumers

Ann Fabian

While Levi's® jeans began as practical clothing for gold miners, the designs of Ralph Lauren are, from the outset, conscious fashion statements. Like other artists who want not only to create but also to sell, Lauren draws on motifs that speak powerfully to the American audience. His re-creation of the Western image thus provides testimony to the importance of the frontier to the psyche of the American public.

The son of a Russian immigrant mural painter, Ralph Lauren began his fashion career as a tie salesman after dropping out of City College of New York. He started designing his own line of ties in 1967, then advanced to menswear in 1968, women's wear in 1971, perfume in 1978, luggage and handbags in 1981, and home furnishings in 1983. Like Levi Strauss & Co., his is a privately held company. Lauren has 125 stores, 2,000 employees, and a personal net worth of almost a half-billion dollars. Though his

Ann Fabian, "History for the Masses: Commercializing the Western Past." Reprinted from *Under an Open Sky: Rethinking America's Western Past*, edited by William Cronon, George Miles, and Jay Gitlin, by permission of W.W. Norton & Company, Inc. Copyright © 1992 William Cronon, George Miles, and Jay Gitlin.

may seem a classic urban success story, Lauren has turned increasingly to the West for inspiration. It has been suggested that his vision of the Old West was originally inspired by the movies; his ranch near Ridgway, Colorado, was where John Wayne's *True Grit* was filmed. Like Levi Strauss, Lauren is also a philanthropist, whose special projects include the local schools near his ranch and the Nina Hyde Center for Breast Cancer Research in Washington, D.C. In the following selection, writer Ann Fabian, author of *Card Sharps, Dream Books, and Bucket Shops: Gambling in Nineteenth-Century America*, analyzes Lauren's re-creation of a Western image.

The popular West has not been confined to texts and images; it has had its moments in advertising and in fashion. And in this vein the most skilled recent exponent of popular western imagery has not been a historian, a filmmaker, or a novelist but a clothing designer—Ralph Lauren. The popular West successively has represented ideologies of expansion, conquest, manhood, progress, virtue, independence, possibility, prosperity, and democracy, and Lauren has built upon them all. He has made a fashion empire out of a magnificent pastiche, out of materials culled from British imperialism, native American aesthetics, and working westerners' rugged wear. Rather than the history of the West Lauren has used the long history of representations of the West, choosing freely from the art of Frederic Remington and from the devices of Madison Avenue and Hollywood. His adept manipulation of a repertoire of mixed images makes him a great figure of the postmodern West. In the late 1970s Lauren adopted all the white male cowboy paraphernalia filmmakers had recently abandoned, added a whiff of the trail, and mixed them all to market a men's perfume he called Chaps. Lauren knew he had a ready audience well schooled in the vocabulary of the West, and he pitched his particular vision to customers shaped by the special combinations of greed and nostalgia that characterized America in the 1980s. Lauren has been very successful.

Lauren is the latest in a long line of entrepreneurs who have been able to turn a profit with metaphoric evocations of a frontier past. Several things about his career suggest that western history and its popular representation still have much to offer both scholars and entrepreneurs. Lauren began by elaborating on the Marlboro Man. In the 1950s the R.J. Reynolds Tobacco Company appropriated images of western manliness to sell effeminate filter cigarettes to male smokers. When Lauren launched his western ventures, he built on the long labor not of white western settlement but of Marlboro advertising. He gave the man on horseback a well-dressed female companion and a well-furnished interior.

Lauren's play with western images has a biographical side. He says he was inspired to create a line of western clothes when he had trouble finding a snap-button cowboy shirt in Denver. Like so many other tourists, Lauren had been deceived by what he thought he knew of the western past. He had seen himself, perhaps, traveling to a Denver that was a nineteenth-century cow town, not the financial center of the mountain West. Since that first disappointing excursion Lauren has more than compensated for our lack of western wear. But he did not stop with the production of perfume, fashion, and images. In the grand style of his western predecessors he turned to a western landscape to refashion himself. Like pioneers before him and like the pioneer entrepreneurs of western images—Theodore Roosevelt, Owen Wister, and Frederic Remington— Lauren used the West to market himself. In so doing, he made a fortune, and transformed himself from eastern entrepreneur to rugged westerner.

Lauren Remakes Self and Surroundings

Lauren, a native New Yorker, first made himself into his own best western model. Not content to wear his western clothes in the city, he and his wife created a ranch on thirteen thousand acres in southwestern Colorado. The ranch, redecorated to his exacting standards, has become the setting for his collection of the "real" antiques that have inspired his clothes and furniture. Lauren has been able to design and build the structures of the western past on his own land, he has been able to hire cowboys whose rugged good looks complement his dramatic landscapes, and he has begun to produce steaks, a mythic food of the western diet, to feed his well-dressed customers. If he succeeds with his meat line, Lauren will have extended his empire from his own imagination to the outsides of bodies, from the bodies to the Colorado landscape, and from the landscape back to the insides of the bodies he has clothed. Just as professional historians began to turn western legend into fact, Lauren resurrected the legend for hungry customers. Moreover, he has had the wherewithal to try to turn the facts of the Colorado present back into carefully elaborated fictions. Along the way he has sharpened the tools of taste and style that in an aesthetic universe serve to enhance the cultural power of the moneyed.

Lauren has sometimes found the real twentieth-century West a bit truculent. Considering the town of Ridgway, Colorado, to fall below his aesthetic standards, he offered to redesign it at his own

Like western clothes, country & western music and dancing has taken America by storm in the 1990s. These patrons of a country & western bar set their beers aside to learn one of the staples of the country & western experience: line dancing.

expense. And when *Vanity Fair* sent Brooke Hayward to interview Lauren, she succumbed to his vision and gushed over the beauty of his ranch, describing him as a "real godsend to Ouray County. He set the tone for the new look of it—really beautiful, well-kept land." Coloradans may have had their doubts about the tone he set. Yet in his very failure to consult the locals, Ralph Lauren once again proved himself a fit heir to traditions of the West. With Lauren in charge, decisions about the economic and aesthetic future of Ouray County would be made, as they had been in the past, in New York. Lauren resurrected an older version of western colonialism to go with his clothes. Decades ago John D. Rockefeller pocketed profits from iron and coal mined in southern Colorado, soothing restive locals with the promise of welfare capitalism. We perhaps assumed that Rockefeller's smooth pattern of profit taking belonged to an era long past, but we were wrong. Lauren found the profits in a reinvented past, and he has been busy retelling in fashions and home decorations a story of white male migration, imperial conquest, and American development. At the close of the twentieth century, he leaves to the cultural historian the task of understanding the appeal of his new version of a very old story.

Lauren reopened old channels in the commerce of western history, and his career helps us understand how the same search for profits that had lured men and women to the West could be extended to the presentation of western pasts. Like prospectors who took over abandoned claims, the entrepreneurs of western imagery continue to eke wealth from well-mined sites. Representations of the West, drawn from the past, continue to reshape the present, to alter the economy, ecology, and demography of communities where westerners live and work. In the West the legend continues to become fact.

Lauren envisioned a future for the western past, but his labors in the fields of fashion have also produced materials historians will be able to mine far into the twenty-first century. But Lauren, like all his fellow entrepreneurs of western images, will also pursue the historians, doubling, mocking, and distorting their labors as Buffalo Bill did Turner's and reminding another generation of scholars just how often interest in their interpretations depends on the entrepreneurs of mass culture.

For Discussion

Chapter One

1. How did Frederick Jackson Turner define "frontier"? How did this definition differ from the concept of the frontier held in Europe? What are some of the implications and consequences of this difference?

2. Turner identifies a number of specific American intellectual traits nurtured by the frontier. Do any of these exist today? Have any new traits emerged? To what stimuli can you attribute their development?

3. According to Turner, what effect did an influx of Europeans have on native American society?

4. On a map, examine the U.S. Interstate Highway system, especially the even-numbered routes (I-70, for instance). How would Turner explain their location?

5. Does the fact that George Wilson Pierson was writing in 1942 in any way influence his conclusions? What determining or catalytic event functioned for him as did the Bureau of the Census's announcement that there was no more free land for Turner?

6. What major objections does Pierson make to Turner's thesis? In your opinion, are these valid? What criticisms might you add now, fifty years after Pierson—and one hundred years after Turner?

7. Does Walter Prescott Webb address Pierson's final objections to Turner and his followers? If so, whose "side" is he on?

8. Assess the three essays as to originality, style, and tone. Can you imagine the three authors together in a conversation? Try to formulate such a script.

Chapter Two

1. Does George Armstrong Custer really differ much in attitude from other authors in this chapter? Explain.

2. Does Helen Hunt Jackson appear to believe that native Americans could be assimilated if treated properly? Does she seem to think they should be? Find evidence in her viewpoint that sup-

ports your answers.

3. Both George Armstrong Custer and John Chivington seemed to believe that it was morally acceptable to do whatever was most expedient to make Indians less of a threat to white society. What examples can you think of in the world today of similar attitudes? Do you agree with these people? Explain.

4. How does the experience of cultural exchange or conflict between native Americans and Euro-Americans compare to that of African-Americans or other minorities and Euro-Americans?

5. Try gathering oral history. Ask your grandparents or other friends about their experiences in the American melting pot. Do they believe assimilation or multiculturalism is preferable?

Chapter Three

1. What evidence in the viewpoints shows "the wilderness master[ing] the colonists"? Was this true only on the initial (fur) frontier, or did a similar process occur at each successive frontier? Explain.

2. What kinds of people sought the frontier? What character traits were created or intensified on the frontier? Give evidence to support your answer.

3. Does the man/land relationship remain the same today as it was in the nineteenth century, or is there evidence of changing attitudes toward nature? If there are changes, what causes them? If not, what is the essence of the relationship?

4. How did the introduction of capital and increased technology affect the fur and mining frontiers?

5. Unlike the early frontier people, we today tend to think that with money and technology we can control nature. For what purposes should we do so? Have people ever erred in this attempt? Have we been totally successful in the attempt? What light do the midwest floods of 1993 shed on this issue?

Chapter Four

1. Which of the women in this chapter had the most difficult life? Which the most satisfying? Explain.

2. What character traits were necessary for a successful homesteader? Do you think that there was a natural selection process (a process that results in the survival and reproduction of those best suited to an environment) that determined who chose to take up homesteads?

3. It is important in political debate to know your opponent's position. What evidence is there that Yan Phou Lee does? How

does he use sarcasm and satire as argumentative tools? How does he incorporate statistics? knowledge of American history? Do you think his argument might backfire? Who, apparently, is his audience? How might that audience respond to his article?

4. How does James D. Phelan make use of Ho Yow's arguments to refute him? Do you think it might be important to read *all* of Ho Yow's article? ("Chinese Exclusion: A Benefit or Harm," *North American Review* CLXXIII [September 1901] 314-330.) Examine political debates and editorials in today's press to see whether opposing viewpoints are always accurately quoted in the heat of debate.

5. Were opponents of Chinese immigration in the late nineteenth century patriotic or provincial—or both? Explain. Apply the same question to modern issues such as NAFTA (North American Free Trade Agreement) or, once again, immigration.

Chapter Five

1. Do you think Nat Love met with as little racial prejudice as he claims? Provide evidence to support your conclusion.

2. Do we still have heroes today? If so, who are some of them? How have they attained that status? Is the process similar to or different from that operating for the cowboy and the bandit? Are real people heroes anymore? Why or why not?

3. One of the contributing factors to mythologizing the figures in this chapter was their depiction in a wide variety of media: history books, editorials, ballets, and movies, for example. Choose one of these figures—or a modern hero—and compile a list of all the different treatments you can find. Do the interpretations agree with one another? If not, what reasons can you suggest for the differences?

Chapter Six

1. Examine the West you know. Aside from those presented in this chapter, what other "representations of the West, drawn from the past, continue to shape the present, to alter the economy, ecology, and demographics of communities where Westerners live and work"?

2. Examine contemporary American society for other manifestations of the Western past. (A supermarket might be a good place to start; read the shelves for "Western" brand names. While you're at it, consider the origin of the word "brand.") What conclusions do you draw from this examination of our present?

3. How do the selections on film explore "how minorities participate in and rework the central myths of the dominant culture"?

4. Are Western films realistic or not? Explain. Do the authors agree? with you? with each other? If they are not realistic, what attracts audiences?

General

1. Frederick Jackson Turner wrote that "the existence of an area of free land, its continuous recession, and the advance of American settlement westward, explain American development." Write a brief essay agreeing or disagreeing with this statement. Use specific evidence from this book, your personal experiences, or elsewhere to support your position.

Chronology

1763   Proclamation of 1763. King George III declares all land west of the Appalachian Divide off limits to colonial settlers. The prohibition is futile. The call of good lands over the horizon is far more powerful than the prohibition of a king across the ocean.

1803   Thomas Jefferson purchases the Louisiana Territory from France.

1804-1806 Lewis and Clark expedition to the Pacific and back.

1808   Missouri Fur Company established.

1821   Sequoya develops Cherokee alphabet.

1822   Rocky Mountain Fur Company organized by William Ashley of St. Louis; instead of establishing permanent forts, Ashley institutes the annual rendezvous, where trappers and Indians meet traders to barter furs for ammunition, whiskey, and supplies.

1824   Jedediah Smith discovers South Pass through the Rocky Mountains.

1835   Rev. Samuel Parker and Dr. Marcus Whitman are the first missionaries to travel overland to the West Coast; the following year Narcissa Whitman and Eliza Spaulding are the first white women to cross South Pass en route to Oregon.

1840   The last fur trading rendezvous. Trade shifts from beaver to buffalo, from rendezvous to fort.

1841   Immigration to Oregon begins with a small party moving westward through South Pass.

1843   The first party of "dudes," led by Sir William Drummond Stewart, follows immigrant trail through South Pass to the Wind River Mountains. They are sport hunters on the trail of buffalo, accompanied by hunters, muleteers, and camp servants. The party inaugurates the concept of Western tourism.

1846-1848 War with Mexico; at its conclusion, the United States acquires land which will be Texas, California, New Mexico, Utah, Nevada, and Arizona.

1848   *January 24* James Marshall discovers gold at Coloma, California.

February 2 Treaty of Guadalupe Hidalgo is signed; by it, California becomes a possession of the United States.

1850   Territory of Utah established.

California statehood.

1854   Kansas-Nebraska Act. The United States acquires Indian Territory.

1857-1858 The Utah War between the Mormons and the United States.

1860-1861 The Pony Express runs between St. Joseph, Missouri, and Sacramento, California.

1861-1865 Civil War.

1861   Telegraph connection from coast to coast makes Pony Express obsolete.

Theodore Judah surveys route through Sierra Nevada for a transcontinental railroad.

1862   Homestead Act and Transcontinental Railroad Act are passed by Congress.

1863   Construction begins on the Central Pacific and Union Pacific railroads.

1864   Sand Creek Massacre.

1866   Long cattle drives begin; the first trail herds reach Abilene, Kansas, in 1867.

1868   Battle of Washita. Seventh Cavalry defeats the Cheyenne in Oklahoma.

U.S. treaty with the Nez Percé is the last of three hundred treaties with Indians in one hundred years.

1869   *May 10* The Golden Spike joins the Union Pacific and Central Pacific railroads at Promontory Point, Utah.

December 10 Wyoming's "Female Suffrage Act" is signed into law, granting women for the first time anywhere in the United States the legal right to vote and hold office.

1871   The Indian Appropriation Act nullifies treaties and makes Indians wards of the federal government.

1872   Yellowstone National Park becomes the first nature area designated as a national park and protected by federal law.

1873   Levi Strauss and Jacob Davis patent blue jeans.

Barbed wire is invented, presaging the end of the open range.

The first issue of the Colt .45 revolver.

1875	Anti-Chinese riots in San Francisco.
1876	Battle of the Little Bighorn. The Seventh Cavalry, under Gen. George Armstrong Custer, is soundly defeated.
1881	Billy the Kid is killed by Pat Garrett.
	Gunfight at the OK Corral, Tombstone, Arizona.
1882	Buffalo Bill Cody presents the first Wild West show.
1887	Prentiss Ingraham's *Buck Taylor: King of the Cowboys*, a dime novel, introduces the cowboy hero in fiction.
1888	Theodore Roosevelt's *Ranch Life and the Hunting Trail* is published.
1889	Oklahoma land rush begins on April 22. Settlers rush to claim land bought by the U.S government from the Creek and Seminole Indians, previously relocated West.
1890	Indian Territory becomes Oklahoma Territory.
	Debacle of Wounded Knee, the last major armed conflict between Indians and U.S. forces.
	Wyoming is admitted to the Union as the first state having granted women the vote.
	The Bureau of the Census declares the end of the frontier; there is no longer "free land," as the United States now has at least two people per square mile.
1892	John Muir founds the Sierra Club.
1893	Frederick Jackson Turner presents "The Significance of the Frontier in American History," inaugurating one hundred years of debate among historians.

Annotated Bibliography

Ramon F. Adams, *A Fitting Death for Billy the Kid.* Norman: University of Oklahoma Press, 1960. Critical analysis of various sources of misinformation: dime novels, movies, old timers, biographies, and regional histories.

Eveline M. Alexander, *Cavalry Wife: The Diary of Eveline M. Alexander, 1866-1867.* Ed. Sandra L. Myres. College Station: Texas A & M University Press, 1977. A spunky cavalry wife's diary of travel across Indian Territory to New Mexico and Colorado. Personal portrait of life on the frontier, dodging tarantulas, riding out alone to see buffalo close up, and climbing vertical ladders to visit pueblos.

Thomas G. Alexander, ed., *"Soul Butter and Hog Wash" and Other Essays on the American West.* Provo, UT: Brigham Young University Press, 1978. Includes essays on Mark Twain and frontier religion, the cowboy and the cattleman, and Mormons and ethnicity.

William Marshall Anderson, *The Rocky Mountain Journals of William Marshall Anderson: The West in 1834.* Eds. Dale L. Morgan and Eleanor Towles Morgan. San Marino, CA: The Huntington Library, 1967. A fascinating account of Anderson's 1834 ride-for-health to the Rockies. The volume is especially valuable for its wit, its biographical "galaxy of mountain men," and its bibliography.

James Axtell, *The European and the Indian: Essays in the Ethnohistory of Colonial North America.* New York: Oxford University Press, 1981. Ten essays exploring the reciprocal impact of English and Indian cultures.

James Axtell, *The Invasion Within: The Contest of Cultures in Colonial North America.* New York: Oxford University Press, 1985. Contrasts the English attempt to "civilize" the Indians with the French willingness to accept their culture.

Gunther Barth, *Bitter Strength: A History of the Chinese in the United States, 1859-1870.* Cambridge, MA: Harvard University Press, 1964. Argues that the Chinese lack of commitment to settle and the perception of them as unfree labor were causes as important as racial prejudice for anti-Chinese feeling.

Isaac Haight Beardsley, *Echoes from Peak and Plain; or, Tales of Life, War, Travel, and Colorado Methodism.* Cincinnati: Curts and Jennings, 1898. The personal account of one of the early Methodist ministers in Colorado. Especially interesting is the sanitized biography of J. M. Chivington, a minister before he was a commander at the Sand Creek Massacre.

James P. Beckwourth, *The Life and Adventures of James P. Beckwourth, as Told to Thomas D. Bonner.* Intro. by Delmont R. Oswald. Lincoln: University of Nebraska Press, 1972. Bernard DeVoto was ambivalent about this book, feeling it was neither history nor fiction, but rather myth; at the same time, "it reveals more of Indian human nature than any other book of the time." Anyone interested in mountain men should at least dip into it, though with caution.

Donald J. Berthrong, *The Southern Cheyennes*. Norman: University of Oklahoma Press, 1963. Berthrong updates George Bird Grinnell's previously definitive account of the Cheyenne fight for survival. Focusing on the period before 1875, this book is somewhat less from the Cheyenne perspective than Grinnell's. Includes chapter on Sand Creek.

Samuel Bowles, *Across the Continent: A Summer's Journey to the Rocky Mountains, the Mormons, and the Pacific States*. Ann Arbor, MI: University Microfilms, Inc., 1966. Reproduction of 1865 publication. Bowles, a prominent editor, and Schuyler Colfax, speaker of the U.S. House of Representatives, crossed the continent during the summer of 1865. The account of the physical conditions of travel is intriguing, but of greater significance are comments on social and political affairs: Mormon polygamy and the necessity for a transcontinental railroad are thoroughly discussed.

John Bradbury, *Travels in the Interior of America in the Years 1809, 1810, and 1811. . . .* London, 1819. Vol. 5 Early Western Travels, 1748-1846. Ed. Reuben Gold Thwaites. New York: AMS Press, Inc., 1966. Bradbury went up the Missouri as far as the Mandan villages with Hunt, Crooks, and McKenzie. Especially good vignettes and descriptions of events such as the New Madrid earthquake.

Juanita Brooks, *The Mountain Meadows Massacre*. Norman: University of Oklahoma Press, 1950. Brooks, though a member of the Church of Jesus Christ of Latter-Day Saints, attempts a balanced analysis of the Mountain Meadows Massacre of 120 or so emigrants to California in the fall of 1857. For years the massacre was blamed on the Indians, but Brooks concludes that it was the product of the antagonistic relations between the Mormons and the United States. One conclusion: The atrocity was "a classic study in mob psychology or the effects of war hysteria."

Dee Brown, *Bury My Heart at Wounded Knee: An Indian History of the American West*. New York: Henry Holt and Company, 1970. From first contact to 1890, a corrective to the traditional Western history written from the point of view of Americans of European descent.

Dee Brown, *The Gentle Tamers: Women of the Old Wild West*. Lincoln: University of Nebraska Press, 1958. An excellent examination, well researched, delightfully written, of wives and nurses, miners and boardinghouse operators, whores and schoolmarms, reformers and hurdy-gurdy dancers.

J. Goldsborough Bruff, *Gold Rush: The Journals, Drawings, and Other Papers of J. Goldsborough Bruff, April 2, 1849-July 20, 1851*. Eds. Georgia Willis Read and Ruth Gaines. California Centennial Edition. New York: Columbia University Press, 1949. Bruff, captain of the Washington City and California Mining association, records depressing accounts of miners' hardships. He himself was abandoned when ill by his companions. Despite the subject matter, his sketches provide a sense of whimsy.

Franklin A. Buck, *A Yankee Trader in the Gold Rush*. Boston: Houghton Mifflin Company, 1930. Many of Buck's letters over a thirty-year span (1850-1880) sketch the California life of one who went West seeking gold but made a better life as a trader and farmer. Provides interesting insights on everything from the Civil War's impact on California politics to the future of viniculture.

Edward Gould Buffum, *Six Months in the Gold Mines*. Ann Arbor, MI: University Microfilms, Inc., 1966. Reproduction of an 1850 publication. A member of the Seventh Regiment of the New York State Volunteers, Buffum arrived in Yerba Buena (San Francisco) on March 6, 1847. He provides a clear description of the impact of the gold rush's frenzy on the formerly sleepy Mexican province, and an analysis of California's future potential. He includes an account of his own experiences in the gold fields during the fall, winter, and spring of 1848-1849.

Walter Noble Burns, *The Robin Hood of El Dorado*. New York: Coward McCann, 1932. A romanticized treatment of the California bandit Joaquin Murieta similar to his earlier work on Billy the Kid.

Anne M. Butler, *Daughters of Joy, Sisters of Misery: Prostitutes in the American West, 1865-1890*. Urbana: University of Illinois Press, 1985. Butler argues that the frontier was far more conservative in its social values than is popularly supposed. Thus prostitution, while one form of employment, had many restrictions.

John Walton Caughey, *The California Gold Rush*. Berkeley: University of California Press, 1975. A good analysis of the California gold rush, topically organized. Good bibliography.

Francis A. Chardon, *Journal at Fort Clark 1834-1839*. Ed. Annie Heloise Abel. Pierre: Department of History, State of South Dakota, 1932. Very readable account of life at a fur-trading fort, including daily events (fur pressing, meat hunting, marital problems, incessant war on rats), celebrations such as dances (scalp dance, buffalo dance), occasional skirmishes with hostile enemies, and the catastrophe of the 1837 smallpox epidemic—all told concisely yet vividly.

James Chisholm, *South Pass, 1868: James Chisholm's Journal of the Wyoming Gold Rush*. Lincoln: University of Nebraska Press, 1960. Ed. Lola M. Homsher. A delightful account of the Wind River gold rush. Chisholm, a correspondent for the Chicago *Tribune*, provides a greenhorn's fresh insights with the polished prose of a journalist.

Hiram Martin Chittenden, *The American Fur Trade of the Far West*. 2 vols. Stanford, CA: Academic Reprints, 1954. Reprint of 1902 publication. The preeminent early work on the fur trade; used and praised by such historians as Frederick Jackson Turner and Ray Allen Billington. Biographies of major traders and analysis of social and economic consequences of the fur trade.

Louise Amelia Knapp Smith Clappe (Dame Shirley), *The Shirley Letters from the California Mines, 1851-1852*. Ed. Carl I. Wheat. New York: Alfred A. Knopf, 1949. Dame Shirley's letters to her sister provide some of the best detailed descriptions of mining on the Feather River at Rich Bar: mining techniques, attitudes toward foreigners, and the rise of crime and vigilante justice.

C. M. Clark, *A Trip to Pike's Peak & Notes by the Way. etc.* San Jose, CA: The Talisman Press, 1958. A wonderfully vivid contemporary account of the 1859-60 Colorado gold rush; Clark captures people and places so concretely that the letters often read like short stories.

John Conron, ed. *The American Landscape: A Critical Anthology of Prose and Poetry.* New York: Oxford University Press, 1973. An anthology of writers, including poets, explorers, scientists, and novelists, on the American landscape as it changes from a new world Eden to a landscape of ruin. The authors' responses to nature range from awe to exploitation, from coexistence to dominance, from nature as inspiration to nature as antagonist.

Elizabeth B. Custer, *"Boots and Saddles" or, Life in Dakota with General Custer.* Norman: University of Oklahoma Press, 1961. Reprint of 1885 edition. Elizabeth Clift Bacon Custer accompanied her husband to many of his postings. In this book, she describes their life on the plains, including life at Fort Abraham Lincoln, from which General Custer set out on his last, ill-fated expedition. Clearly in love with the general, Libbie Custer provided many of the details from which the image of Custer as hero was formulated. For additional insights into his military career and their life together, see *Following the Guidon* (1890) and *Tenting on the Plains* (1887), also by Libbie Custer.

George Armstrong Custer, *My Life on the Plains, or, Personal Experiences with Indians.* Norman: University of Oklahoma Press, 1962. Covering the years 1867-1869, Custer tells of the Seventh Cavalry's operations on the frontier, including the Battle of Washita of 1868. He denounces "humanitarians" who advocated an "Indian peace policy."

Vine Deloria, *Custer Died for Your Sins: An Indian Manifesto.* London: Collier-Macmillan Limited, 1969. Facets of the relations between Indians and others—Indian humor, the Red and the Black, problems of Indian leadership, the impact of missionaries and anthropologists.

Dan de Quille (William Wright), *Big Bonanza.* New York: Alfred A. Knopf, 1947. Dan de Quille, a journalist with the Virginia City *Territorial Enterprise*, was encouraged by his friend Mark Twain to write a history of the Comstock Lode. This description of the mining techniques, local characters (including major investors and Indians and Chinese) is the result. First published in 1876, the book is a bonanza of primary materials on the early days on the Comstock.

Bernard DeVoto, *Across the Wide Missouri.* Boston: Houghton Mifflin Company, 1947. An enthusiastic history of the Missouri fur trade, illustrated with paintings by Alfred Jacob Miller, Karl Bodmer, and George Catlin.

Michael Dorris, *The Broken Cord: A Family's Ongoing Struggle with Fetal Alcohol Syndrome.* New York: Harper & Row, Publishers, 1989. Dorris recounts the problems of his adopted son and places them in the larger context of a major contemporary medical problem and the even larger context of alcohol having been introduced to the native American population as an item of trade.

Clifford Merrill Drury, *First White Women over the Rockies: Diaries, Letters, and Biographical Sketches of the Six Women of the Oregon Mission Who Made the Overland Journey in 1836 and 1838.* Glendale, CA: Arthur H. Clark Company, 1963. The subtitle tells it all.

J. P. Dunn Jr., *Massacres of the Mountains: A History of the Indian Wars of the Far West.* New York: Harper & Brothers, 1886. Contains a chapter on Sand Creek remarkably pro-Chivington and anti-Indian.

Philip Durham and Everett L. Jones, *The Negro Cowboys.* New York: Dodd, Mead & Company, 1965. One of the first full treatments of a frontier population that had largely faded into anonymity.

Charles Alexander Eastman (Ohiyesa), *The Soul of the Indian.* Boston: Houghton Mifflin, 1911. Rpt. Johnson Reprint Co., 1971. A member of the Santee Sioux who fled into Canada in the 1860s, Eastman was sixteen before he had seen a white man. Later he attended Dartmouth College and got his M.D. from Boston College; he returned to the Sioux to practice medicine. There he met and married Elaine Goodale.

Elaine Goodale Eastman, *Sister to the Sioux: The Memoirs of Elaine Goodale Eastman, 1885-91.* Lincoln: University of Nebraska Press, 1978. Elaine Goodale went West in the 1880s to establish day schools among the Brulé Sioux. Witness to the increase of white settlement, the emergence of the Ghost Dance religion, and the tragedy at Wounded Knee, she married Charles Eastman (Ohiyesa) in 1891.

Anne Ellis, *The Life of an Ordinary Woman.* Boston: Houghton Mifflin Company, 1929. Anne Ellis, born into poverty, spent most of her life at hard work, outlived two husbands, but never lost her sense of humor nor her desire to make the world better: walls carefully papered with newspapers, curtains stitched from nightshirts, books around to read. Wonderfully concrete, sometimes outrageous, observations on mining towns in late nineteenth-century Colorado.

John Mack Faragher, *Women and Men on the Overland Trail.* New Haven, CT: Yale University Press, 1979. Faragher writes from a feminist perspective, that "an important step in creating a society of free and equal women and men is the creation of a history of women and men in their real connectedness." He applies this philosophy in examining gender and family on the way West.

Matthew C. Field, *Prairie & Mountain Sketches.* Eds. Kate L. Gregg and John Francis McDermott. Norman: University of Oklahoma Press, 1957. Field, the assistant editor of the New Orleans *Daily Picayune*, accompanied the British William Drummond Stewart on a "party of pleasure to the Rocky Mountains" from St. Louis to the Green River Rendezvous in 1843. Selections from Field's diary and his sketches from the *Picayune*.

Christiana Fischer, ed., *Let Them Speak for Themselves: Women in the American West, 1849-1900.* Hamden, CT: Archon Books, 1977. Army wives, ranch wives, working women, and travelers describe the West; a good collection of documentary materials.

Mary Hallock Foote, *A Victorian Gentlewoman in the Far West: The Reminis-*

cences of Mary Hallock Foote. Ed. Rodman W. Paul. San Marino, CA: The Huntington Library, 1972. Foote, writer of short stories and serialized novels and illustrator for *Century Magazine* and *Atlantic Monthly,* followed her husband, Arthur DeWitt Foote, a mining and irrigation engineer, to the New Almaden mercury mines, to Mexico and Idaho, and back to Grass Valley, California. Wallace Stegner's *Angle of Repose,* a fictionalized version of her life, provides interesting comparison.

Joe B. Frantz and Julian Ernest Choate Jr., *The American Cowboy: The Myth & the Reality.* Norman: University of Oklahoma Press, 1955. The authors present the cowboy as "part of the whole Western panorama, instead of looking at him . . . in isolation from his larger environment."

Wayne Gard, *Frontier Justice.* Norman: University of Oklahoma Press, 1949. An informal study of the varieties of law and order developed to deal with the range of conflict on the various Western frontiers.

Pat F. Garrett, *The Authentic Life of Billy the Kid, the Noted Desperado of the Southwest, Whose Deeds of Daring and Blood Made His Name a Terror in New Mexico, Arizona, and Northern Mexico.* Norman: University of Oklahoma Press, 1954. A reprint of the 1882 book. Pat Garrett, the sheriff who killed Billy the Kid, sketches the desperado's fall from innocence (avenging bad language toward his mother; killing a Mexican gambler who refused to pay up and who insulted gringos). Garrett also defends himself against media second-guessers.

Marion S. Goldman, *Gold Diggers & Silver Miners: Prostitution and Social Life on the Comstock Lode.* Ann Arbor: The University of Michigan Press, 1981. While concentrating on the demographic, economic, legal, and personal causes of prostitution on the Comstock Lode from the 1860s to the 1880s, the book links the microcosmic details to larger regional, national, and archetypal causes of prostitution. Excellent research from contemporary primary sources makes sections as readable as a novel.

Charles Goodrum and Helen Dalrymple, *Advertising in America: The First 200 Years.* New York: Harry N. Abrams, Inc., 1990. Excellent illustrations supplement a very readable, analytical text.

Horace Greeley, *An Overland Journey from New York to San Francisco in the Summer of 1859.* New York: Alfred A. Knopf, 1964. The man who admonished "Go west, young man. . ." tells of his trip. Includes major passages on Mormons and Brigham Young, the American desert, California tourist attractions and mines, and Kansas, which he likes far better than he had expected.

Bailey C. Hanes, *Bill Pickett, Bulldogger: The Biography of a Black Cowboy.* Norman: University of Oklahoma Press, 1977. Bill Pickett, c. 1860-1932, born in Texas, had two older cousins, working cowboys involved in the long trail drives. Willie dreamed of emulating them and worked the 101 Ranch in the Cherokee Strip of Oklahoma, a ranch on which Tom Mix, the cowboy film star, also worked. Pickett invented the rodeo sport of bulldogging and in 1971 became the first black cowboy to be inducted into the National Rodeo Cowboy Hall of Fame.

Robert V. Hine, *Community on the American Frontier: Separate but Not Alone.* Norman: University of Oklahoma Press, 1980. Explores the sense of community in a nation often characterized as individualistic. From the New England town to modern communes, with stopovers at Mexican rancheros, trappers' rendezvous, and settlers' barn raisings along the way.

Stan Hoig, *The Sand Creek Massacre*. Norman: University of Oklahoma Press, 1961. An excellent analysis of the events leading up to the massacre, with close attention to the character of Col. John M. Chivington. A balanced account of probably the greatest tragedy of U.S.-Indian relations.

J. S. Holliday, *The World Rushed In: The California Gold Rush Experience*. New York: Simon and Schuster, 1981. A monumental thirty-three years of research, primarily in diaries and letters of the Argonauts, resulted in this extraordinarily personal, vicarious experience of the gold rush.

Ovando J. Hollister, *Boldly They Rode: A History of the First Colorado Regiment of Volunteers*. Lakewood, CO: Golden Press, 1949. Hard-fighting, hard-drinking, hard-living Coloradans in battle with Texans during the "civil convulsions" of the 1860s. Sidebar comments (mostly bigoted and pejorative) of Indians and Mexicans.

Washington Irving, *The Adventures of Captain Bonneville*. Eds. Robert A. Rees and Alan Sandy. Boston: Twayne Publishers, 1977. Another illustration of Irving's fascination with history's movers and shakers.

Washington Irving, *Astoria; or, Anecdotes of an Enterprise Beyond the Rocky Mountains*. New York: G.P. Putnam and Son, 1869. An admiring description of John Jacob Astor's plans for the American Fur Company and of the men in the field; good mix of adventure and manifest destiny.

Donald Dale Jackson, *Gold Dust*. New York: Alfred A. Knopf, 1980. Tells the story of the gold rush "through the experiences, feelings, and thoughts of the people who participated in it."

Donald Dale Jackson, "Sojourners Who Came to Stay," *Smithsonian* 21 (February 1991) 114-125. Examines Chinese immigrants from the gold rush era to the twentieth century; activists' efforts at commemorating their ancestors' struggles against oppression are especially interesting.

Francis Jennings, *The Invasion of America: Indians, Colonialism, and the Cant of Conquest*. New York: W. W. Norton & Company, 1975. Rejecting the concept of transplanting the seeds of European civilization into a "virgin land," Jennings views the process as conquest.

Howard Mumford Jones, *O Strange New World. American Culture: The Formative Years*. New York: The Viking Press, 1964. Explores his belief that "the profound and central truth [is] that American culture arises from the interplay of two great sets of forces—the Old World and the New."

Teresa Jordan, *Cowgirls: Women of the American West*. Garden City, NY: Doubleday & Company, Inc., 1982. Interviews with dozens of modern cowgirls; inserts from novels, journals, and magazine articles of and by Western women of the past.

Charles Larpenteur, *Forty Years a Fur Trader on the Upper Missouri*. 2 vols. Ed. Elliott Coues. New York: Francis P. Harper, 1898. In 1833, Larpenteur planned to make a brief trip to the Rockies with William Sublette and Robert Campbell. Instead, he stayed forty years, much of it with the American Fur Company, though toward the end of his life he was an independent trader and a sutler at various forts. A readable autobiography of his life from 1832 to 1872.

David Lavender. *The Fist in the Wilderness.* Garden City, NY: Doubleday, 1964. A thorough examination of the Canadian and American influences on the fur trade, centering on Fort Mackinac.

David Lavender, "Some American Characteristics of the American Fur Company," in *Aspects of the Fur Trade: Selected Papers of the 1965 North American Fur Trade Conference.* St. Paul: Minnesota Historical Society, 1967.

William H. Leckie, *Buffalo Soldiers: A Narrative of the Negro Cavalry in the West.* Norman: University of Oklahoma Press, 1967. Examines the roles of the Ninth and Tenth Cavalry on the Plains after the Civil War.

Robert E. Levinson, *The Jews in the California Gold Rush.* New York: Ktav Publishing House, Inc., 1978. As "the world rushed in" to California, Jews added to the state's ethnic diversity. Based strongly on primary documents, this book recounts civic, mining, mercantile, and religious activities of the Jewish community.

Patricia Nelson Limerick, *The Legacy of Conquest: The Unbroken Past of the American West.* New York: W. W. Norton & Company, 1987. Views the problems and the virtues of the West as part of a continuum, not interrupted in 1890 with the "closing of the frontier." Based, in large part, on business considerations.

Nat Love, *The Life and Adventures of Nat Love, Better Known in the Cattle Country as "Deadwood Dick."* Ed. William Loren Katz. New York: Arno Press and *The New York Times*, 1968. The autobiography of a black cowboy, from his days as a slave to life as a Pullman porter.

Joseph G. McCoy, *Historic Sketches of the Cattle Trade of the West and Southwest.* Kansas City, MO: Ramsel, Millett & Hudson, 1874. This account by an observant and opinionated cattle shipper describes ranches, cattle drives, railheads, and packing houses, and provides thumbnail sketches of contemporaries in the cattle business.

Frank Marryat, *Mountains and Molehills or Recollections of a Burnt Journal.* London: Longman, Brown, Green, and Longmans, 1855. If you can read only one account of the gold rush, Marryat's is the one. Having arrived via the Isthmus route in 1850, he provides vivid descriptions of Spanish ranch customs and San Francisco fires, fleas and clipper ships, as well as the mines. Humorous and informative.

Maximilian, Prince of Wied, *Travels in the Interior of North America.* Part 1. Vol. XXII, *Early Western Travels, 1748-1846.* Part 2, Vol. XXIII; Part 3, Vol. XXIV. Ed. Reuben Gold Thwaites. New York: AMS Press, Inc., 1966. From 1832 to 1834, Prince Maximilian traveled overland from Boston to St. Louis and thence up the Missouri, making notes and collecting specimens of American flora and fauna. He was accompanied by the Swiss painter Karl Bodmer whose Indian portraits provide important ethnographic data. Especially good descriptions of the Sioux, Mandan,

Crow, Assiniboine, and Arikara, as well as of Forts Clarke, Pierre, and Union.

Mary Jane Megquier, *Apron Full of Gold: The Letters of Mary Jane Megquier from San Francisco, 1849-1856.* Ed. Robert Glass Cleland. San Marino, CA: The Huntington Library, 1949. Mary Jane Megquier, reputedly the first American woman to cross the isthmus and frankly in search of money, accompanied her physician husband to California in 1849. Her accounts of running a boarding house, of local entertainment (from Lola Montez's spider dance to the public execution of a murderer) and of natural catastrophes (fire, flood, and earthquake) reflect her enthusiasm for life in San Francisco.

Dale Morgan, ed., *Overland in 1846: Diaries and Letters of the California-Oregon Trail.* Georgetown, CA: The Talisman Press, 1963. A collection of diaries (including some of the ill-fated Donner party and their rescuers), maps, newspaper reports, and guides. Well edited; readable.

Sandra L. Myres, *Westering Women and the Frontier Experience, 1800-1915.* Albuquerque: University of New Mexico Press, 1982. A major reinterpretation of the role of pioneer women based on letters, journals, and reminiscences. A wide spectrum of roles: The "gentle-tamer," the "sun bonnet saints," and the "silent partners" are joined by some lusty characters and rousing reformers.

Sandra L. Myres, ed., *Ho for California! Women's Overland Diaries from the Huntington Library.* Informative annotation and editing of diaries of women traveling to California via three routes: across the Isthmus of Panama in 1849, the California Trail, 1850-1859, and Southwestern Trails 1869-1870.

Peter Nabokov, ed., *Native American Testimony: An Anthology of Indian and White Relations.* New York: Harper & Row, 1978. Thematically organized, the anthology brings together important commentaries on the interactions between native Americans and newcomers.

Victor G. Nee and Brett DeBary Nee, *Longtime Californ': A Documentary Study of an American Chinatown.* Boston: Houghton Mifflin Company, 1974. A portrait of the people of San Francisco's Chinatown, from the Exclusion Act of 1882 to the 1970s; extensive interviews.

Roger Nichols, ed., *American Frontier and Western Issues: A Historiographical Review.* New York: Greenwood Press, 1986. An anthology of fourteen bibliographical and historiographical essays on frontier topics, ranging from agriculture to urbanization and frontier women to the frontier army.

Nelson C. Nye, *Pistols for Hire: A Tale of the Lincoln County War and the West's Most Desperate Outlaw William (Billy the Kid) Bonney.* New York: The Macmillan Company, 1943. A novel.

Peter Skene Ogden, *Peter Skene Ogden's Snake Country Journals, 1827-28 and 1828-29.* London: The Hudson's Bay Record Society, 1971. Provides insight into the British point of view in the competition with Americans for control of Oregon country and its natural resources, here primarily fur.

Glenn Ohrlin, *The Hell-Bound Train: A Cowboy Songbook*. Urbana: University of Illinois Press, 1973. Some classic cowboy songs; some modern rodeo songs, good discography.

Rodman W. Paul, *California Gold: The Beginning of Mining in the Far West*. Lincoln: University of Nebraska Press, 1965. One of the most frequently cited analyses of the gold rush: scholarly, succinct, and readable.

Roy Harvey Pearce, *Savagism and Civilization: A Study of the Indian and the American Mind*. Berkeley: University of California Press, 1988. An examination of the conflict between the notion of the noble savage and the urge to Christianize the heathen, in the process seizing their land and nearly exterminating them.

William Perkins, *Three Years in California: William Perkins' Journal of Life at Sonora, 1849-1852*. Eds. Dale L. Morgan and James R. Scobie. The journal of an arrogant, bigoted, opinionated Canadian storekeeper with a good eye for detail.

Francis Paul Prucha, *The Great Father: The United States Government and the American Indians*. Lincoln: University of Nebraska Press, 1986. The definitive work on the subject.

Bessie Rehwinkel, as told to her husband Alfred M. Rehwinkel, *Dr. Bessie*. St. Louis, MO: Concordia Publishing House, 1963. The life and adventures of a woman doctor in homesteader Wyoming in the first decade of the twentieth century. Though the setting is a generation later, the experiences are frequently similar to those of the 1993 television show "Dr. Quinn, Medicine Woman."

Don Rickey Jr., *Forty Miles a Day on Beans and Hay: The Enlisted Soldier Fighting the Indian Wars*. Norman: University of Oklahoma Press, 1963. A fascinating study of the everyday life of the enlisted man from 1865 to the 1890s.

John Rollin Ridge (Yellow Bird), *The Life and Adventures of Joaquin Murieta, the Celebrated California Bandit*. Norman: University of Oklahoma Press, 1955. A popularized and positive treatment of a man many viewed an outlaw and others saw as an ethnic hero.

Kenneth Roberts, *Northwest Passage*. Greenwich, CT: Fawcett Crest, 1936. A sweeping novel centered on Robert Rogers's search for the Northwest Passage.

Theodore Roosevelt, *Ranch Life and the Hunting Trail*. Lincoln: University of Nebraska Press, 1983. Theodore Roosevelt knew the West firsthand; from 1884 to 1886 he built up his ranch on the Little Missouri in Dakota Territory, relishing the physical challenges as well as the characters of the Badlands. The book is illustrated by his friend, the famous Western artist and sculptor, Frederic Remington.

Osborne Russell, *Journal of a Trapper*. Lincoln: University of Nebraska Press, 1955. Mountain man, member of the Oregon Territorial Provisional Government, miner, boardinghouse operator, and judge on the Placerville Vigilance Committee, Russell here describes life in the Rocky Mountain fur trade from 1834 to 1843.

Elmer Clarence Sandmeyer, *The Anti-Chinese Movement in California*. Urbana: University of Illinois Press, 1973. The classic study of the roots of agitation which led to restriction and then exclusion of Chinese.

Mollie Dorsey Sanford, *Mollie: The Journal of Mollie Dorsey Sanford in Nebraska and Colorado Territories, 1857-1866.* Lincoln: University of Nebraska Press, 1959. Describes life on the prairies: the trip west, homesteading, the Colorado gold rush, and the impact of the Civil War.

William W. Savage Jr., *The Cowboy Hero: His Image in American History & Culture.* Norman: University of Oklahoma Press: 1979. A study of the cowboy of history as well as the cowboy as prototype of American character. A variety of media—literature, film, music, advertising, and psychology—is employed in the analysis.

William W. Savage Jr., *Cowboy Life: Reconstructing an American Myth.* Norman: University of Oklahoma Press, 1975. A collection of contemporary accounts by cowboys, cattlemen, and journalists, of the life of the cowboy, primarily on the southern Great Plains from the 1860s to 1900.

Howard L. Scamehorn, ed., *The Buckeye Rovers in the Gold Rush.* Athens: Ohio University Press, 1965. Diaries of two emigrants from southeastern Ohio, 1849-1852.

Lillian Schlissel, *Women's Diaries of the Westward Journey.* New York: Schocken Books, 1982. An analysis of 103 women's diaries of the overland journey, divided by period: 1841-1850, 1851-1855, and 1857-1867. A woman's point of view without blatant feminism. Short portions from four diaries.

Charles Howard Shinn, *Mining Camps: A Study in American Frontier Government.* Ed. Rodman W. Paul. Gloucester, MA: Peter Smith, 1970. First published in 1884, *Mining Camps* is a series of studies on social organization and government in early California.

Duane A. Smith, *Rocky Mountain Mining Camps: The Urban Frontier.* Lincoln: University of Nebraska Press, 1974. The Rocky Mountain mining frontier (1859-1880) differed from other frontiers because it was urban before it was rural, less individual than cooperative, more rapidly developed, with concomitant luxuries and social problems, and more dependent on the rapid acquisition of ready cash.

Henry Nash Smith, *Virgin Land: The American West as Symbol and Myth.* Smith examines material from many disciplines, primarily history and literature.

Roberta Reed Sollid, *Calamity Jane: A Study in Historical Criticism.* Helena: The Historical Society of Montana, 1958. Separates fact from legend.

Frank Soule, John H. Gihon, and James Nisbet, *The Annals of San Francisco.* Facsimile. Palo Alto, CA: Lewis Osborne, 1966. A history of early San Francisco through 1855. Daily events reported with occasional longer analyses. Excellent contemporary source material.

Kent Ladd Steckmesser, *The Western Hero in History and Legend.* Norman: University of Oklahoma Press, 1965. A brilliant analysis of the transformation of Kit Carson, Billy the Kid, Wild Bill Hickok, and George Armstrong Custer from fact to something else.

Elinore Pruitt Stewart, *Letters of a Woman Homesteader.* Lincoln: University of Nebraska Press, 1961. Widowed by a railroad accident, Elinore Rupert left her job as a washlady in Denver to become a housekeeper for a Wyoming rancher; she sought a homestead and found a second husband.

John E. Sunder, *Bill Sublette, Mountain Man.* Norman: University of Oklahoma Press, 1959. A biography that analyzes its subject's varied roles and argues that American politics, geography, and business all bear Sublette's mark.

Bayard Taylor, *Eldorado, or Adventures in the Path of Empire.* 2 vols. Glorieta, NM: The Rio Grande Press, Inc., 1967. Motivated neither by a lust for gold nor wealth from trade, Taylor recognized California in the latter half of 1849 as a society "as transitory as it was marvelous"; he tries to capture its "fleeting images"—of fleas and floggings, of the California horse and the California political convention, of disease and the diggings.

William H. Truettner, *The West as America: Reinterpreting Images of the Frontier, 1820-1920.* Washington, DC: The Smithsonian Institution Press for the National Museum of American Art, 1991. An exhibit catalog, this is a wonderfully rich compendium of American art, with a somewhat revisionist text.

Mark Twain, *Roughing It.* Twain's rambling through the West, including Hawaii, in the 1860s provides a cross-section: miners, Mormons, stage drivers, desperadoes, and speculators. The book has been called "Twain's rejection of the mythic, romanticized image of the West, and his autopsy of the American dream."

Robert M. Utley, *Frontier Regulars: The United States Army and the Indian, 1866-1891.* Bloomington: Indiana University Press, 1977. A balanced, scholarly overview exploring the post-Civil War conquest of the Plains.

Robert M. Utley, *High Noon in Lincoln: Violence on the Western Frontier.* Albuquerque: University of New Mexico Press, 1987. A thorough treatment of the events surrounding Billy the Kid's exploits.

Robert M. Utley, ed., *Life in Custer's Cavalry: Diaries and Letters of Albert and Jennie Barnitz, 1867-1868.* New Haven, CT: Yale University Press, 1977. Through the diaries and letters of a literate, loving couple, everyday life in the Seventh Cavalry, as well as frank assessments of officers, including Custer, are vividly presented.

Herman J. Viola, *After Columbus: The Smithsonian Chronicle of the North American Indians.* Washington, DC: Smithsonian Books, 1990. A comprehensive history of the native American for half a millennium; lavish illustrations complement clear exposition.

Elliott West, *The Saloon on the Rocky Mountain Mining Frontier.* Lincoln: University of Nebraska Press, 1979. An examination of the saloon, "the most complex and versatile retail business of the Rockies" during the mountain mining frontier—1858 to the early 1890s. Includes some astonishing details: The annual consumption of alcohol just after 1860 equalled two gallons for every man, woman, and child in the country.

Edward L. Wheeler, *Deadwood Dick on Deck, or Calamity Jane, the Heroine of Whoop-Up*. Ed. Philip Durham. New York: The Odyssey Press, Inc., 1966. A classic illustration of the dime novel version of the American West.

Lonnie J. White, et al., *Hostile and Horse Soldiers: Indian Battles and Campaigns in the West*. Boulder, CO: Pruett Publishing Company, 1972. Examination of warfare on the Plains from 1864 to 1886, including essays on the Sand Creek Massacre, the Wagon Box Fight, and the Bannock-Piute War of 1878.

Richard White, *"It's Your Misfortune and None of My Own": A New History of the American West*. Norman: University of Oklahoma Press, 1991. Drawing on new historical research emphasizing issues of environment, gender, and urban development, the book argues that "as succeeding groups have occupied the American West, they have done so without regard for present inhabitants."

David J. Wishart, *The Fur Trade of the American West, 1807-1840: A Geographical Synthesis*. Lincoln: University of Nebraska Press, 1979. Probably the definitive study of the Upper Missouri Fur Trade and the Rocky Mountain Trapping System from 1807 to 1840. A readable, scholarly account of ecological, cultural, and economic consequences of Euro-Americans engaged in the fur trade in the trans-Mississippi West. Good bibliography.

Owen Wister, *The Virginian: A Horseman of the Plains*. 1902. Boston: Houghton Mifflin Company, 1968. Reprint of the 1902 novel that created the fictional prototype of the cowboy.

Daniel B. Woods, *Sixteen Months at the Gold Diggings*. New York: Harper and Brothers, 1851. Reprinted by Arno Press, Inc., 1973. Having embarked in February 1849 for the gold fields, Woods grew wealthy, not from gold but in experience. He demonstrates a concern for morality without being stuffy, and he offers good advice: Don't go, but if you must, be strong and moral.

Walter Woods, *Billy the Kid, in The Great Diamond Robbery and Other Recent Melodramas*. Ed. Garrett H. Leverton. Volume VIII of *America's Lost Plays*. Bloomington: Indiana University Press, 1940. The melodrama presents the idealized version of Billy, the mythic hero.

Walker D. Wyman, ed., *California Emigrant Letters*. New York: Bookman Associates, 1952. Letters from California emigrants sent back to hometown newspapers, recounting the journey, methods of mining, life in the mines, and the quick-sprouting new Western cities.

Index